Building Middle Class Nations

Ahmed Tahiri Jouti

Building Middle Class Nations

Inclusive Economic Development for the Global South

palgrave
macmillan

Ahmed Tahiri Jouti
Casablanca, Morocco

ISBN 978-3-032-02133-5 ISBN 978-3-032-02134-2 (eBook)
https://doi.org/10.1007/978-3-032-02134-2

This Palgrave Macmillan imprint is published by the registered company Springer Nature Switzerland AG
The registered company address is: Gewerbestrasse 11, 6330 Cham, Switzerland

Competing Interests The author has no competing interests to declare that are relevant to the content of this manuscript.

Introduction of the Book

In an era of rapid disruptive changes, increasing inequalities and growing political instability, the prosperity of a nation is not exclusively linked to economic indicators such as Gross Domestic Product growth rate, or the Gross Domestic Product per capita or the urban expansion. These indicators are no longer sufficient and cannot prevent countries from being fragile in the absence of strong institutions and sound composition of societies.

Indeed, it is not only about being high performers in terms of economic indicators but it is also about sustaining these performances and making them profitable to every member of the nation. It is about providing the opportunity to everyone in the nation—whether he is a citizen or a migrant, a resident, or a foreign investor—to convert their ideas and dreams to a reality that would be beneficial for the nation. Sustainability consists of making everyone contribute to the welfare of the whole nation and make the nation take care of every member.

The abundance of natural resources can boost the Gross Domestic Product of a nation for decades while the wealth accumulated does not benefit the nation itself but a minority of people that can enjoy a better life to the determinant of the majority. At the opposite, nations with limited natural resources have developed their capacities, their governance, and their public policies in order to create real socio-economic models that leave no one behind and where everyone has the opportunity to contribute to social and economic development.

The main difference between both nations is the ability to reduce inequalities and make the gaps invisible between the different clusters of the society by providing equal rights, equal access to resources, and encouraging entrepreneurship and innovation initiatives. Indeed, it is about building middle-class nations.

From another perspective, most of the developing countries have a high GINI Index while most of developed countries have a low GINI Index. Obviously, there are some exceptions such as the United States, a wealthy developed country that has a high GINI Index (between 0,41 and 0,45) which is comparable with most other developing nations and can be comparable to Latin America countries. Such a situation is due to factors such as a less redistributive tax system, weaker social security systems, large inequalities in terms of wages and wealth.

The GINI Index is a statistical measure of income or wealth inequality within a population. It ranges from 0 (perfect equality where everyone has exactly the same income) to 1 (perfect inequality where one person has all the income and everyone else has none).

Some economists defend the idea that the focus should be on growth first to create enough wealth before thinking about equal distribution mechanisms to reduce inequalities while other economists defend the idea that no real growth can be achieved without equity and fairness.

Indeed, the first group of economists believe that the fair redistribution is a consequence of growth while the second group of economists believe that the fair redistribution is not the consequence of growth but a condition for it.

For the first group of economists, a superior GINI Index in most developing countries reflects the level of maturity of the nation that is still looking for growth levers and that has not reached yet the stage where it needs to think about redistribution. Moreover, the model of the United States, one of—if not—the strongest economies in the world has never been concerned with the redistribution of wealth and still leading the world economy. Therefore, the equal distribution of wealth has never stopped the growth and prosperity of a nation.

For the second group of economists, the data shows that the growth potential of a nation is limited by the increasing inequalities among the society. If people are not empowered and cannot access natural and financial resources to be productive, they would be left behind and if the public policies are not supporting these people, disparities and gaps would keep increasing. Therefore, underdevelopment is not only a matter of fair distribution of wealth but this fair distribution is a way to growth and prosperity and there may be exceptions for particular reasons.

From this book perspective, the middle-class feature of a nation is not limited to economic indicators such as the GINI Index but is extended to social, cultural, educational and political aspects that, combined, will ensure the homogeneity of the society while reducing gaps and disparities between the different clusters.

From this perspective, evaluating the middle-class feature exclusively on the basis of the economic indicators makes it inaccurate. For instance, a country like the United States could seem as a non-middle-class nation if the analysis is limited to the GINI Index, but when the analysis is enlarged to include various dimensions including free and fair access to business opportunities, the United States can be considered as a middle-class nation falling behind in terms of social opportunity, and basic well-being.

To better understand this perspective, the book is divided into three parts and nine distinct chapters:

The first part of the book defines the foundations and the methodology that guides the entire work, it introduces—the Lifts and Nets Framework—and the conceptual groundwork for detailed discussions in the other parts of the book. The first part is composed of two chapters:

- Chapter 1 discusses how a nation's social homogeneity affects the effectiveness of the governance system and political regimes, advocating for balanced diversity. It introduces the idea of a middle-class nation—where equitable access, fair distribution, and opportunity reduce disparities—and sets the stage for the Lifts and Nets Framework to support sustainable development.
- Chapter 2 presents the Lifts and Nets Framework, a comprehensive approach that promotes upgrading mechanisms and protect individuals from economic downturns. It stresses the importance of a coordinated approach across key sectors—education, housing, healthcare, and financial system—to achieve fair homogeneity and reinforce the middle-class feature of the nation, while introducing the book's overall methodology.

The second part of the book explores the application of the Lifts and Nets Framework to the social sphere to reinforce the middle-class feature of the nation, focusing on education, housing, transportation, and healthcare. Combined, these chapters demonstrate how inclusive, well-integrated social policies can reduce visible gaps between population clusters, enhance homogeneity, and sustain the middle-class feature of the nation. The second part of the book is composed of three chapters:

- Chapter 3 examines the social structure of nations by identifying distinct social clusters and their impact on the homogeneity of the nation. It highlights how reducing disparities and promoting upgrade mechanisms, especially through access to quality education, are essential to building a balanced middle-class nation. Effective public policies must address these social dynamics, including education reform and equal educational opportunities, to foster inclusion and long-term stability.
- Chapter 4 emphasizes the impact of housing and transportation on social inclusion and urban development. It shows how unequal access to transportation network and smooth mobility networks can reinforce poverty and limit economic inclusion. By applying the Lifts and Nets Framework, the chapter advocates for integrated policies that promote affordable, smart cities and urban poles, aligned with broader strategies in education, health, and infrastructure to build cohesive and prosperous urban communities.
- Chapter 5 underscores the vital role of public health policies on national stability and social equity, positioning them as key drivers in building middle-class nations. It highlights how inclusive, preventive, and regionally adaptable health systems can reduce inequalities and protect societies during crises like COVID-19. The chapter also stresses the need for cross-sector coordination—particularly with education and urban planning—to foster healthier environments and support long-term social resilience.

The third part of the book examines the critical interactions between social public policies, economic competitiveness, and the financial system in shaping a middle-class nation. This part is composed of two chapters:

- Chapter 6 highlights how weak social public policies—especially in education, healthcare, housing, and transportation—create hidden costs that undermine economic competitiveness. These inefficiencies reduce productivity, increase operational burdens for businesses, and erode trust in public institutions. Over time, this dynamic reinforces inequality, fuels tax avoidance, and weakens the foundation needed to build a stable middle-class nation.

- Chapter 7 examines how financial systems, while designed to support economic inclusion, often exacerbate inequality through risk transfer models that disproportionately burden low-asset individuals. In non-middle-class nations, this dynamic results in financial exclusion and exploitative lending conditions for vulnerable populations. The chapter argues that only when financial reforms are aligned with cohesive public policies and risk-sharing paradigm can financial systems genuinely contribute to building a resilient middle-class nation.

The fourth part of the book highlight that strong, accountable institutions and an institutional approach to political governance are fundamental to building and sustaining a middle-class nation. This part is composed of two chapters:

- Chapter 8 highlights the essential role of political governance in reinforcing a nation's middle-class feature by ensuring power is exercised inclusively and accountably. It contrasts institutional governance—which promotes equity, innovation, and strong public policies—with rent-based systems that concentrate power between the hands of a group of individuals and weaken cohesion. The chapter stresses the importance of resilient institutions, meritocratic leadership, and transparent rules and balances in sustaining stable and adaptable middle-class nations.
- Chapter 9 argues that only institutional governance—rooted in fairness, accountability, and adaptability—can sustainably build a middle-class nation. It contrasts this with individualistic systems that entrench inequality and resist reform, stressing that middle-class nations thrive on empowered institutions and coordinated public strategies. The chapter calls for a renewed social contract based on equity, innovation, and political will, positioning the middle class as the backbone of national prosperity.

Contents

About the Author

Dr. Ahmed Tahiri Jouti holds a Ph.D. in Finance and Economics. He is the Managing Partner of Green for South, a consulting firm specializing in sustainable finance, public policies, and climate finance. He is also the co-founder of NeuronAIze, a startup in the field of artificial intelligence. His work lies at the crossroads of innovation, development, and equity, with a strong emphasis on designing inclusive financial systems that support long-term transformation.

With a particular focus on the Global South, Dr. Tahiri Jouti has led numerous consulting assignments across Africa, the Middle East, and Southeast Asia, advising governments, development institutions, and financial stakeholders on sustainable development strategies. Through both his advisory work and public contributions, he promotes a vision of empowerment, social justice, and the expansion of a resilient middle class in emerging economies. Contact E-mail: a.tahiri@greenforsouth.com.

List of Figures

List of Tables

PART I

The Lifts and Nets Framework for Middle Class Nations

CHAPTER 1

The Middle-Class Nations

Introduction of the Chapter

A nation is a large aggregate of communities and individuals united by factors such as language, culture, history, or occupation. As part of a nation, a community is a group of people living in the same place or having a particular characteristic in common (Oxford English Dictionary). Indeed, the concept of a nation covers the area or space and its inhabitants having common interests (language, culture, history, ownership, values, and responsibilities, religion, occupation, or any other form of interest).

In reality, the concepts of nation and government are totally independent. In fact, a nation can cover large areas under the control of multiple governments, borders (Hastings & Wilson, 1998) and vice versa, a government can control several nations in a specific territory. In this book, the concept of "nation" would be directly linked to the different communities under the control of a central government where public policies are applied to ensure stability, growth, and prosperity. Indeed, the concept of nation is directly linked to a central political power.

From another perspective, it is obvious that the more homogeneous a nation and its various communities are, the easier it is to design consistent and effective public policies (Adelino & Blake, 2010). Indeed, the contagion effect of the different policies is easy to handle if certain features and characteristics between the different components of a nation are nearly identical or close. On the opposite side, the more heterogeneous a nation

A. Tahiri Jouti, *Building Middle Class Nations*,
https://doi.org/10.1007/978-3-032-02134-2_1

and its underlying communities are, the harder it is to design consistent and effective public policies. Indeed, the complexity level of public policies depends on the degree of heterogeneity of a given nation in terms of features and characteristics.

Moreover, public policies are not only impacted by the level of heterogeneity of the nation they are serving but they are also supposed to improve the nation homogeneity as well. In fact, the homogeneity of a nation can be measured through several indicators and dimensions and can be impacted through different public policies.

This chapter addresses the concept of heterogeneity/homogeneity degree of nations from different perspectives and dimensions. It also shows that totally homogeneous or heterogeneous nations are not necessarily good indicators of soundness and prosperity. In this context, middle-class nations appear to be a relevant target for public policies and governmental action plans and strategies. Indeed, middle-class nations are a smart combination of factors and actions that ensures a global balance from economic, social, and political perspectives.

Finally, this chapter also describes the targeted global balance in a given nation from the economic, social, and political perspectives.

The Concept of Middle-Class Nations

Heterogeneity vs. Diversity

As it may be understood from the introduction of this chapter, heterogeneity is not looked upon favorably and some readers may confuse it with the concept of diversity that is considered as a key driver of innovation and performance. Indeed, diversity is, in general, related to criteria such as gender, ethnic background, religion, and other similar elements (Leo Parvis, 2005). It goes without saying that diversity has always contributed to the creation of strong nations and the reinforcement of their economic and political power.

On the other hand, heterogeneity is linked to elements and criteria other than those related to diversity. Indeed, the education level, the average income, the housing standard are all examples of factors that can define the heterogeneity of a nation. For instance, a highly diverse nation may be homogeneous and vice versa, a heterogeneous nation can be poorly diverse.

From this perspective, there are four categories of nations:

Leading Nations: Highly Diverse and Homogeneous Nations
These are nations that gather a diversity of social groups belonging to different ethnicities, religions, and races but for social progress, economic advancement, and political stability, all the indicators show an acceptable level of homogeneity.

Such a configuration reflects the capacity of these nations to achieve inclusion in its various facets (economic, political, social) for all people regardless of their origin, race, or any other factor. In this category of nations, every component (cluster or group of people) contributes to common stability and progress.

These nations are leading because of their ability to attract the most talented people and provide them with the most attractive economic opportunities in a fair and equitable system.

Opportunistic Nations: Highly Diverse and Heterogeneous Nations
These are nations that gather a diversity of social groups belonging to different ethnicities, religions, and races but indicators related to social progress and economic advancement show that there is a strong heterogeneity.

In such a configuration, public policies are not inclusive at all and are serving the interests of a social group to the detriment of the others. This can occur in the case of nations that welcome immigrants by granting them special status without giving them the possibility of obtaining the citizenship or by considering them second-class citizens even if they do obtain the citizenship. This can also happen in the case of nations where the regime is supported by a social group (that can constitute a majority) benefiting from the favors of this regime. In this case, heterogeneity is the consequence of discriminatory public policies where access to economic resources and opportunities is limited to certain segments of the nation.

Generally, these nations cannot rely exclusively on their own people to achieve growth and prosperity because they do not have the necessary skills or maybe they have a reduced size of population. Therefore, immigration is an opportunity to attract people and fill the gaps.

Fair and Closed Nations: Poorly Diverse and Homogeneous Nations
These are nations whose social structure has remained stable for decades, if not centuries with no major shifts or significant migratory flows that can impact their diversity. The migratory flows can be due to economic

incentives (*people looking for better opportunities*), political reasons (*colonialism, migration due to armed conflicts*), or environmental conditions (*drought, natural catastrophes*). In this configuration, indicators related to social progress and economic advancement show an acceptable level of homogeneity.

In such a configuration, homogeneity is a sign of fair distribution of wealth and resources, fair and equitable access to economic opportunities for all the members of the nation.

These nations have sufficient size of skilled people and do not have any specific strategies or public policies to encourage immigration. They can rely on their own people and achieve economic growth and prosperity.

Autocratic Nations: Poorly Diverse and Heterogeneous Nations
These are nations with stable social structure in the absence of any significant migratory flows or any other turbulences as mentioned earlier but all the indicators related to the economic, social, or political spheres show that there is a high level of heterogeneity.

This heterogeneity is a sign of an autocratic regime where a minority is dominating the whole nation. This domination can be explained by various reasons such as lobbying practices, colonialism, religious beliefs, etc.

Such heterogeneous nations cannot attract immigrants and do not provide any interesting economic opportunities for foreigners because of the minority domination. Therefore, people know that this is a highly controlled market.

The following scheme represents the four categories of nations depending on their diversity and their heterogeneity (Fig. 1.1):

Heterogeneity vs. Homogeneity

From the previous paragraph, heterogeneity is considered negative, totally different, and independent from the concept of diversity. On the opposite side, homogeneity or what is called "an acceptable degree of homogeneity" was promoted as an interesting target of public policies and governmental action. In this context, a serious question arises: *What degree of homogeneity is considered acceptable for a given nation?*

To provide an appropriate answer, let us adopt the following assumptions:

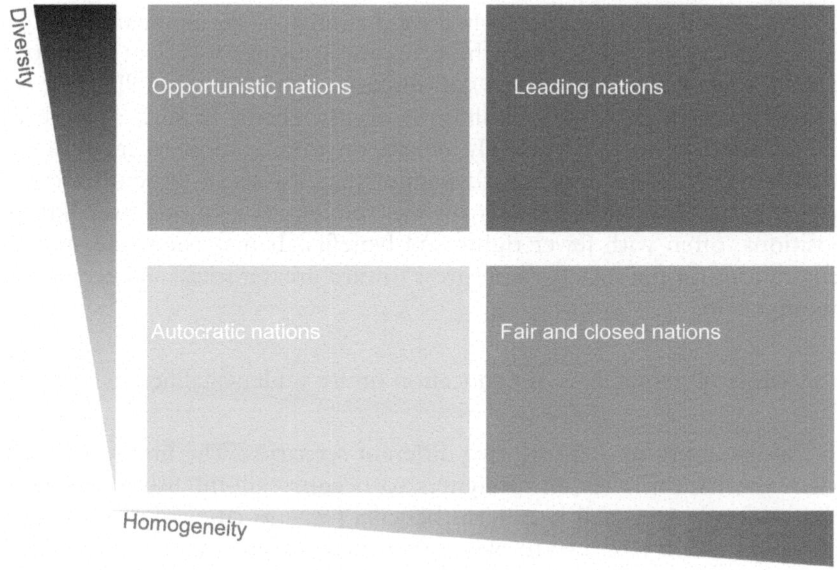

Fig. 1.1 The matrix of nations based on their diversity and homogeneity

One Factor Homogeneity or Heterogeneity

Let us assume that the education degree is the only factor of homogeneity under study, a highly homogeneous nation can take one of the following forms:

- Most of people have higher-education degrees

In this context, several scenarios may unfold, which will be discussed in detail in this section. The first scenario arises when job opportunities for highly educated individuals are limited. As a result, they accept positions below their qualifications, leading to a phenomenon known as (*degree inflation*). In such a situation, the oversupply of qualified candidates pushes employers to increase their educational requirements for less skill-intensive jobs, while keeping wages unchanged.

This situation would lead to frustration and people would prefer to migrate abroad for better job opportunities or quit school since the employment market under-evaluates people's capabilities.

The second scenario arises when the majority of the population holds higher-education degrees and the economy provides sufficient opportunities for all. Consequently, less skill-intensive jobs remain unfilled due to a shortage of local workers willing to occupy them. In such a context, the nation becomes increasingly reliant on immigration to meet labor market needs. Over time, this dynamic creates a social structure dominated by highly educated citizens while immigrants take on lower-skilled positions, often with fewer rights and benefits. It may then take several generations for the society to progress toward greater social and economic homogeneity.

- Most of people have no education or are under-qualified

In this assumption, there are two different scenarios. The first scenario is when the nation relies on foreigners to occupy skill-intensive jobs with high wages but no real long-term benefits (*such as citizenship or at least rights equivalent to locals*) to obviously protect locals. Indeed, if the need is temporary and these foreigners would be replaced gradually by highly competent local people, it is fair enough. Nevertheless, if there is no plan to replace foreigners by local people and the country will keep hiring foreigners, this orientation would lead to a heterogeneous nation in the middle term.

The second scenario is when the nation would allocate jobs to local people even if they do not have the necessary capabilities and education. In this context, there would be a real issue in terms of leadership credibility and competence and the minority of highly qualified people would not find themselves in a comfortable position in a non performing nation with less effective public policies.

Indeed, a high degree of homogeneity can lead to an unbalanced nation with scenarios that can lead to the other extremity—a highly heterogeneous nation. Now, based on one factor—education—a degree of homogeneity is considered acceptable when the nation is constituted of all the education levels and in all the specialties while the gap between a level and the other is not significant.

To better understand the concept of acceptable degree of homogeneity, let us use some plots (Fig. 1.2):

Indeed, an acceptable degree of homogeneity for a given nation consists of a variety of clusters with a large middle-class cluster and

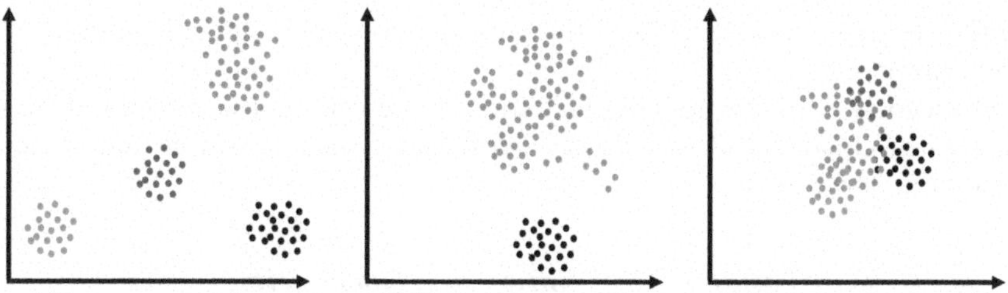

Fig. 1.2 Plots representing different degrees of homogeneity of nations

very small gaps between the different clusters. For instance, a nation needs a small cluster of highly qualified people to occupy top management functions, a large cluster of middle-class qualified people to ensure middle management functions and jobs, and finally an important cluster of low-skilled people to occupy the less skill-intensive jobs.

In this context, homogeneity consists of small gaps in terms of education between the different clusters. Such a configuration would make communication easier between the different clusters and the upgrade efforts less hard. This conclusion would be discussed earlier in details.

If these conclusions are valid for the education factor, they can be valid for all the other factors such as health, income, housing, etc. Nevertheless, in practice, such an approach is not realistic since the homogeneity of a given nation never relies on a unique factor.

Multi-Factors Homogeneity or Heterogeneity

The combination of many factors would create more clusters with the possibility to have sub-clusters inside the same cluster. Therefore, the fair homogeneity should be ensured between the different clusters and inside each cluster.

For instance, a nation can be composed of two clusters mainly the highly qualified people cluster and the low-skilled people cluster. In both clusters, there are two sub-clusters; the high-income people and the low-income people sub-clusters. A fairly homogeneous nation is when the gap in terms of income between all the sub-clusters is reduced and the gap in terms of qualification and education between both clusters is getting lower. In other words, highly qualified people must have roughly and fairly similar income levels and the gap with low-skilled people should be minimized.

Indeed, a fairly homogeneous nation is the one that is composed of a myriad of clusters and sub-clusters with fairly similar features and socio-economic indicators.

Middle-Class Nation vs. Homogeneity

A middle-class nation is a fairly homogeneous nation where the different clusters are close to each other in terms of social and economic indicators. Such a definition, in spite of its reliability, does not reflect accurately the real image of the concept.

The 5-Stars Hotel Example

To better understand the middle-class nation concept, let us take the example of a 5-Stars Hotel that has very expensive and large suites but also affordable and comfortable single or double rooms. In this hotel, there are enough rooms and suites to make the cost affordable for everyone and once you have the necessary means to access a single/double room, you can enjoy shared spaces such as the swimming pools, the Gym, and other equipments the same way someone who booked a suite will.

In this example, there are two perspectives: the perspective of suites' customers and the perspective of single/double room customers.

- Perspective of Suites' Customers

Generally, suites' customers have the financial capacity to afford all the costs, and in return they require a very pleasant and luxurious treatment and company. Obviously, they will be sharing some shared spaces in the hotel with other customers and they would like to feel no gap in terms of manners, cleanliness, and behavior. Otherwise, they would not appreciate their stay and can leave at any moment the hotel.

Hotel managers would have to raise the prices of single/double rooms as a filter to admit only people that have the financial capacity and the necessary living standards to be in line with suites' customers. Indeed, it is not only about the financial capacity but also about homogeneity of the standards of life. Moreover, suites' customers would also need to pay an extra for this filter.

– Perspective of Single/Double Room Customers

Obviously, people staying in suites have some extra advantages but the minimum offered to single/double rooms customers is fair enough. Indeed, once you get access to this hotel, gaps become totally invisible. If customers of single/double rooms do not share the same standards of living, the prices will go up as a filter. Therefore, the access to the hotel will be costly and a lot of people would be left behind. Indeed, a fairly homogeneous nation would reduce the costs for everyone to get access to this hotel.

A middle-class nation can be assimilated to this 5-Stars Hotel where people can get access to a single/double room with an affordable cost (***equivalent to the possibility to access to resources and wealth fairly***) and can enjoy highly valuable public services (***equivalent to the hotel shared spaces***) without feeling any visible gaps with people enjoying large suites.

What Is and What Is Not

The following statements can illustrate more accurately the concept of a middle-class nation:

- A middle-class nation is not a nation dominated by the middle class. In fact, it is a nation where there are several clusters but they are all close to each other in terms of social and economic indicators.
- A middle-class nation is when the minimum quality of life is good enough to make any gaps between the different clusters and classes invisible.
- A middle-class nation does not mean that high net worth individuals are inexistant or would have to pay more contributions to the nation. It is a nation that fights against inequalities and where nobody is left behind and at the same time, creating wealth is encouraged.
- A middle-class nation is fairly homogeneous not only in terms of economic indicators but also in terms of education level, health, housing, transportation, and this homogeneity also applies to basic elements such as hygienic standards, good manners, etc.
- Public policies are more efficient in the context of middle-class nations and all the public policies are supposed to reinforce the middle-class nation features.

- In this book, the concept of middle-class nations is not linked exclusively to the economic features. It integrates other elements related to education and social status.

Translating Concepts into Metrics

The Middle-Class Nation Metrics

Since the middle-class nation concept is not relying exclusively on economic indicators, the following metrics can be also used to position the different nations accordingly:

- From a Pure Economic Perspective: At least 60–70% of the population falls within a defined middle-class income band—between 0,75 and 2,5 times—the national median income per capita, adjusted for purchasing power parity.
- From a Social Perspective: the access gap between lowest and highest income quintiles to key public goods (education, healthcare, housing, digital access) does not exceed 20 percentage points. The lowest income quintile represents the poorest 20% of the population and the highest income quintile represents the richest 20%. If 95% of the richest 20% have access to quality healthcare, and 78% of the poorest 20% do, then the access gap (95–78% = 17%) is equal to 17 percentage points which is within the acceptable range (less than 20%)
- From a Well-Being Perspective: Subjective well-being or life satisfaction indices (such as the World values survey, Gallup world Poll) have to show a low variance across income deciles (Standard deviation below 0,8 on a 10-point scale). This means that people's life satisfaction scores don't differ much between income groups.

The Fair Homogeneity Metrics

A fair homogeneity means that socio-economic clusters are distinct but the gap between them is narrow enough to allow cohesion and mutual understanding. The fair homogeneity concept can be assessed through the following thresholds:

- The Gini coefficient for income and wealth should remain below 0.30.
- The *education attainment gap* between the top and bottom quintiles should be less than 1.5 years of schooling. The richest 20% have, on average, 11.2 years of schooling, and the poorest 20% have 10.0 years. Therefore, the gap is 1.2 years which satisfies the target (less than 1.5 years).
- The health outcome gap (e.g., life expectancy difference between richest and poorest quintiles) should not exceed 5 years.
- *Housing quality disparity* (share of population living in substandard dwellings) should be under 10%.
- *Intergenerational mobility index* (OECD metric) above 0.70 reflects that children's outcomes are not rigidly determined by parents' socio-economic status.

The Data Strategy to Measure Homogeneity

Effective management begins with effective measurement. The more precise the measurement, the greater the ability to design policies that are relevant, consistent, and impactful. Indeed, without reliable measurement, public action operates in uncertainty, reducing both efficiency and accountability.

Measurement precision depends on the quality and reliability of the data collected. This requires identifying and gathering the most relevant variables, ensuring data accuracy, and building robust systems for aggregation and verification. Reliable data collection creates the foundation for evidence-based policymaking, allowing decision-makers to translate complex social dynamics into actionable insights.

To achieve this, it is essential to integrate all existing databases—covering education, health, income, and other key dimensions—into a unified data system. Once integrated, advanced machine learning techniques such as DBSCAN, K-Means, or K-Medoids can be used to identify the main clusters that constitute the social structure. Time-series tracking can then capture trends and evolutions over time, enabling a continuous evaluation of public policies and interventions. Finally, international benchmarking offers a broader comparative perspective, allowing governments to reposition their policies and assess their effectiveness in a global context.

The Relevance of Middle-Class Nations

Middle-Class Nations Main Features

As mentioned previously, middle-class nations do not exclude high net worth individuals as a way to ensure a fair distribution of wealth among its members. At the opposite, from one side, it encourages rich people to become richer and to create more opportunities but not at the expense of the other social strata and from the other side, it fights against poverty while reinforcing the middle-class. Therefore, to better understand the features of middle-class nations, it is important to explore the concept of poverty and its various facets.

Poverty and its Various Facets

Poverty is about not having enough money to meet basic needs such as food, clothing, health expenses, and shelter. The cost of these basic needs varies from a country to another and from an era to another. Moreover, what is considered as being basic needs can vary as well. Therefore, the poverty threshold is a moving target and it depends on the context. Hence, if this cost increases and if the basic needs expand to include more elements, more people would be considered as poor.

For instance, having access to electricity and to sanitation is considered nowadays as basic needs and those who are deprived of these services are considered poor. Nevertheless, two centuries ago, electricity did not exist back then which means that at that time, electricity or sanitation were not considered as basic needs.

Fighting against poverty is a common responsibility of the nation and its members. Indeed, a nation must implement mechanisms to assist and help its members to escape from poverty, and at the same time, individuals must have the necessary willingness and capacity to do so. Before exploring the different facts of poverty, it is important to address first the concept of price stability and inflation.

– Vertical Inflation vs. Horizontal Inflation

The magic square of the economy represents the four major variables of a country's economic policy that are economic growth, price stability, employment, and external balance. There are very strong interactions between the different variables. For example, as suggested by Philips curve, when employment rates decrease, prices go up and vice versa.

Throughout the world, governments and central banks are trying to control the inflation that is defined as a general increase in prices and a fall in the purchasing value of money. In practice, there are two types of inflation. First, the vertical inflation which occurs when prices go up of a defined basket of basic goods and services and the horizontal inflation which occurs when what is called the basket of basic needs expands to include more elements. In practice, governments and central banks are only focusing on the vertical inflation and do not update constantly the composition of the basket of basic goods and services.

In reality, inflation is a personal experience that everyone lives by his own for many reasons. First, the composition of a defined basket varies from a person to another and from a home to another. Secondly, prices also vary from a region to another and sometimes from a neighborhood to another. Thirdly, not everyone can behave in a way that decreases its own inflation rate. Indeed, some people would look for alternative goods while others would keep consuming the same goods and quantities. For example, people would start to drink coffee instead of tea if its price goes up while others would keep drinking tea and complaining about it.

All in all, to ensure a better monitoring of inflation, central banks shall consider horizontal inflation as well and understand the different factors leading people to poverty.

– Forms of Poverty

Poverty can have various facets and forms. Governments and financial authorities should estimate the portion of each form in the nation to elaborate appropriate strategies (Lanjouw, 2001). Indeed, there are four facets that can be summarized as follows:

- *Poverty Related to Inflation* (Cardoso, 1992): it is when there are very high rates of inflation (hyperinflation) that a part of the population finds itself with a revenue that does not satisfy all their basic needs (this is the vertical inflation as explained previously). It is also the case when the basket of basic needs gets larger and a part of the population does not have the access to these needs (this is the horizontal inflation). This form of poverty is much easier to handle.

Indeed, governments and financial authorities need to stabilize prices meanwhile they can grant subsidies to the most vulnerable people.

- *Economic Poverty*: it is when people have the necessary skills and ideas but do not have the necessary resources to satisfy their basic needs and cannot start their own business or enroll in training courses to get access to the labor market. This form of poverty is also easy to handle. Obviously, governments and financial authorities can grant subsidies, free loans and can also rely on microfinance schemes to support income-generating activities and projects.
- *Skills Poverty* (King & Palmer, 2006): it is when people do not have the necessary financial resources to satisfy their basic needs but they do not have any skills that can generate a decent revenue. This form of poverty is harder to tackle and requires empowerment mechanisms to develop the capabilities of the population to be productive and generate income.
- *Poverty of Will*: it is when people do not have the necessary financial resources to satisfy their basic needs, they do not have any skills to generate a decent revenue and they do not have any will to change their situation even if there are appropriate programs of empowerment and assistance. This situation can occur when there is a way to generate some revenue without any effort or with very humble efforts or when there are subsidies that are paid by the government. This form of poverty is the hardest to deal with for many reasons. First, it reduces the efficiency of public policies especially when it comes to empowerment mechanisms and instruments since few people would endorse them. Secondly, some people could satisfy partially their needs and they are so happy with it. Nevertheless, such a situation cannot be improved and the target of creating a middle-class nation would be hard to achieve.

From another perspective, the poverty of will includes the absence of willingness of people to improve their quality of life and their standard of living. Sometimes, people have the necessary resources but refuse to improve their way of life, their hygiene, their manners, and their standard of living. In this context, poverty evolves beyond a mere economic condition to become a mindset and a way of life, making social integration across clusters particularly difficult. This phenomenon is often referred to by economists as the poverty trap (Azariadis & Stachurski, 2005).

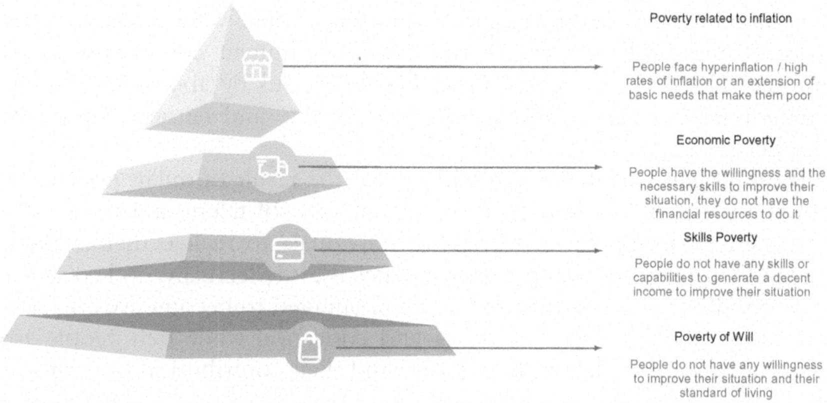

Fig. 1.3 Facets and forms of poverty

The following figure summarizes the various facets of poverty and the interactions between each layer (Fig. 1.3):

It goes without saying that every layer and facet of poverty requires a different approach. A one size fits all solution is not possible in this case. For instance, when people do not have the necessary skills or they do not have the willingness to improve their situation, providing microfinance loans or even subsidies cannot be efficient and effective.

Moreover, even when individuals achieve a decent level of income, if they lack the willingness to improve their quality or standard of living, public policies may appear ineffective, as a certain degree of heterogeneity would persist within the population.

Features of a Middle-Class Nation

In heterogeneous nations, wealth often emerges as the consequence of unfair—or even discriminatory—policies and regimes. This pattern has appeared repeatedly across regions and historical periods, shaping how societies perceive the wealthy. In many contexts, affluent individuals are seen as beneficiaries of an unequal distribution of national resources—such as land ownership, monopolistic privileges, or state favoritism—and are therefore viewed as having received more than their fair share as members of the nation.

Indeed, the existence of different social classes dates back to the time of the ancient Egypt with the rulers' class, the elite class who were literate and wealthier, then common people who constitute the majority and finally slaves. From that time, human communities and nations happened to become more homogeneous by abolishing slavery, reinforcing governance, and promoting equality and fairness among its members.

In homogeneous nations, wealth is not the result of unfair policies or a biased social order. Rather, it is the outcome of talent and hard work within an environment that enables individuals to realize their visions, pursue their projects, and progress financially, intellectually, and socially.

In middle-class nations, people are encouraged to become wealthy and to improve their standard of living and education while rich people are appreciated for their talent, hard work, and their contribution to reinforce the power of the nation by creating new brands, new activities, growth drivers, new jobs for people, and in some cases a new life style. For this purpose, public policies are supposed to support wealthy people to grow more and create more impact.

In heterogeneous nations, people are fighting against wealthy people and in fact, in their mind, they are fighting against a regime or a political model that favors a group of people over the nation.

Another major difference between middle-class nations and heterogeneous nations when it comes to wealthy people is that in middle-class nations, everybody can get access to appropriate opportunities depending on their talents and willingness to improve their situation and become wealthy. In heterogeneous nations, unless you are part of lobby groups, the elite, or privileged clusters, becoming wealthy is just a wish.

In middle-class nations, public policies try to protect wealthy people from economic downturns, otherwise, they would invest less, take less risks and would not fully play their role as major contributors to the welfare of the nation as a whole.

In parallel, middle-class nations fight against all forms of poverty discussed earlier. Indeed, public policies should understand the causes and the intensity of every form and help people to grow and evolve to remove all the poverty traps.

For instance, subsidies and social assistance should be designed to preserve individual dignity while encouraging active participation in the labor market. In practice, the minimum wage should provide higher income than government subsidies—along with the added benefits of social recognition and self-respect.

Moreover, empowerment programs and mechanisms are also necessary to help people to evolve and grow, find a job, or get ready to seize an economic opportunity to generate more income. Empowerment includes the upgrade of the standard of living and quality of life as well.

From another perspective, interest-free loans and microfinance products are valuable instruments to support individuals who possess the necessary skills but lack the financial means to start or expand their businesses. However, this alone is not sufficient. Such mechanisms should be designed to assist the poor while preparing them to eventually engage directly with the banking system once they reach a certain threshold. Microfinance clients are not meant to remain dependent on these institutions indefinitely; if they do, it would indicate a failure of public policy.

Finally, combating poverty or encouraging wealth creation and civic contribution is not solely a matter of designing dedicated public policies or implementing specific mechanisms. In reality, all other areas of public policy—including education, housing, transportation, healthcare, and access to clean water—can directly improve people's lives. Consequently, every public policy domain is relevant and should contribute both to poverty reduction and to fostering the capacity of individuals to grow, prosper, and contribute to the nation.

Underlying Drivers of Middle-Class Nations

There is a myriad of reasons that justify the need to create middle-class nations and reinforce them. As defined earlier, middle-class nations are not nations who are necessarily dominated by middle-class but these are nations that have homogeneous clusters having common features and similar indicators. Moreover, these are nations where rights and access to economic opportunities and social services are equal and guaranteed.

This being said, it is important to understand the reasons behind building middle-class nations and reinforcing their homogeneity through public policies and different instruments to upgrade the mindsets of people.

Middle-Class Nations Are Easier to Serve

As mentioned earlier, middle-class nations make public policies more effective and easier to elaborate since there are homogeneous clusters that have common features and similar indicators. Therefore, when dealing with a specific issue, governments and authorities would find it easier to tackle.

For example, in a middle-class nation, a housing shortage can drive up market prices. To address this, governments can develop new satellite towns connected to major cities via efficient public transportation. With a high number of users finding the transport both affordable and convenient, such investments become more profitable. Housing quality in these satellite towns can match that of central urban areas, while prices remain lower due to the greater distance from downtown.

In a non-middle-class nation, when there is a housing deficit, governments tend to prioritize low-income populations. As a result, they often develop new zones with low-standard buildings to minimize housing costs. However, public transportation is not necessarily expanded in these areas, as low-income residents may be unable to afford transportation fares unless heavily subsidized—a policy that is difficult to sustain over time.

From another perspective, the middle-income class may find limited housing options that match their expected standard of living. Consequently, they are often forced either to pay more for housing designed for higher-income groups or to purchase lower-standard units in these new zones, often lacking adequate infrastructure and transportation. In such cases, policies initially intended to support low-income groups end up benefiting the middle class instead. Nevertheless, the middle class remains dissatisfied, as their standard of living declines as a result.

Such a situation can be extended to any other issue or public policy. Indeed, middle-class nations are easier to serve and to govern.

Middle-Class Nations Are More Stable Politically (Hall, 2013)

As previously discussed, middle-class nations are characterized by a high level of homogeneity, which extends beyond economic indicators. One of the most distinctive features of such nations is the widespread awareness among their citizens, and their capacity to comprehend future challenges and national or global issues—such as climate change. This collective awareness strengthens governance systems and enhances the accountability framework of political leaders and all individuals entrusted with public responsibility.

In this context, the public opinion is not easy to control and manipulate, and everyone is accountable for his actions depending on his status and the responsibility he is assuming. Such configuration makes middle-class nations more stable politically, economically, and socially.

Indeed, people's awareness makes accountability frameworks even stronger and more efficient in the long run. Political leaders are selected wisely for their capabilities, talent, and vision, and no one can be left without punishment if he betrays the nation.

Middle-Class Nations Are More Attractive Economically

Middle-class nations generally enjoy higher purchasing power, making them attractive markets for investment. Local businesses benefit from a large consumer base with significant spending capacity. At the same time, foreign investors are drawn to these markets, eager to capitalize on the economic opportunities they offer.

The attractiveness of middle-class nations is not limited to the size of their markets or the purchase power of its people, it is extended to their standard of life that provide better conditions. Moreover, these middle-class nations have better education outputs, therefore, foreign businesses could seek and find much more easily talents to hire in order to develop their capabilities.

Middle-Class Nations Are More Secure Socially

When public policies prove ineffective, individuals often must bear additional costs to meet their needs. For instance, in a country where health sector governance and strategy are weak, public health services may be inadequate, forcing people to pay for private care to receive proper treatment. In contrast, in a middle-class nation with a well-functioning public health system, access to quality services is guaranteed, relieving citizens from extra fees and ensuring equitable care for all.

Consider another example: a government may promote the construction of satellite towns without simultaneously developing adequate public transportation infrastructure. Families relocating to these towns to benefit from affordable housing are then forced to spend extra on private vehicles to meet their commuting needs. Furthermore, if insufficient resources are allocated to local policing, residents may also incur additional costs by hiring private security services.

In non-middle-class nations, whenever the government fails to provide the necessary services, people would have to pay extra fees to satisfy their needs if they have enough resources otherwise, they would remain deprived of these services.

Indeed, middle-class nations are more secure and stable socially because of the effective public policies that provide people with all the necessary services without paying extra fees.

Conclusion of the Chapter

Whenever I visit a new country, I often gauge its level of development using two informal indicators. First, during the drive from the airport to the hotel, a stark contrast between affluent and poor neighborhoods signals underlying development challenges. Second, the availability and cleanliness of public restrooms can serve as a proxy for the nation's overall standard of living; poorly maintained or scarce facilities suggest a lower level of public service provision and living conditions.

Indeed, the middle-class nation concept is not exclusively linked to the economic situation. It is extended to all the other indicators such as property and standard of living, education, access to basic services such as clean water, sanitation, etc.

Middle-class nations are easy to serve and do not imply a high degree of complexity when elaborating public policies. They are politically stable since the high degree of awareness reinforces the country's Governance and accountability frameworks. Moreover, economically speaking, they can attract investors who would find the standard of living convenient and the administrative requirements easy to handle while having access to a valuable labor market.

Moreover, middle-class nations are socially secure and stable. Indeed, all the public policies are supposed to reinforce the features of middle-class nations to ensure an acceptable degree of homogeneity in a way that economic gaps would seem invisible. In other words, people have access to basic services without any extra cost such as housing, public transportation, education, health, etc.

Now that the concept of middle-class nations is clearer, many questions arise. First, is there any appropriate approach to transform nations to middle-class ones? Second, who are the stakeholders of such a transformation? Third, how this approach should be applied to public policies?

The next chapter in this first part would address these questions in a way that presents the transformative approach to middle-class nations called in this book "The Lifts and Nets approach" that applies to all the public policies.

References

Adolino, J. R., & Blake, C. H. (2010). *Comparing public policies: Issues and choices in industrialized countries*. SAGE Publications.

Azariadis, C., & Stachurski, J. (2005). Poverty traps. *Handbook of Economic Growth, 1*, 295–384.

Cardoso, E. (1992). *Inflation and poverty (Working Paper No. 4006)*. National Bureau of Economic Research. https://doi.org/10.3386/w4006

Donnan, H., & Wilson, T. M. (1998). *Border identities: Nation and state at international Fontiers*. Cambridge University Press.

Hall, J. (2013). Africa's middle-class: A factor favouring political stability. *Africa Conflict Monthly Monitor, 2013*(4), 4–7.

King, K., & Palmer, R. (2006). *Skills development and poverty reduction: The state of the art*. Postbasic education and training working paper, 7.

Lanjouw, J. O. (2001). *Demystifying poverty lines. UNDP Series on Poverty Reduction*. United Nations Development Programme.

Parvis, L. (2005). *Understanding cultural diversity in today's complex world*. lulu.com

CHAPTER 2

The Lifts and Nets Framework for Public Policies

Introduction of the Chapter

As discussed earlier in the previous chapter, the target of any nation that wishes to become a middle-class nation is to develop a fair degree of homogeneity and maintain it throughout time. Indeed, this can be achieved through a myriad of public policies that make the different clusters and segments of people close to each other in terms of social and economic indicators.

Having the transition toward a ***middle-class nation*** as a major national objective, public policies must adopt a common approach and shared paradigm to ensure governmental action is consistent, comprehensive, and effectively contributes to achieving this goal.

Indeed, this common approach should equip the different clusters and segments of the population with the necessary tools and incentives to continuously improve their living conditions and capabilities. For instance, people should have opportunities to keep learning and acquiring new skills and knowledge—including those with limited educational backgrounds. Moreover, since each individual has unique capacities, strengths, and weaknesses, the education system must ensure that no one is left behind. Everyone should have the chance to be guided and supported according to their own learning pace, so they can acquire the skills needed for their personal and professional development.

A. Tahiri Jouti, *Building Middle Class Nations*,
https://doi.org/10.1007/978-3-032-02134-2_2

This approach should be adopted in all the other sectors and public policies such as housing, financing, healthcare, etc. Therefore, it needs to provide people with opportunities to access to the necessary means to upgrade their situation and conditions (these mechanisms are called "lifts mechanisms") and in case people's situation gets impacted negatively, they have the necessary support to reduce the impact and gets them back where they were initially through the "nets" mechanisms.

This chapter aims at defining the general framework of the approach to adopt to achieve the middle-class nation target. This approach is called "The Lifts and Nets" approach. It would describe in a precise and concise manner the public policies components to adjust in order to be in line with this approach.

Moreover, this chapter would describe the mechanisms to adopt when implementing public policies with real life examples in order to understand the relevance of this approach and its impact on the structure and homogeneity of a given nation. In parallel, this chapter would also address the case of middle-class nations when elaborating public policies and how to improve their fair homogeneity degree.

Finally, the chapter would describe the methodology adopted in this book and the main concepts addressed in each of the remaining chapters.

The Lifts and Nets Approach

General Framework of the Lifts and Nets Approach

The Lifts and Nets approach consists of three main elements. First, it consists of improving people's quality of life and living standards to reach at least the national standard if not more. Second, it aims at improving the national standard by upgrading the different segments and clusters of the nation and improving the various social and economic indicators. Third, it also assists people during random life events to protect them and provide them with the opportunity to maintain their standard of living.

Indeed, the first and second elements constitute both the "Lifts Mechanisms" since they are supposed to upgrade people and the different segments of the nation to reach a certain threshold. For instance, improving people's health can be achieved through different mechanisms such as the general medical coverage (Anderson et al., 2012) for people who cannot contribute to the fund, encouraging telemedicine practices for people living in rural areas without the necessary medical infrastructure to host them locally (Preston et al., 1992).

When it comes to upgrading the national standard of health, the government can encourage sport among the different segments of the population (Van der Veken et al., 2020) by investing in neighborhoods parks and gyms while adopting preventive health measures.

The third element constitutes the "Nets Mechanisms" that are supposed to provide people with the necessary support and assistance in difficult days. For instance, people who lost their homes during a natural disaster and who used to belong to the middle-income class are supported by different mechanisms to build new houses while having a free access to a healthy home during the construction phase. These assistance mechanisms should not be improvised. Indeed, the government is supposed to create a national insurance scheme for natural disasters (McAneney et al., 2016) with appropriate emergency and back up plans.

The general framework is not limited to a range of mechanisms isolated from each other. It is a framework that applies to each public policy that should implement its own Lifts and Nets mechanisms while taking into account the interactions that could occur with other public policies already implemented or under implementation.

Indeed, the general framework is structured around three interrelated layers. The first layer consists of the mechanisms themselves—the lifts and nets. The second layer corresponds to public policies, each embedding its own specific Lifts and Nets Mechanisms. The third layer encompasses the interactions between these various public policies and mechanisms, assessing their combined impact and overall efficiency.

The following figure describes the Lifts and Nets Mechanisms in a simplified manner (Fig. 2.1):

Main Components of the Lifts and Nets Approach

To better understand the framework, some concepts need to be addressed in details such as the national standard level, the targeted national standard level, the lifts mechanisms, and the nets mechanisms.

The National Standard Level

Today's universal approach toward poverty consists of identifying poverty lines, elaborate policies to reduce the number of people living below

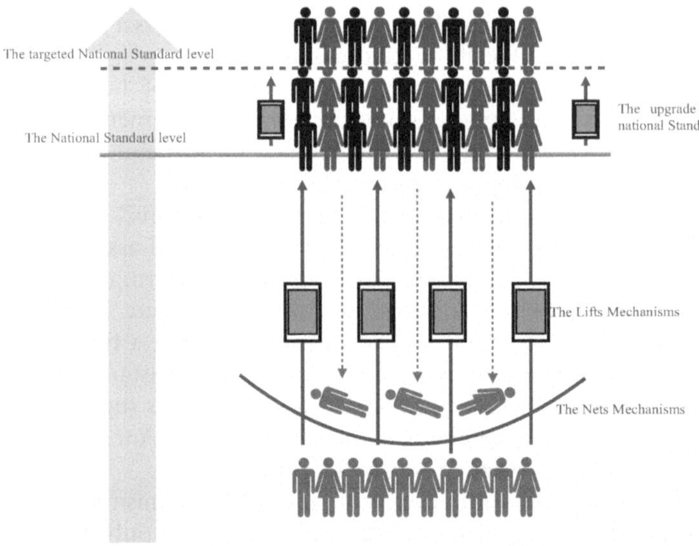

Fig. 2.1 The general scheme of lifts and nets mechanisms

these lines and to implement them in the hope of improving the global situation.

According to the World Bank data, the extreme poverty line in 2022 was estimated at 2.15 USD per day with more than 648 million people globally in this situation in 2019.

It is worth noting that this line was previously estimated at 1.90 USD per day but was adjusted based on the global price levels across the globe. This level needs to be updated regularly to take into account the price levels and the inflation rates globally.

Based on this indicator, governments have sought to lift as many people as possible above the poverty line (Mahembe et al., 2018). Nevertheless, individuals moving from USD 1.6 to USD 2.2 per day remain highly vulnerable, as any increase in price levels can easily push them back below the poverty threshold. Consequently, such progress is fragile, and public policies that rely solely on this minimalist approach fail to genuinely enhance people's quality of life.

For instance, in order to improve the quality of life of people in extreme poverty, some governments have created social housing zones with very low-quality standards compared to average housing standards. These zones have a very high density, and in some contexts, people living in these neighborhoods are still labeled as poor people.

Indeed, such public policies just try to lift people out of extreme poverty to position them in a vulnerable situation where they can be easily recognized as former extremely poor people and in some cases where they can be downgraded easily to extreme poverty line again.

Therefore, lifting people out of extreme poverty does not necessarily mean that they have to remain in its borderline. Moreover, it does not mean that they have to access exclusively to low-quality services. In addition to this, the traditional approach focuses only on the economic indicators mainly the daily income. Nevertheless, extreme poverty often evolves into a mindset—a specific set of behaviors and a distinct culture (World Bank, 2004).

For instance, it is understandable that people without access to clean water may face challenges related to hygiene and cleanliness. However, it becomes less understandable when individuals who have gained access to clean housing and water still fail to adopt basic hygiene standards. This illustrates that a slight improvement in economic conditions, if not accompanied by behavioral support and social assistance, cannot lift people out of poverty in a sustainable way.

Extremely poor people need a process of integration in the nation. They need to adopt the same living standards in terms of education, good manners, hygiene, preferences, and culture than any other cluster. Indeed, they need to be part of a fairly homogeneous nation where the gaps, if there are any, would be invisible.

For this purpose, public policies need to lift people out of poverty and bring them closer to the national standard level in terms of social and economic indicators. This means that if an average citizen has an apartment of seventy square meters, a car, a retirement plan, a medical coverage, and a monthly income of at least 1100 USD, all the public policies should provide extremely poor people with efficient mechanisms to reach that threshold. Moreover, public policies should also help poor people to upgrade their standards of living in terms of basic elements such as kids schooling, hygiene and cleanliness, and the art of living in community.

For instance, to improve the hygiene standards of people, public policies can improve the access to clean water and to public baths at a very low price and everywhere. These public policies have to promote the daily showers and cleanliness. Some people will argue that such objectives cannot be assigned to governments, which have more important things to worry about.

Nevertheless, such aspects are very important since they improve the homogeneity of the nation which makes, as explained earlier, public policies more efficient and issues less complicated to handle.

The national standard level reflects the real situation of a nation and serves as a benchmark for assessing its overall development. It can be multifactorial, combining both sectoral indicators and composite multidimensional indices.

To measure this standard accurately, two complementary dimensions are considered: the median level, which captures the central tendency, and the gaps, which reveal inequalities across different population segments.

As outlined in Chapter 1, from an economic perspective, the national median income per capita, adjusted for purchasing power parity, represents the central reference, while the share of the population within the defined middle-class income band—between 0.75 and 2.5 times the median—illustrates the dispersion.

In the field of education, the median number of years of schooling defines the standard, and the education attainment gap between the top and bottom quintiles reflects inequality. Similarly, in health, the median life expectancy serves as the central measure, while the health outcome gap—the life expectancy difference between the richest and poorest quintiles—indicates disparity.

In addition, complementary indicators can enrich the analysis. Consumption deciles divide the population into ten equal groups according to household consumption levels, allowing comparisons between lower and higher segments. Asset indices measure the ownership of durable goods, housing quality, and access to basic services, providing a proxy for long-term wealth. Multidimensional indicators combine several dimensions—such as education, health, and living standards—into a single composite measure of well-being or deprivation. Finally, each chapter of this book includes a list of indicators designed to measure these gaps and track progress toward fairer and more cohesive national development.

The Targeted National Standard Level

Confucius, the famous Chinese philosopher, once said that those who do not move forward moves backward. Indeed, it is important to improve the national standard level and to set new targets on a regular basis.

In practice, within every nation, the elite continues to advance in terms of wealth, economic conditions, tastes and preferences, social indicators, and overall living standards. This continuous advancement tends to widen the gap between the elite and other population segments, reinforcing the heterogeneity of the nation. This does not imply that the evolution of the elite should be limited or slowed down; rather, it highlights the need to enable other social segments to evolve as well. Such a dynamic would raise the national standard level and allow the entire nation to progress together.

Now, consider the opposite scenario: while the elite continues to advance, the government focuses its efforts primarily on lifting the poor or addresses only economic aspects, leaving the middle class unsupported. In this situation, the middle class could be squeezed between the advancing elite and the struggling poor, losing ground in terms of living standards and social influence. As a result, the nation would fragment into three distinct clusters, reducing the overall efficiency of governmental policies and undermining the relevance of the national standard level, given the widening gaps between groups.

Therefore, it is not about setting a targeted national standard level, it is more about defining the ways and means of advancing all the components and clusters of the nation by further reducing disparities.

From another perspective, it is important to know that this approach is not focusing on individuals but on householders and families. Obviously, sound families would create a sound nation. Therefore, targets should take into account the interests of families to stabilize the present and the interests of their children to prepare the future.

The evolution of the standards, culture, way of life from a generation to another should be closely observed and analyzed in a way that would keep the concept of "family" alive to be used as the main mechanism to ensure the sound evolution of the nation. Indeed, when setting targets, we should keep in mind that we are serving families and households and not individuals (Willis, 1987).

Moreover, to shape the future of the nation and raise the standards of living, public policies should focus on kids and provide them with a stable and peaceful environment to grow and, in their turn, build stable families and households while improving their situation.

With a bit of hindsight, people from middle-class families can easily recognize that their standard of living is far superior to that of their parents. They generally benefit from better education, broader economic opportunities, and improved living conditions. The real challenge, however, lies in generalizing this experience: ensuring that each new generation feels that they enjoy a better situation than the previous one and that they can continue to improve their own circumstances while providing their children with the same opportunities.

All in all, the targeted national level represents the benchmark that public policies aim to achieve. It is an estimated value of progress that reflects the desired improvement compared to the current situation, defined as the national standard level. While the national standard level describes the existing conditions and performance of a nation across different dimensions, the targeted national level sets the forward-looking objectives that guide policy action and resource allocation toward achieving higher standards of equity, well-being, and development. These targets encompass both median values, which capture the central position of the population, and gaps, which measure disparities across different socio-economic groups.

The Lifts Mechanisms

A *lift mechanism* refers to an institutional, economic, or social component within a national system that enables individuals to improve their circumstances and elevate their standard of living. It can be implemented by the government or by any actor pursuing the public good. While it is designed to be universally accessible, the extent and pace of each person's progress depend on their own motivation, effort, and capacity to evolve.

Indeed, the lifts mechanisms is a combination of opportunities accessible to people to upgrade individually and conceived for the nation to achieve the targeted national standards as defined earlier.

Lifts mechanisms can be implemented and encouraged through different public policies. Indeed, governments undertake the role of implementing policies that facilitate the evolution of people and at the same time encourage third parties such as non-governmental organizations to contribute to the efforts of helping people and making them evolve.

Therefore, there are two categories of lifts mechanisms that need to be implemented. First, there are direct lifts mechanisms that help people directly through a myriad of instruments and supporting tools. Second, there are indirect lifts mechanism that help all the third parties that want to contribute to the national efforts through incentives and supporting mechanisms.

It is worth noting that more than simple instruments and supporting tools to the nation and its underlying communities, the lifts mechanisms are designed to match a vision that is clear and that can achieve the targeted national standard in a more efficient way.

Finally, throughout time, lifts mechanisms can become obsolete and outdated with a very limited impact on the nation. Therefore, conceiving and implementing lifts mechanisms is not a one-time job. Obviously, the efficiency and the relevance of these lifts mechanisms must be assessed regularly based on their capacity to reach all the members of the nation and to help them improve their situation while minimizing the cost of such a mechanism.

When lift mechanisms fail to reach all members of society, lose their capacity to create meaningful impact in people's lives, or become excessively costly, policymakers must recognize that such mechanisms are not meant to be permanent. They should evolve, adapt, or be replaced by more effective and inclusive alternatives capable of restoring upward mobility and societal progress.

Examples of lifts mechanisms abound. For instance, the free access to education, either through a highly performant and inclusive public education system or through a system of subsidies to the private education sector, is a very interesting lift mechanism provided that it helps people acquiring the necessary skills to be productive and generate an income.

The Nets Mechanisms

A net mechanism refers to a component of a system that would help people maintain and safeguard their situation in the face of life's hazards. As per lifts mechanisms, this component can be implemented by the government or any other party that serves the common interest of the nation. Nevertheless, unlike Lifts Mechanisms, the access is given exclusively to people facing life's hazards.

In practice, Nets Mechanisms is a combination of systems and instruments to help people safeguard and maintain their position and situation while leaving no one behind. Such a mechanism reduces the gap between the different clusters and gives a second chance to people who failed.

As per lifts mechanisms, nets mechanisms are implemented and encouraged through different public policies. Governments should implement instruments and tools that assist directly people facing life hazards and in parallel, encourage third parties to contribute to these efforts.

These nets mechanisms are an expression of a clear vision that safeguards and protects the nation's achievements and average level and need to be regularly updated in order to maintain their efficiency and effectiveness and enable them to play fully their role.

Nets mechanisms should not take the exclusive form of financial subsidies and aids. In practice, they can take a variety of forms. For instance, in the education sector, nets mechanisms can serve as a way to provide technical assistance to students who cannot achieve a minimum standard of knowledge and learning with extra lessons of reinforcement or through a dedicated e-learning platform. Moreover, the education system can provide apprenticeship pathways for different technical capabilities and skills that would enable people to be productive and generate income while contributing to the country's economic growth. Indeed, education programs and system should not focus only on highly qualified pathways such as engineering, medical studies, or business schools.

In practice, nets mechanisms should identify all cases where people would be rejected by the system or will not be able to reach certain thresholds in order to support them in an inclusive and efficient manner.

Finally, it is worth noting that nets mechanisms cannot be conceived or implemented separately from lifts mechanics. From a conceptual perspective, they are complementary mechanisms to an interesting national average level. Lifts mechanisms support people to achieve more growth and prosperity while nets mechanisms support those who fail to do so in order to safeguard the homogeneity of the nation.

The Public Policies Component

Apart from the national standards (the actual and the targeted) that constitute the main objectives of this framework, public policies are the impact vehicle and the contagion mechanism in a nation that can change the life of people. Most of the time, when talking about reducing gaps in any governmental program, the main focus is on economic indicators. Nevertheless, and as explained earlier, it is a combination of indicators other than those related to the economic situation that should be improved.

For instance, education public policies should adopt the right mechanisms and approaches in order to provide people with appropriate education backgrounds depending on their vocations and talents while not leaving anyone behind. Education can be used as a lift to change people's life. It can be considered as a net that provides people with the minimum of knowledge to be productive and have a decent income.

The same reasoning can be applied to other sectors and public policies such as housing, health, and transportation. Indeed, economic and social inclusion does not rely only on financial indicators and instruments such as subsidies and free services. It is about connecting people to real economic opportunities and providing them with the necessary tools to improve their situation by themselves.

For example, a government can reduce taxes and provide people with subsidies but the positive impact of these mechanisms can be easily offset by failing public policies. A household that receives monthly a subsidy of 30 USD per kid has to pay more than 100 USD per month in private schools because of the failure of the public education system. A family would prefer to not receive any subsidies but to have their kids in highly qualified and free public schools.

Therefore, there are two main considerations related to the role of the public policies component in the Lifts and Nets Framework. First, all the public policies are concerned with the middle-class nation target and it should not be limited exclusively to economic indicators. Secondly, a particular attention must be paid to the combined effects of public policies. In certain cases, the positive impacts of a public policy can be easily offset by a failing public policy that did not take into account the middle-class nation target.

The Lifts and Nets Methodology

The General Framework of the Lifts and Nets Methodology

The main target of the Lifts and Nets approach is to reinforce the middle-class feature of the nation. Therefore, all the public policies are concerned by this approach whether directly or indirectly, individually or collectively. Indeed, the approach is applied at the level of each public policy separately while keeping an eye on the interactions between the different policies.

For a better understanding of the methodology to be applied, here is a concise summary of the steps to take:

Step 1: Define the Scope of the Public Policy Concerned by the Approach

The scope of a public policy covers aspects such as the area of intervention, the beneficiaries, the partners and different stakeholders, the targets to be achieved, the budget or the funding, the power of decision and execution, the power of control and supervision, and the interactions with other public policies.

For instance, a public policy related to housing covers the area of providing people with healthy homes at a convenient cost (rent, purchase). Moreover, the beneficiaries of this public policy are all the citizens and foreigners allowed to purchase houses or to rent them. The partners and different stakeholders are real estate developers, local and regional authorities, real estate registry, tax administration, and many other partners. The power of decision and execution lies with the ministry of housing while the power of control and supervision rests with the parliament.

Finally, there are many interactions with other public policies such as education (to provide kids with education in all the old and new zones), transportation (to provide people with common transportation regardless of how far the new zones are from the economic and commercial centers), tax policy (to reduce the tax cost of real estate transactions), finance policy (to offer appropriate financing rates to people purchasing their own homes while creating sufficient financial vehicles to channel funds into this sector), and security policy (to offer secure and safe neighborhoods for all).

Step 2: Identify the Targeted National Average Level

In a holistic approach, governments shall identify the targeted national average level for the nation on the basis of multiple indicators such as income, education level, housing standards, health, etc. Then, based on that target and while taking into account the interactions with other public policies, governments shall identify the targeted national average level for a certain public policy.

For instance, the targeted national average level consists of a national average income of 1300 USD per month and per household, a house of 75 m^2 costing less than 800 USD per m^2, a score of 440 for the education level according to the Program for International Student Assessment, a life expectancy of 78 years with −10% of people suffering from cancer.

Obviously, other indicators can be added to define and describe accurately the targeted national average level. Based on these targets, when elaborating the housing public policy, it is not only the indicators related to housing that should be taken into account but all the other indicators.

Indeed, providing houses costing less than 800 USD per square meter would require the creation of new urban zones. This will involve the creation first of a dense common transportation network at an affordable cost. Therefore, people with limited income can get access to affordable housing while using common transportation and without the need to buy a car or more. But it is not all, the housing public policy should take into account other aspects such as education and health to achieve the national targets. Thus, the government or/and the local authorities should build schools and hospitals and attract investors and doctors to the new zone in collaboration with the education and health departments. The entity in charge of developing these new zones needs to take into consideration all the other aspects such as education, security, entertainment, health, public transportation while respecting the targeted average level of each indicator and each aspect.

Step 3: Identify the Lifts Mechanisms to Implement

In this step, the government must identify the necessary instruments and tools to upgrade and improve the quality of life of people and this includes people who are above the average. For instance, the government in partnership with the local authorities can build parks that have sports zone and libraries inside. The aim is to raise the level of people and to improve their health condition. Indeed, people of all ages can pick up a book or an e-book, read it, or listen to it while walking in the park.

Moreover, such infrastructure would include snacks, worshipping spaces, and cultural events. This is to raise the awareness and the education levels of people while improving their health through the practice of sports. Therefore, the housing policy should take into account such projects in collaboration with other public policies such as education, environment and health.

It is worth noting that public policies should not be designed or implemented in isolation. They ultimately serve the same people, interests, and overarching goals. Therefore, they must be coordinated to ensure coherence and effectiveness, taking into account all societal clusters—including those above the average.

Indeed, in classic public policies, governments tend to think that rich people are not supposed to get served and that taxes they use to pay is a contribution that has to be exclusively allocated to poor people to reduce the gap.

In practice, these public policies would need to create a certain degree of cohesion in the nation. To do so, rich people need to benefit from the budget and the impact on their daily life should be clearly visible in order to sustain their contributions to the budget. Moreover, these rich clusters are part of the nation and should be integrated in all these approaches.

For instance, if the targeted national average for housing is set at 800 USD per square meter, this benchmark should also apply to wealthier groups. While they may own larger homes with bigger surface areas, the base price per square meter should remain roughly the same once luxury-related expenses are excluded. In this sense, public policies should not only focus on lower-income groups but also ensure that upper clusters benefit from fair and balanced measures.

Step 4: Identify Cases Where People are Left Behind or are Facing Life's Hazards

Once the lifts mechanisms are identified and included in the different public policies, the government needs to identify cases where people may be left behind or lose their status and wealth. Then, for each case, the government needs to understand the causes and roots of all the problems leading to such a situation and as well as the consequences.

For instance, individuals who have taken out mortgages to purchase their homes may lose their jobs and sources of income during a severe economic downturn, putting them at risk of losing their homes as well. Such circumstances can contribute to the impoverishment of the population. Similarly, when natural disasters destroy thousands of homes, many people lose both their shelter and financial stability, leading once again to increased poverty. These examples illustrate individuals affected by life's unforeseen hazards. However, there are also those who are left behind from the very beginning, excluded from opportunities before such shocks even occur.

For example, people living in remote or hard-to-reach rural areas often struggle to access essential medical care when needed. Public policies should therefore take their specific circumstances into account. Similarly, in the field of education, students who fail to keep up with the academic curriculum may be expelled from school and left without further learning opportunities. These are examples of individuals who are left behind from the start and whose needs must be addressed through inclusive policy design.

Step 5: Identify the Nets Mechanisms

For people facing different life hazards and those left behind, nets mechanisms need to be conceived and implemented to help them absorb the shocks, reduce their impacts, and gradually benefit from the lifts mechanisms to upgrade and improve their situation.

If elaborating nets mechanisms to leave no one behind is mainly oriented to poor people, elaborating nets mechanisms to assist and support people who are facing life hazards is oriented to the other clusters and segments of the population including rich people. Therefore, as per lifts mechanisms, nets mechanisms are also oriented to all the different clusters of the nation.

From another perspective, nets mechanisms are not necessarily expensive and costly. There is always a different way to do things with better outputs and results. Indeed, embracing new technologies may be very rewarding to solve basic problems. For instance, Distributed Ledger technologies can provide an effective solution for school wastage through a platform that can record the number of hours of presence at school before granting tokens to be converted to local currencies.

It is worth noting that both Lifts and Nets Mechanisms need to serve all the segments of the nation and in all the circumstances.

Step 6: Define the Interactions with Other Public Policies

As mentioned earlier, public policies should not be designed or implemented in isolation from one another. In most cases, there are strong interconnections among the various mechanisms, tools, and instruments promoted by each policy area. For example, the quality of life does not depend solely on the availability of high-standard housing at affordable prices; it also encompasses factors such as safety, the quality of nearby schools, access to healthcare, air quality, and the presence of parks and green spaces.

Therefore, strong interactions exist among different public policies, all of which should work toward the same overarching objectives. The benefits generated by one policy should not be undermined by the drawbacks of another. For example, efforts to develop new urban areas on the outskirts of cities—in partnership with real estate developers to provide more affordable housing—can be easily offset by the lack of public transportation, local economic opportunities, and leisure facilities. As a result, residents may be forced to purchase one or more cars to commute to the city, where most economic activities remain concentrated.

Indeed, gaps or inconsistencies in public policies often compel individuals to compensate for what the system fails to provide. In such cases, the intended target groups may not receive the expected benefits, leading to two possible scenarios. In the first scenario, the policy and its associated projects fail entirely, and none of the intended beneficiaries are effectively served. In the second scenario, other population segments—different from those initially targeted—end up benefiting from the policy, resulting in a misallocation of resources and a deviation from the original objectives.

Clearly, the interactions among different public policies should produce positive outcomes for citizens. However, when gaps remain unaddressed, individuals are often forced to bear the resulting costs themselves. In such situations, public trust and participation may decline, leading people to disengage from governmental initiatives and projects.

Step 7: Adjust the Lifts and Nets Mechanisms Accordingly
Understanding the interactions with the other public policies would have an impact on the Lifts and Nets Mechanisms to be implemented. First, they may be some common mechanisms to be relied on in the different public policies. Second, some Lifts and Nets Mechanisms can complement existing mechanisms and then they would either cost less or achieve more impact for the community.

For example, the national security public policy has already implemented a mechanism for issuing identity cards to children as soon as they are born. Such an instrument can be used to combat school wastage in a more effective way. In some rural areas, parents send their children to school just to get the subsidies. Once cash is collected, they bring them back to work. In some countries, they implemented a Distributed Ledger technology-based platform connected with an application used by teachers and schools to clock ID cards at the start and end of each session. Once, the kid reaches a threshold of minimum hours of presence, tokens are generated for both the school and the parents. These tokens can be converted to the local currency.

As per this example, the absence of identity documents for children would have made this project ineffective. Therefore, it is important to understand the tools and instruments already implemented to build additional mechanisms or at least to check the feasibility of the mechanisms to implement.

The Book Approach and Chapters

The book addresses the issue of creating middle-class nations based on the Lifts and Nets Mechanisms. It is divided into four parts. Each part is constituted of two to three chapters.

PART 1: The Lifts and Nets Framework for Middle-Class Nations
The first part is focusing on the main concepts and frameworks promoted by the book mainly the concept of middle-class nations and the Lifts and Nets Mechanisms. This part is composed of two chapters. The first chapter tries to define accurately the concepts related to middle-class nations such as homogeneity/heterogeneity and diversity.

Moreover, the first chapter seeks to identify the defining features of middle-class nations in terms of political stability, social security, and economic attractiveness. In this regard, building middle-class nations can be viewed not only as an ultimate goal but also as an effective pathway toward sustainable and inclusive growth. Indeed, societies with a strong and broad middle class are generally easier to serve, as their needs are more homogeneous, and public policies become simpler to design, coordinate, and implement.

The second chapter of the book presents the Lifts and Nets Mechanisms general framework while defining its major components and concepts such as the national standard level, the targeted national standard level, the lifts mechanisms and the nets mechanisms. It also presents the methodology to adopt when implementing the Lifts and Nets Mechanisms in a particular context and the different steps leading to it.

The second chapter of this first part presents also the methodology adopted and the remaining parts and chapters of this book as well as the links between them. It is worth noting that for simplification purposes, the remaining chapters are divided into three parts covering the social sphere, the economic sphere, and the political sphere. In practice, the boundaries between these spheres when implementing the Lifts and Nets Mechanisms are very thin.

PART 2: The Lifts and Nets Framework in the Social Sphere

The second part of the book is focusing on the social sphere but without isolating it from the other spheres and perspectives. Whenever there are interactions with the other fields and spheres, they are included. Such an approach would help us to draw a general scheme in an easier way.

In the social sphere, the book focuses on the main areas providing welfare to people that are education, housing, and transportation as well as health.

The third chapter of this book would be addressing the education public policies and how they can contribute to building a middle-class nation while implementing Lifts and Nets Mechanisms. The chapter also defines the interactions with other public policies and highlights the necessity to have an ongoing process of updating and upgrading the framework and the different policies related to education since it is a central point in the global strategy.

Moreover, in the book's approach, education is considered as a way to build a middle-class nation in terms of knowledge, practices, and awareness toward the major issues and challenges facing the different components and clusters of the nation. Education provides the nation with the necessary capabilities to shape its future and safeguard its interests and the interests of the next generations.

The fourth chapter of this book addresses housing and transportation policies. Within the general framework, housing is considered the second most critical factor in building a middle-class nation. From this perspective, it is always possible to provide citizens with high-standard housing at affordable prices by strategically adjusting and managing the various price-determining factors. However, for such an approach to be effective and sustainable, it must be supported by complementary public transportation policies that ensure accessibility, connectivity, and spatial equity.

It is worth noting that housing policy interacts closely with many other public policies—not only to achieve its own objectives but also to ensure that progress in the housing sector is not inadvertently undermined by the unintended consequences of other policy areas.

The fifth chapter examines public health policy from multiple perspectives, encompassing both physical and mental health dimensions. It goes beyond the curative approach—addressing issues such as access to healthcare, inclusion in national insurance schemes, and medical infrastructure—to emphasize the preventive dimension. This includes leveraging technology, promoting healthy lifestyles, and fostering a positive collective mindset in which individuals share the belief that tomorrow can be better than today.

From this perspective, the impact of health policies on building a strong middle-class nation is evident, as preventive approaches not only save lives but also do so at a lower cost. Consequently, effective coordination with other public policies—such as education, housing, employment, and social protection—is essential to achieve sustainable and inclusive health outcomes.

PART 3: The Lifts and Nets Framework in the Economic Sphere
The third part of the book is focusing on the economic perspective while shedding light on mechanisms that can promote the Lifts and Nets approach in the economy. Unlike the second part that addresses the fields related to social public policies, this part discusses the mechanisms that can impact the structure of the economy in a way that creates lifts for people to upgrade and improve their economic situation and implements nets to protect their wealth and assets and then maintain their welfare.

The sixth chapter covers the issue related to the social cost on economies. Indeed, there is no need to demonstrate the impact of failing public policies on the economic growth and prosperity. For instance, an underperforming health sector can lead to economic downturns especially in the case of pandemics. A failing education policy can have long-term impact on the capacity of the nation to shape its own future and reinforce its capabilities.

In addition to this, this chapter addresses the impact of failing public policies on the competitiveness of businesses particularly. Starting the analysis from an individual perspective, people tend to fill the gaps of public policies and this has a cost. For instance, a family can enroll the kids in private schools if the public school is not performing well. Moreover, a family would have to buy more than one car to ensure the mobility of its members if the public transportation is not available or is not secure enough.

Indeed, at an individual level, living in a country with failing public policies can be costly, as citizens are forced to cover gaps themselves. This situation can lead to two scenarios. In the first, people demand higher wages to compensate for the deficiencies in public provision. They require additional financial resources to cover expenses such as their children's education, healthcare, security, and other essential services that the government has failed to provide adequately.

The second scenario is that people would be less productive and unhappy in their jobs because of the frustration they have and the things they need to handle in their daily life. In some cases, people would put the blame on their employers that do not cover all their financial needs.

These two scenarios are not necessarily independent. Citizens may become less productive while simultaneously demanding higher wages to compensate for gaps in public services. Even with increased income, maintaining a higher standard of living in the absence of effective public policies often requires more resources than in countries with well-functioning systems. Consequently, this creates a vicious cycle of reduced productivity and economic underperformance, where both individual and national well-being are undermined.

Actually, this chapter shows that failing public policies in the social fields have a very big impact on the economy and on the competitiveness of businesses that would need to deal with an increasing level of wages and a decreasing level of productivity at a national level.

The seventh chapter examines modern financial systems built on the principle of risk transfer. Under this model, fund providers are largely insulated from risk, while those utilizing the funds are expected to generate sufficient returns to cover both principal and profit. If the investments fail to yield the anticipated returns, the borrowers or fund users bear the resulting losses themselves.

Such a principle would help reducing the agency conflicts between the fundraisers and the lenders. Nevertheless, in the long run, this principle would lead to a transfer of wealth from failing fundraisers to lenders who are always protected even during the worst economic downturns.

Indeed, a financial system or economy based on the principle of risk transferring can easily offset all the other efforts made by the social public policies to reduce the gap between the different clusters and create a middle-class nation.

Therefore, this chapter sheds the light on the financial mechanisms based on the principle of risk transferring to replace them with a risk-sharing economy where profits and losses are shared between the different components. In this case, the financial system would be perceived as a neutral vehicle that connects fundraisers and fund providers but does not have any impact on transferring wealth from a segment to another in a way that widens the gap between them.

Moreover, a risk-sharing economy is also a wealth sharing economy where economic inclusion is the main principle governing all the economic public policies. Indeed, the lifts mechanisms consist of connecting people to real economic opportunities while providing them with social services that would reduce the social cost and improve the overall productivity of the nation. The nets mechanisms consist of providing people with the technical assistance and the necessary financial support to people who could not maintain their position.

Finally, this third part would give real life examples in a very simple and straightforward approach to fully understand the economic mechanisms to introduce in the different public policies to create middle-class nations.

PART 4: The Lifts and Nets Framework in the Political Sphere

The fourth part of the book explores the political dimensions of the Lifts and Nets Framework, focusing on how governance structures must be adapted to enhance the effectiveness and efficiency of public policies in the pursuit of a middle-class nation.

The eighth chapter specifically examines the governance system required to implement the Lifts and Nets mechanisms without constraints or limitations. It also identifies the essential prerequisites for ensuring that public policies operate effectively and efficiently within the context of middle-class nation-building.

It is important to recognize that implementing the Lifts and Nets mechanisms may encounter resistance from individuals who are invested in maintaining the status quo or protecting their own interests. In such cases, public policies based on this framework may become less effective and less efficient. Consequently, addressing governance structures and fostering a positive culture and mindset are essential prerequisites to ensure that the framework delivers meaningful and sustainable outcomes.

The final chapter discusses the impact of creating middle-class nations on the political stability and on the fluidity of transition toward new models and schemes. The chapter also addresses the issue of maintaining the middle-class feature of a nation throughout time in spite of the new factors and disruptions affecting the society, the economy, and the governance.

Conclusion of the Chapter

Building a middle-class nation seems to be a very relevant target for countries that want to create a competitive advantage and emerge as a new power. Nevertheless, the processes of achieving such a target can give rise to several debates in terms of methodologies and implementation frameworks.

This chapter put forward two major principles governing the methodology and processes related to building a middle-class nation. The first principle consists of implementing in each public policy the lifts mechanisms that support people in their quest of improving their life in its various facets as well as nets mechanisms that maintain their position and situation.

The second principle is related to the combination of the different public policies when adopting the Lifts and Nets mechanisms. Indeed, those in charge of elaborating the different public policies need to pay attention to the combined effect of the instruments and tools implemented so that the positive impact would not be offset by a failing policy or instrument.

Now that the general framework and the implementation methodology are defined, the next parts and chapters of the book would discuss in details the different aspects and elements to make the whole approach clearer and more accurate. Indeed, the implementation framework would be discussed from different angles such as the social perspective, the economic dimension, and the political sphere.

The analysis would cover public policies, economic models, and governance systems to ensure the effectiveness and the efficiency of the different instruments and tools implemented based on the Lifts and Nets Framework while not forgetting the ultimate objective of such an approach that is to build and maintain middle-class nations.

References

Anderson, M., Dobkin, C., & Gross, T. (2012). The effect of health insurance coverage on the use of medical services. *American Economic Journal: Economic Policy, 4*(1), 1–27.

Mahembe, E., & Odhiambo, N. M. (2018). The dynamics of extreme poverty in developing countries. *Studia Universitatis "Vasile Goldis" Arad–Economics Series, 28*(2), 18–35.

McAneney, J., McAneney, D., Musulin, R., Walker, G., & Crompton, R. (2016). Government-sponsored natural disaster insurance pools: A view from down-under. *International Journal of Disaster Risk Reduction, 15*, 1–9.

Preston, J., Brown, F. W., & Hartley, B. (1992). Using telemedicine to improve health care in distant areas. *Psychiatric Services, 43*(1), 25–32.

Van der Veken, K., Lauwerier, E., & Willems, S. J. (2020). How community sport programs may improve the health of vulnerable population groups: A program theory. *International Journal for Equity in Health, 19*, 1–12.

Willis, R. J. (1987). What have we learned from the economics of the family? *The American Economic Review, 77*(2), 68–81.

World Bank. (2004). *Mind, heart and soul in the fight against poverty*. The World Bank.

PART II

The Lifts and Nets Framework in the Social Sphere

CHAPTER 3

Lifts and Nets Mechanisms Applied to Education

Introduction of the Chapter

As discussed earlier in the previous chapters, the middle-class nation concept is not linked directly and exclusively to economic indicators. Indeed, a fairly homogeneous nation does not rely only on indicators such as the average income or the GDP per capita, it is a combination of indicators covering different areas creating a certain degree of homogeneity inside a defined nation.

Therefore, the Lifts and Nets mechanisms framework should be applied to different spheres and improve all the relevant indicators starting with the social sphere that has so many interactions with all the other areas. Indeed, as social public policies can have an impact on the economic and political public policies, the latter can also have an important impact on the social public policies.

Obviously, one of—if not—the most important social sector(s) that can be impacted by economic indicators and political trends and at the same time, can impact positively or negatively these indicators and trends is the education sector.

Education is a cross-cutting sector that enables a nation to build its capabilities and strengthen collective awareness. It can serve as a key source of competitive advantage by attracting foreign investment and fostering human capital. Through education, nations cultivate

A. Tahiri Jouti, *Building Middle Class Nations*,
https://doi.org/10.1007/978-3-032-02134-2_3

entrepreneurs, engineers, doctors, and a wide range of emerging professionals who together shape the nation's future and drive sustainable development.

Moreover, education improves people's sense of responsibility toward their countries (Astin, 1998), communities, families, and religions. It creates people who are aware of the challenges and issues facing them and provide them with the necessary tools and instruments to contribute effectively to the collective efforts.

This chapter explores the key mechanisms to be implemented in the education sector within the framework of the Lifts and Nets approach, aiming to strengthen the fair homogeneity of a nation. It addresses universal education issues such as ensuring access to appropriate schooling and lifelong learning opportunities for all, as well as guaranteeing quality education where no one is left behind in acquiring the skills and capabilities necessary to contribute to the nation's advancement.

Finally, it is worth noting that raising and harmonizing education levels across a nation is one of the most powerful factors in narrowing disparities between different social clusters. When educational attainment becomes broadly shared, many other divides—particularly economic ones—tend to diminish or even become less visible.

Education Sector and Its Major Issues

The General Framework of Issues Related to the Education Sector

To illustrate the structural disparities that characterize education systems in middle-income countries compared to high-income countries, the table below presents a comparative snapshot of key indicators related to educational attainment, out-of-school rates, and the legal guarantees of free and compulsory schooling. These metrics provide an empirical foundation to assess how effectively each system supports access, progression, and excellence. They also help reveal the extent to which education functions as a "lift" for the majority of the population—or, conversely, reinforces elitism and social segmentation (Table 3.1).

The data confirms significant differences between middle-income and high-income countries in terms of higher-education attainment. The share of adults completing a Master's degree remains extremely low in Egypt (0.38%), Tunisia (3.82%), and Jordan (2.43%), compared with much higher levels in Sweden (16.97%), Switzerland (19.13%), and Türkiye

Table 3.1 Education indicators between middle-class and high-income countries (*Source* UNESCO Institute for Statistics[1])

	Middle income countries			*High income countries*		
	Tunisia	*Egypt*	*Jordan*	*Sweden*	*Switzerland*	*Turkiye*
Educational attainment rate, completed doctoral or equivalent education, population 25+ (%)	0,86 (2019)	0,36 (2017)	1,44 (2023)	2,38 (2023)	4,09 (2024)	3,01 (2023)
Educational attainment rate, completed master's or equivalent education, population 25+ (%)	3,82 (2019)	0,38 (2023)	2,43 (2023)	16,97 (2023)	19,13 (2024)	15,83 (2023)
Out-of-school rate for children and adolescents of primary and lower-secondary school age, both sexes (%)	Not available	4,48 (2024)	1,92 (2023)	0,4 (2023)	0,04 (2023)	0,18 (2022)
Number of years of free primary and secondary education guaranteed in legal frameworks	11	12	12	12	13	12
Number of years of compulsory primary and secondary education guaranteed in legal frameworks	9	12	10	9	10	12

(15.83%). The pattern is even more pronounced at the doctoral level, where middle-income countries remain below 1.5%, while Switzerland surpasses 4%. Such disparities indicate a limited capacity in middle-income systems to nurture advanced human capital, thereby restricting social mobility and reinforcing the divide between an intellectual elite and the rest of the population. Out-of-school rates further reflect structural challenges: while high-income countries approach universal access, Egypt still faces a non-negligible 4.48% out-of-school rate, signaling persistent issues in ensuring continuity and completion of primary and lower-secondary education.

[1] UNESCO Institute for Statistics. (n.d.). *UIS Data Browser—SDG 4 monitoring (Indicator 4.5.1).* Retrieved [Month Day, Year], from https://databrowser.uis.unesco.org/browser/EDUCATION/UIS-SDG4Monitoring/t4.5/i.4.5.1.

Although the legal frameworks guaranteeing free and compulsory education appear broadly similar across the two groups, the outcomes diverge sharply. Tunisia, Egypt, and Jordan legally guarantee between 9 and 12 years of free or compulsory schooling—comparable to Sweden, Switzerland, and Türkiye—yet the educational results differ substantially. This demonstrates that legal guarantees alone are insufficient without robust governance, adequate financing, and high-quality school environments.

Therefore, the education system needs to be conceived in a way that reduces the gaps between the different components of the nation and gives more than just a second chance to those who cannot be part of the elite people.

From another perspective, when observing and analyzing the outputs of the education sector in developing countries, two major findings arise. First, in these countries, despite the education sector's issues, there is an elite that stands out and is comparable to the elites of developed countries that have better education systems (Speciale, 2007).

In developing countries, education systems are more appropriate for two elite categories, the intellectual elite and the economic elite for countries that have private education sector (Doherty & Pozzi, 2017). Indeed, in terms of content, structure, and pathways, public education is more adapted to talented people that have enough capabilities and willingness to achieve higher results. These people constitute the intellectual elite and all the other people are left behind with few appropriate pathways or would select domains and fields that are not really inspiring them.

The economic elite is constituted of people who do not have the necessary capabilities to achieve higher results in public education but have the necessary financial resources to enroll in private education institutions that generally provide better conditions and assistance to those who are not part of the intellectual elite.

Second, if a person is not part of the intellectual or the economic elites, they are left behind in a way that would limit their professional and personal horizons and would not let them fully exploit their potential (Heleta & Magus, 2021). Moreover, some people would be rejected by the public education system and in the absence of the necessary financial resources, they would have no promising future.

Hence, the problem of the education sector in most of the developing countries is not related only to the contents delivered but to the fact that the system creates a gap in the society between the elite and those who are left behind. Consequently, the education sector public policies need to contribute to the efforts of creating and reinforcing the middle-class nation philosophy and not the opposite.

From this perspective, the following scheme summarizes the issues related to the education sector that limit its contribution to build a middle-class nation (Fig. 3.1).

The figure shows that due to the different issues in the education system, there are three categories of people. First, people with no educational background because they did not have access to schools or to any other educational alternative (Access issues), or they had to leave school since they could not keep up with the existing educational program (reinforcement and accompaniment issues) and when leaving, they had no alternative pathways.

The second category consists of individuals who are unable to achieve the results required to enter elite universities or programs in business, engineering, law, medicine, and other prestigious fields. Typically, alternative branches or programs are available for those who do not gain access to these elite pathways. This situation generates two significant gaps. First, there is a gap in final outputs between graduates of these alternative programs and those from prestigious institutions, reflecting differences in knowledge, skills, and opportunities. Second, there is a gap between

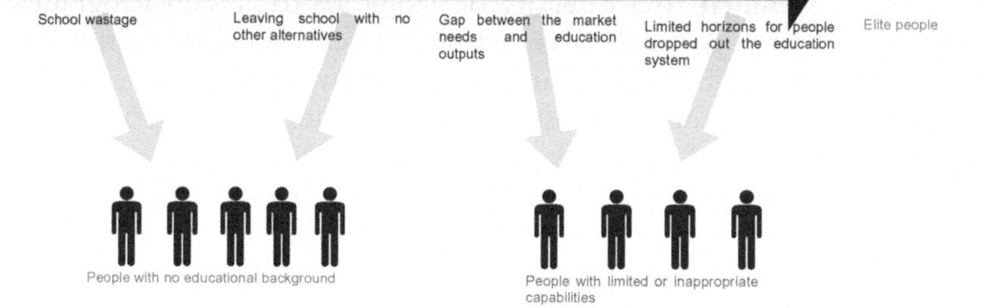

Fig. 3.1 The education outputs and gaps in developing countries

the capabilities of graduates and the actual demands of the labor market, meaning that many individuals may have skills that are either limited or misaligned with market needs, reducing their employability, and potential contribution to national development.

The third category are elite people who had the chance to join elitist education programs and are comparable to elite people in other countries. This category of people has enough opportunities in the labor market and may also be seduced by job offers abroad, leading in some cases to the brain drain.

Moreover, the third category also integrates average people that had the chance to join private sector institutions providing more support and assistance in the different stages of learning until they become part of the elite people.

Indeed, seen from this perspective, in most cases, private education sector fills two major gaps. First, it expands the capacity of schools and education institutions in terms of number of students. Secondly, it ensures a better follow-up for students and provides better outputs.

The Major Issues Related to Education for a Middle-Class Nation

According to the general scheme related to major issues related to the education sector, there are mainly four main issues: the access to education, the learning difficulties, the absence of alternative pathways, and the elitist learning system.

The Access to Education Issues

The access to education is a universal human right that needs to be provided to everyone and at all ages (Mc Cowan, 2010). Education should not be limited to a category of people or to certain geographic zones or through a particular channel. Moreover, education institutions and channels should be open to anyone and at any time.

In developing countries, most of the education public policies are focusing exclusively on the children's access to education; thus, ignoring the needs of the other age groups of the population including those who were out-of-school in the absence of alternative pathways. Therefore, this part will address the access issues of children separately from those of other age groups.

Generally, children may have no access to education for different reasons:

– A Limited Geographic Coverage

In many rural areas, educational infrastructure is incomplete, with limited availability of primary schools, middle schools, and high schools. In some cases, children must walk tens of kilometers each day to reach schools that often lack basic conveniences such as proper food, climate control (e.g., heating or air conditioning depending on the weather), and safety measures. Beyond these basic deficiencies, the quality of pedagogy and the availability of technical materials required for effective education are often insufficient, further limiting students' learning opportunities (Vasconcellos, 1997).

Most of the education public policies consist of building schools in rural areas with basic equipments and no regular maintenance. Indeed, the limited geographic coverage of education institutions also limit the access of children to appropriate education (Balsamo, 2000).

In some cases, primary schools are available locally, but higher-education institutions, such as high schools, are absent. Consequently, children of younger ages must relocate to other villages, living far from their parents and siblings. Families are often required to provide financial support for their children studying in distant regions, while schools are expected to offer mental health support to help young students cope with the challenges of being separated from their families.

From a high-level perspective, when schools are built in rural areas, children often leave their villages to attend universities in cities. Subsequently, many of them work and settle in these urban areas. Therefore, even if rural schools provide full access and high-quality education to all children, in a decade or two, these schools may become underutilized if there is no corresponding job creation in the villages, leading to gradual depopulation (Mensah et al., 2016).

Therefore, the advantage of this approach is that migration from rural areas to cities would be smoother and easier to manage. However, the downside is that the government would be investing in educational institutions that may no longer be needed after a couple of decades.

– Economic and Social Reasons

Economic Reasons: Boys and girls are also facing common challenges. For instance, they are expected to help the family in economic activities such as farming or cattle breeding. In this case, schooling and education become accessory. From another perspective, advanced schooling would mean that children may leave the village and the family would have no free labor. Moreover, the family would need to support their kids financially during all the schooling process.

Safety Issues: In addition, when schools are located in another village, safety concerns arise for both boys and girls during their daily commute. As a result, families may decide to keep their children at home to ensure their safety, rather than risk the hazards of traveling long distances to school (Oluyomi, 2014).

From another perspective, access to appropriate education is equally essential at later stages of life for several reasons—such as the need to advance in one's career, to transition into a new field, or simply to pursue personal growth and self-improvement. Lifelong learning opportunities enable individuals to adjust and upgrade their socio-economic situation, particularly for those who were not fortunate enough to benefit from quality education during childhood (Ritt, 2008).

For older people, the limitations regarding their access to education can be summarized as follows:

- *Education Policies Focusing on Younger Population*: In general, education public policies are focusing more on younger people to provide them with the necessary access and the appropriate skills and education they need in their life. Older people who did not have the chance to get access to schooling are not part of the policy.
- *Absence of Bridges*: Even those who had the chance when they were children to get appropriate schooling, when they have a conversion plan to move to another field or sector, they do not find bridges in universities or in the technical training institutions to develop their capabilities.

Such mechanisms are very important to implement since the only available and necessary skill in the next century and decades is fast learning and the capacity to learn different and new things at any age (Redecker, 2010). Public policies in the education sector should consider the access issue for all the age groups of the nation and not focus only on children.

The Issues Related to Learning Difficulties

Providing access to education for all age groups and at any time is an essential first step, but it is not sufficient on its own. Indeed, individuals who have the opportunity to access educational institutions must also remain engaged in the learning process and complete their training programs in order to fully achieve the intended objectives.

In practice, learning difficulties may be related to the learning process itself or to the limited capabilities of people as they could be related to other factors such as economic downturn, deep changes in the social situation or any other factor. These factors are impacting children but also older people in their capacity to go through all the education program and obtain their diploma.

- *Learning Difficulties Related to the Learning Process Itself*: As discussed earlier in this chapter, in less effective education systems, programs and curricula are more adapted to elite people while average people are left behind especially when it comes to subjects such as STEM (Science, Technology, Energy, and Mathematics). Generally, the curricula do not take into account the different understanding levels of people to deal with the variety of subjects and do not integrate any support and reinforcement mechanisms to accompany people who are not comfortable with the process (Weedon, 2018).

In less effective education systems, children are exposed to a variety of subjects as a way to test their interests and hobbies. If they are comfortable with STEM subjects, for example, they may select a pathway where they can specialize in one of these subjects. Otherwise, they need to select another pathway.

This approach is fundamentally unfair and flawed for two main reasons. First, a child's dislike for a particular subject may stem not from the subject matter itself, but from the teacher's inadequacy whether due to poor pedagogical skills, lack of motivation, or negative behavior toward students. Second, for children and young learners, exposure to a broad range of subjects should not merely serve as a means of identifying individual interests, but rather as an essential foundation for acquiring basic knowledge across multiple domains. Therefore, the educational approach should be complemented by support and reinforcement mechanisms to guarantee that all students develop the minimum required competencies and capabilities.

In the first approach, people who are not good at school would need to leave the school. Even, redoing the year only serves to expose the student to the same level of difficulty and incomprehension without adapting the learning approach to them. Therefore, the chances to bring them back on the learning track are very low in this case.

- *Economic Downturns*: this factor can impact the learning process of people at all ages (Jordan et al., 2008). In rural areas, for example, lucky children who have the access to education because the school is not far, their families have enough financial resources to encourage their members to get to school and they have no difficulties regarding the learning process may at any time be the victims of an economic downturn where they need to leave the school and be part of the family workforce.

Moreover, talented students at later stages (high school and universities) may select a less interesting and rewarding branch because it requires fewer years and then provides them with a salary as quickly as possible.

- *Deep Changes in the Social Situation*: a death, a divorce, or any other family event can lead to an economic downturn. For instance, a father's death means that part—if not all—of the family income and revenue would disappear. Nevertheless, changes in the social situation can have no impact on the economic capacity of the family but can have a negative impact on the mental health of the family members (Table 3.2).

A divorce can have very bad consequences on the learning journey of children with feeling of dissatisfaction, unsafety, and loss of confidence. Such events can lead to learning difficulties even for talented students (Anthony et al., 2014). Indeed, the stability of the mental health of children is very important to ensure an enjoyable learning journey and experience for all.

The table highlights a major weakness in middle-income countries: many homes, especially in Morocco and to a lesser extent Egypt, do not provide sufficiently positive or stimulating early learning environments for

Table 3.2 Education indicators between middle-class and high-income countries; Source: UNESCO Institute for Statistics[2]

	Middle income countries			*High income countries*		
	Morocco	*Egypt*	*Jordan*	*United States*	*South Africa*	*Turkiye*
Percentage of children under 5 years experiencing positive and stimulating home learning environments, both sexes (%)	36,20 (2018)	73,40 (2018)	91,60 (2018)	N.A	N.A	N.A
Existence of funding mechanisms to reallocate education resources to disadvantaged populations	No	No	N.A	Yes	Yes	No

young children. Such early disadvantages accumulate over time, shaping weaker foundational skills and widening learning gaps as children progress through school. Combined with the absence of targeted funding mechanisms for disadvantaged groups, these early home-based inequalities risk solidifying long-term educational inequities across society.

The Absence of Alternative Pathways

Generally, in the education systems of developing countries, apart from the elitist education programs such as business schools, law schools, engineering schools, and medical schools, the other alternatives are absent or weak.

- *Absence of Sufficient Alternative Pathways*: for students dropped out the education programs for all the reasons mentioned above (Pharo, 2012), there are no sufficient alternative pathways that can provide

[2] UNESCO Institute for Statistics. (n.d.). *UIS Data Browser—SDG 4 monitoring (Indicator 4.5.1)*. Retrieved [Month Day, Year], from https://databrowser.uis.unesco.org/browser/EDUCATION/UIS-SDG4Monitoring/t4.5/i.4.5.1.

them with a better future. Indeed, the education system does not cover all the technical trainings needed to practice professions such as plumbing, carpentry, electrician, and so on. Most of the time, for these professions to be practiced in these countries, you just need to join a practician and learn from him. It is worth noting that the practician himself learnt by practicing and does not necessarily have diplomas in the field.

In this context, such professions are underpaid compared to developed countries where practitioners have appropriate trainings. This situation leads automatically to significant gaps in terms of income between elite people and people that have no alternative pathways.

Moreover, such professions are not considered noble like those practiced by elite people for two main reasons. First, they are underpaid, and secondly, they do not require any specific trainings which throw people with these professions at the bottom of the pyramid.

The data shows that upper-secondary completion rates remain significantly lower in middle-income countries, especially Morocco and Jordan, compared with high-income countries like Sweden and Switzerland, where completion exceeds 80–90%. Participation in vocational education also follows this pattern, with middle-income countries enrolling far fewer youth in TVET-Technical and Vocational Education and Training-pathways—often below 12%—while high-income countries have much stronger uptake and more established systems. These gaps suggest that middle-income countries face structural limitations in both retaining students through upper-secondary schooling and offering high-quality, attractive vocational options, which together can restrict young people's transition into skilled employment.

- *Weakness of the Few Existing Pathways*: Apart from the Elitist learning programs which access requires passing the selection exams and procedures, there are other branches that are open to public with no strict prerequisites but have two major issues. First, the training provided in these branches is not always appropriate with the market needs and requirements. Second, the number of graduates is very high and the market cannot absorb all of them.

In this context, graduates from these branches can never compete with elite people and the abundance of graduates would lead to a decrease in the average wage of this category of people. Even if you get a Ph.D. in a specific branch, you would not be considered the same way a graduate from an elitist program would be (Table 3.3).

Moreover, graduates from these branches and specialties may find themselves occupying positions inferior to their degrees because employers would prefer hiring someone who holds a Master degree rather than someone who holds a Bachelor degree with the same wage because of the abundance of graduates and because of the significant gap between the market needs and the outputs of these branches.

Table 3.3 Education indicators between middle-class and high-income countries; Source: UNESCO Institute for Statistics[3]

	Middle income countries			*High income countries*		
	Morocco	*Egypt*	*Jordan*	*Sweden*	*Switzerland*	*Turkiye*
Proportion of 15–24 years olds enrolled in vocational education, both sexes (%)	8,5 (2024)	11,03 (2024)	2,41 (2024)	13,59 (2023)	22,70 (2024)	22,79 (2022)
Completion rate, upper secondary education, both sexes (%)	46,86 (2017)	76,06 (2017)	56,73 (2017)	81,45 (2021)	92,69 (2021)	73,21 (2022)

[3] UNESCO Institute for Statistics. (n.d.). *UIS Data Browser—SDG 4 monitoring (Indicator 4.5.1).* Retrieved [Month Day, Year], from https://databrowser.uis.unesco.org/browser/EDUCATION/UIS-SDG4Monitoring/t4.5/i.4.5.1.

Education: Lifts and Nets Mechanisms

The Consequences of Elitist Educational Systems

An elitist educational system is based on selection and screening during all the stages of the learning journey. It consists of selecting the most talented people to join elitist programs while all the other people do not have alternative pathways or have weak alternatives.

A middle-class nation education system channels talent to different specialties and tries to find the right balance between the needs of the market and people's tendencies. As explained in the first chapter, it is not about moving all the classes and clusters in a nation to a unique cluster but it is more about having the gaps between these clusters narrower.

Analyzing the different issues related to education programs in developing countries gives an exact idea of the way these programs can impact negatively the quest to build and maintain middle-class nations. This part addresses the consequences on society and on the quest to create and maintain middle-class nations.

From what has been discussed earlier in this chapter, there are two major phenomena. First, the reinforcement of a non-middle-class nation and the inflation/deflation of diplomas.

The Reinforcement of a Non-Middle-Class Nation

The reinforcement of a non-middle-class nation through elitist education programs and systems is achieved through two phenomena:

- *Focusing on the Elite People* (Van Zanten, 2009): A nation without elite that would guide people toward a safe future can lead to a chaotic situation. At the same time, focusing exclusively on the elite and leaving behind all those who are not can lead to a worse situation. Indeed, in the education system, the gaps between the elite and the other segments of people should be invisible to make any transition easier to conduct. Indeed, a performant education system is the one that creates learning opportunities for everyone with the same high quality and never leaves someone behind.

Indeed, focusing on the elite people would create three different classes in the nation with significant gaps between them. Therefore, instead of contributing to a fairly homogeneous nation, education can be a source of profound heterogeneity. In such a system, education would be the exclusive lift for both the intellectual and the economic elites.

In this context, education clearly plays the role of a lift mechanism, offering pathways of upward mobility to talented individuals who may come from disadvantaged backgrounds. Through access to quality education, such individuals can transform their life trajectories and contribute significantly to national development. Conversely, for the economic elite, education often acts as a preserving mechanism, maintaining their privileged position through access to prestigious, fee-paying schools and universities. This dual dynamics highlights the importance of designing education policies that balance opportunity and equity—ensuring that education serves not only as a lift for the most capable but also as a net that prevents others from being left behind.

Nevertheless, the large majority of people do not belong either to the intellectual or the economic elites. In this sense, education often functions as a dysfunctional lift—one that fails to elevate the majority and instead keeps them distant from the elite circles. The system tends to be structured around competition rather than cooperation.

- *Noblesse Classification*: In such systems, what matters most is the profession one practices rather than the way it is practiced. People tend to classify certain professions as "noble" and others as less prestigious, which reflects a deep-seated cultural bias. This mindset reinforces social and cultural divides between the different clusters and segments of the nation, undermining cohesion and mutual respect among citizens.

A direct consequence of such a mindset is that individuals are no longer valued for their performance or achievements but rather for the positions they hold or the professions they practice. Respect becomes tied to status instead of merit, which fosters complacency and weakens the culture of accountability. In many ways, this form of social bias is even more damaging than discrimination based on income or economic situation, as it erodes the very foundations of fairness and collective progress.

In reality, professions are merely a means to achieve greater purposes, to serve others and contribute to the well-being of the community, not a way to set oneself apart or seek personal distinction.

The Inflation or Deflation of Diplomas

A labor market cannot stand with only the elite. The outputs of the education system matter a lot to respond to all the needs of the labor market and achieve the expected growth. Otherwise, two phenomena can happen:

- *The Inflation of Diplomas*: it is exactly when the number of graduates from non-elitist schools and universities is very important with a significant gap in terms of expected skills. Therefore, people would be hired for under-sized and underpaid jobs.

Actually, people would need to spend more time at university to occupy the same functions their parents could be hired for with lower wages and diplomas. This is exactly the inflation of diplomas phenomenon and it occurs when the government wants to improve some Key Performance Indicators of the education sector and starts to allow more people to enroll in educational programs without focusing on the quality of the contents and their capacity to meet the labor market expectations.

Therefore, employers would choose to hire people with higher diplomas to occupy inferior jobs with lower wages and train them to upgrade their qualifications and meet their expectations. As a matter of fact, it is a good deal for employers to make graduates bear the cost of the education sector dysfunctions.

- *The Deflation of Diplomas*: This phenomenon occurs when the elitist programs do not produce a sufficient number of graduates. Therefore, some jobs would be attributed to less qualified people promoting incompetence.

In this context, the elite people may choose to boost their careers and move to developed countries to work in inspiring environments with highly ambitious plans. Moreover, multilateral institutions and large supranational organizations may compete to hire the elite people from developed countries and then compete with local employers. Such a situation can lead to the deflation of diplomas.

The Lifts and Nets Mechanisms for a Middle-Class Nation Educational System

The application of the Lifts and Nets Framework to the education sector gives rise to three distinct mechanisms: The Access mechanisms (the lifts), the Reinforcement and support mechanisms (the Nets), and the Alternative pathways (upgrade mechanisms).

The Access Mechanisms (The Lifts)
Education can change the life of people, ensure a stable and sound future for them and for their children. For this purpose, ensuring the free access to education for all is about fairness and equality between the different segments and clusters of the nation.

The public policies related to the access to education should take into account the following elements:

- *Externalizing Education to the Private Sector*: The public education sector often exhibits multiple structural deficiencies. First, strong teacher unions can create a comfort zone that protects staff even when their performance is inadequate. Second, school administrators typically lack autonomy in staffing decisions, as hiring and firing are managed centrally, limiting accountability and responsiveness. Third, public schools are designed to be standardized, with minimal differentiation or competitive mechanisms, which reduces incentives for innovation and excellence. These factors collectively undermine the ability of public education to serve as an effective lift for the broader population.

Therefore, the education department can externalize education to the private sector according to three principles guiding the new governance of the sector:

- *A Government Support for All the Children*: The education department defines the budget per child that the government undertakes to pay to the private sector for each child, rich or poor. Everybody deserves the support of the government for their education even rich families. Such a financial support would create a connection between children and their country.

- *A Classification for Schools*: The education department defines a certain classification for schools based on their performance (for instance, 3 stars, 4 stars, 5 stars). Based on this classification, the cost will differ from a school to another. Therefore, the government financial support covers the cost for 3 stars schools. The gap between the cost (according to the classification) and the education department financial aid would be borne by the parents. This classification requires a follow up and an effective control by the Education department.
- *A National Education Mapping*: The education department would define a national education mapping defining per region the number of establishments, the number of students and the future evolution of the needs. Therefore, any investment in the education sector by the private sector needs to be approved by the education department and based on the national education map.

Indeed, the education department would become a pure regulator and not a player investing in infrastructure to provide education services. This transformation would require a shift in mindsets. Moreover, public schools can be sold to the education private sector or given to them in return for a rent that is deducted from the annual subsidy amount paid per child by the education department.

- *Limiting Foreign Mission Schools to Foreigners*: Initially, these schools were for the foreigners' children settling in the country. They aim at providing the same learnings as in the mother country. For locals, these schools create young people that may be disconnected from their own identity (language, history, culture, etc.) and more connected with the mother country's identity which creates a new cluster in society.

Generally, the access to these schools is very expensive but it facilitates the enrollment in prestigious universities in the mother country.

When there is a high demand from locals for these schools, it is considered as a sign of the national education system failure. To limit the access of local people to the foreign mission schools, it is necessary to implement a performant national education system that can compete with all the international systems and impose a tax for those who still enroll their children to the foreign mission schools.

Two key performance indicators of a national education system are its ability to both support the average student and provide pathways for children to access prestigious universities at later stages. If the system fails to meet either of these requirements, families will increasingly turn to foreign or mission schools, reinforcing the elitist nature of the education system and perpetuating social inequalities.

- *Focusing on the Rural Areas*: In developing countries, the percentage of people living in rural areas is generally high. Therefore, it is necessary to conceive and deploy a specific strategy for rural areas and there are many elements to consider. Indeed, delivering education in rural areas and giving access to all the children means that a high percentage of the next generation of people will move to the city to get suitable opportunities for their education but also for their careers.

Moreover, gradually, the number of children to join the schools in rural areas will decrease throughout time. Hence, it is important to think about the sustainability of the investments to be made in terms of education infrastructure in rural areas. At the same time, having schools in villages will definitely encourage teachers, doctors, and even highly educated young people originally from these villages to settle down with their families and create an economic dynamic in these rural areas.

From another perspective, as the gap between rural and urban areas widens, the complexity of public policy increases. At the same time, education can be considered as part of a global strategy to reduce the gap between rural and urban areas in the nation. For this purpose, here are some hints in order to achieve higher results when it comes to the rural world:

- *Relying on Mobile Schools*: The problem with the education policy in rural areas is that the same solutions are used to solve the same problems with the same sources of funding. Albert Einstein once said that "Insanity is doing the same thing over and over again and expecting different results." Therefore, it is important to try new and different things. For instance, instead of building schools, it is possible to rely on mobile schools that can cover many villages at once. Indeed, instead of children walking to schools, these schools would drive to these children. Therefore, the children of these villages will study alternately in these schools that are moving every week from a village to another. Such a solution can provide kids with more safety (instead of walking everyday to school) and more time to help their parents. The other remaining time, children can get access to digital learning platforms alternating physical and online learning.

In practice, many solutions can be implemented. For instance, a mobile school can spend 3 days per village per week. The children would have 4 days without school but they can have access to digital platforms for homework and complementary content and help their parents as well.

- *Using Technology for Learning*: As mentioned earlier, mobile schools would not spend a whole week in one village or zone. Therefore, digital platforms are necessary to accompany children during days without school. These digital platforms would serve as a basis for complementary explanations and homework as well as for learning through gamification. Moreover, the department of education would encourage home schooling for parents who would prefer this mode of learning provided that the curriculum covers all the national program. Finally, the department of education needs to implement bridges between traditional schooling and home schooling for parents who would like to move from a mode to another.

To ensure the success of this policy, the department of education needs to work with telecom operators to ensure a full internet coverage in the rural areas as well as the distribution of tablets with a free internet connection to digital learning platforms.

- *Using Technology to Solve Access Issues*: Among the most complicated access issues is the school wastage in the rural areas. To solve this issue, governments pay a monthly income to parents to let children go to school. In practice, this solution seems to be ineffective because most of the time, once the parents get the subsidy, they do not let their children go to school anymore. In South Africa, a blockchain-based solution was provided to make the solution more effective and efficient. Children in South Africa have self-sovereign digital identities that are encrypted within an individual's personal data store that is controlled only by them and their parents. The digital data of children including their identity data and their education history are recorded on a ledger. When a child arrives at school and when he leaves school, the teacher uses the mobile application to record the child's attendance. Once the child reaches a certain threshold of attendance, a smart contract generates an impact token that both parents and the school can convert to subsidies from the government.

Indeed, blockchain made the solution of financial support to parents more effective to guarantee that children get access to schooling. Actually, technology can be used to solve access issues and make solutions more effective and more efficient.

For access issues, there are two major elements to consider. First, the significant gap between the different segments (for instance, children in rural areas and children in urban poles) makes it harder to elaborate and implement effective public policies. Once this gap is reduced, public policies would be cost effective. Second element is that technology offers opportunities and solutions that were not available a decade ago. Therefore, opening the door to new entrants and to new business models can be rewarding and cost effective as well.

To measure the advancements in deploying effective access mechanisms in the education sector, here are some indicators to be monitored (Table 3.4):

The Reinforcement and Support Mechanisms (The Nets)

If someone fails at taking advantage of the lifts mechanisms in terms of access or cannot keep up with the learning journey, public policies should implement nets mechanisms that leave no one behind. This part addresses mechanisms to let nobody leave the school. For this purpose, the public policies in the education sector should take into account the following hints and elements:

- *Adopting a Holistic Approach*: This approach consists of providing the necessary support at the whole person that considers their physical, emotional, social, and spiritual well-being (John, 2017). Indeed,

Table 3.4 Main indicators to measure the effectiveness of access mechanisms

Dimension	*Indicator*	*What it measures*
Access and equity	Enrollment rate (rural/urban)	Extent to which children—Especially in rural areas—Access schooling
	Completion rate (primary, lower sec, upper sec—Rural vs. urban)	Whether students finish compulsory stages
	Gender parity index for access (rural and urban)	Equality between boys and girls in access
Public–private governance	Share of students in public vs. private schools	Degree of externalization to private sector
	Government Subsidy per child (actual vs. planned)	Implementation of the "support for all children" model
	% of schools classified (3/4/5 stars)	Progress in introducing the school quality ranking system
System governance	National Education Mapping Coverage (%)	Whether each region has updated mapping of needs and school locations
	Ratio of approved investments aligned with National map	Alignment of private investments with national planning
Mission schools policy	% of local students in foreign Mission schools	Degree to which the national system retains families
	Tax revenue from local Enrollment in Mission schools	Effectiveness of measures discouraging unnecessary foreign-school enrollment
Rural strategy	School availability per 1000 rural children	Infrastructure adequacy in rural areas
	Migration rate of rural youth to urban areas	Indicator of rural opportunities and future population needs
Mobile and digital solutions	Number of Mobile schools deployed	Adoption of flexible education delivery
	Number of villages served by Mobile schools	Reach of alternative rural access solutions
	% of rural households with access to digital learning devices	Integration of technology as a complement to mobile schooling
	Rural internet coverage rate	Infrastructure enabling digital learning

(continued)

Table 3.4 (continued)

Dimension	*Indicator*	*What it measures*
Attendance monitoring	Attendance compliance rate with digital ID/Blockchain systems	Efficiency of technology-driven attendance verification
	Conversion rate of "impact tokens" into subsidies	Effectiveness of conditional financial support systems

if the access mechanisms are interested in numbers and quantitative indicators such as the number of people getting access to education, the number of people that reached university, etc., the reinforcement and support mechanisms focus on quality education and the impact generated.

This approach relies on the idea that education is not only about the intellectual aspects and sharing knowledge but it is extended to different areas of life such as dealing with natural disasters, managing differences, dealing with other cultures without losing their own identity, and different kinds of activities such as learning outside the school walls, gamification, promoting soft skills, civic education, etc.

This holistic approach would have three major impacts on people. First, learning would be more general and assessments would cover a wide range of areas not only knowledge. Secondly, exposing students to different activities and to real life situations would help each participant and student to learn more about their own tendencies and the way they want to contribute to shape the future. Thirdly, such an approach would transform schools from places with a limited space and walls assimilated to a prison where students are tortured to a place that prepares everyone to face life and its contingencies and this is very important because it would make the learning journey more pleasant for everyone.

- *Reinforcement and Support*: The approach does not require from students to be brilliant at all the subjects. If they have a preference for literature and arts, a student should not be required to have deep learnings in terms of STEM (Science, Technology, Energy,

> and Mathematics) and in some cases, reduce the minimum requirements in terms of knowledge and capabilities. In the other way, a student that is brilliant in STEM subjects would not be required to have deeper learnings in literature, arts, and other similar fields. Indeed, once a child finds its own tendencies and preferences, the minimum requirements in other subjects should be reduced to keep him focused on what he wants to do the most. Otherwise, if he does not find his path, it means two things. First, the system does not respond to everyone's needs. Therefore, the approach should be upgraded. Second, the minimum requirements in all fields should not be reduced.

Indeed, the approach is clear: Show me you're good at something, I will exempt you from being good at all the other things. Later, if the student changes his mind and wants to do different things, there are ways to catch up with the minimum requirements and advance. In practice, the approach resembles to a certain kind of matrix that aims at identifying for every child his own preferences and tendencies.

From another perspective, e-learning platforms used to solve access issues can also play an important role in the reinforcement and support mechanisms. For instance, a child that was fascinated by literature and history would not be required to have high grades and knowledge in mathematics and technology. Nevertheless, if the same child explores another field, let's say, artificial intelligence and he decided to change his path, he can catch up in mathematics and other areas through the e-learning platform and move forward.

In different educational systems, if a student picked a certain specialization, he is generally exempted to learn subjects out of this specialization. However, these educational systems do not offer the possibility to students to change their mind and catch up with the necessary requirements.

To monitor the effectiveness of the reinforcement mechanisms, here is a list of indicators to measure (Table 3.5):

The Alternative Pathways (Upgrade Mechanisms)

The upgrade mechanisms rely on three major principles. First, noblesse does not depend on the job itself, it depends on the way someone practice

Table 3.5 Main indicators to measure the effectiveness of reinforcement mechanisms

Dimension	*Indicator*	*What it measures*
Holistic education	Number of schools implementing holistic programs	Adoption of whole-person development models
	Hours per week of non-academic activities	Exposure to soft skills, arts, civic education, etc
	Student well-being index (physical/emotional/social)	Impact of holistic support
Personalized learning	% of students with individual learning pathways defined	Ability to tailor learning to preferences
	Student satisfaction with their chosen pathway	Alignment between student interests and learning paths
	% of students using e-Learning platforms for Catchup	Flexibility of the system for late specialization
Learning flexibility	% of students allowed reduced requirements in non-preference areas	Implementation of the "show me you're good at something" approach
	Number of pathway Transitions (e.g., STEM → arts)	System's flexibility for changing fields
Inclusive retention	Dropout rate (national and rural)	Effectiveness of nets in keeping students in school
	Re-entry rate after dropout	Ability of the system to re-integrate struggling students

it. Therefore, the education system needs to cover all the jobs and occupations. Indeed, everything requires trainings and these trainings contribute to enhancing the value of the different jobs and professions. For example, a plumber who learnt everything just by practicing would not be as efficient as someone who had special trainings. Indeed, the first plumber would not be respected the same way the second one would and this would have an impact on his pricing policy.

Secondly, people can start a career without going deeper in the learning process. They can start working in this field and then later, they would like to learn more and go further in the learning journey. Therefore, the education system has to provide the necessary pathways for that as upgrade mechanisms.

Thirdly, moving from a discipline to another even after long years of working should be possible. Indeed, conversion pathways can also be considered as upgrade mechanisms for a simple reason. You can feel yourself limited in what you're doing right now and feel that you can do better in another discipline. For instance, an agricultural engineer can have a poor performance in his job and wants to become a comedian because he has talent and more than just a talent, an unconditional love for comedy and acting. In this context, the conversion mechanisms are necessary to upgrade the person from a field where he feels limited to another field where he can be fulfilled.

Based on the three principles mentioned above, the alternative pathways should be designed in a way that enables people to start learning in a particular field, work in this field then, come back to learn more and find a better job while making more impact and later, decide to move to another field where they achieve more and perform better. Indeed, these alternative pathways create a long-life learning journey where people can always do better and do different things.

Table 3.6 Main indicators to measure the effectiveness of upgrade mechanisms

Dimension	*Indicator*	*What it measures*
Vocational and professional skills	Enrollment in vocational programs (youth and adults)	Access to job-linked training
	Certification rate in vocational tracks	Quality and completion of vocational learning
	Employer satisfaction with vocational graduates	Relevance of skilling programs
Pathway upgrades	% of workers returning to study after employment	Efficiency of lifelong learning mechanisms
	Number of bridge programs between fields	Availability of transition routes between disciplines
Career conversion	Number of people changing fields with recognized credit transfer	System's acceptance of late-career reconversion
	Recognition of prior learning (RPL) coverage rate	Ability to validate experience without full schooling
Inclusive lifelong learning	Average age of learners entering Education late	Openness of the system to late learners
	% of population participating in lifelong learning	Culture of continuous upgrade

In practice, people do not have to get a diploma before a certain age, otherwise, they are not able to do it later. Whenever people become aware of their need to learn more and to advance in life, the education system is open to them and can provide them with the necessary opportunities.

Some people can get the diplomas and the necessary trainings and learnings but they have not reached yet the required level of awareness to achieve great things with what they have learnt and vice versa, people can reach the required level of awareness but cannot catch up with time and come back again to school or to university to get the necessary knowledge.

Indeed, awareness and education are both necessary to have motivated learners and performing workers. Therefore, alternative pathways are made for everyone and this would transform the educational system from being elitist to a middle-class system.

To monitor the effectiveness of the upgrade mechanisms, here is a list of indicators to measure (Table 3.6):

Finally, to measure the fair homogeneity of the nation in terms of education policies and outputs, the following list of indicators is relevant (Table 3.7):

The Summary of Lifts and Nets Mechanisms for a Middle-Class Nation Educational System

See (Table 3.8).

Conclusion of the Chapter

Raising awareness, shaping the future, preparing tomorrow's leaders and reinforcing the capabilities of a nation are all assignments attributed to education. Providing adequate education for all at all ages is a lift mechanism that enables people to grow and have more impact on their lives and on their communities.

Moreover, a minimum education is a net mechanism that can save people from being useless and out of the economic cycle of the nation. In reality, there are two different perspectives for the education sector. The first perspective is the one promoted by the parents and families that aims at differentiating their children from the others. The second perspective is the government's that aims at providing equivalent and fair chances to everybody. In practice, both perspectives can co-exist only and only if the

Table 3.7 Fair homogeneity indicators in terms of education policies and outcomes

Pillar	*Indicator*	*What it measures*	*Why it matters*
Access homogeneity	Rural–urban access gap	Difference in school attendance or access between rural and urban children (primary, lower secondary, upper secondary)	Large gaps indicate geographic inequality
	Gender parity index (GPI) of access	Enrollment ratios of girls vs. boys (primary → upper secondary)	Shows if one gender is systematically left behind
	Disability inclusion access rate	% of children with disabilities enrolled compared to national average	Ensures no exclusion of vulnerable groups
	Early childhood Enrollment parity	Differences in access to preschool by region and gender	Early inequalities produce long-term learning gaps
Completion and progression homogeneity	Upper-secondary completion gap (gender)	Difference in completion rates between girls and boys	A direct measure of fairness in outcomes
	Rural–urban completion gap	Completion rates in rural vs. urban areas	Rural disadvantage is a structural inequality
	Socio-economic completion gap	Completion among poorest vs. richest quintile	One of the strongest measures of equity
	Dropout disparity	Dropout rates disaggregated by gender, income, region	Reveals who is at risk of exclusion
Resource and funding homogeneity	Per-student expenditure gap	Difference in spending per student between regions and between school types	Funding inequality creates unequal outcomes
	Teacher allocation parity	Teacher–student ratios across rural/urban, disadvantaged/wealthy areas	A proxy for instructional quality fairness

(continued)

Table 3.7 (continued)

Pillar	*Indicator*	*What it measures*	*Why it matters*
	Funding mechanisms for disadvantaged groups	Whether the system has targeted programs (scholarships, conditional cash transfers, rural school funds)	Measures whether the country corrects inequality
	Infrastructure Homogeneity index	Availability of electricity, internet, water, sanitation across regions	Key for quality and safety of learning
Learning outcomes homogeneity	Gender gap in learning proficiency	Differences in reading/math achievement	True equality = equal learning, not only enrollment
	Rural–urban learning gap	Test score differences by region	Reveals structural disparities
	Socio-economic learning gap	Lowest vs. highest wealth quintile achievement	Global standard equity measure
	TVET/vocational inclusion rate	Equal access to technical and vocational tracks by gender and income	Prevents tracking inequality for disadvantaged youth

education system guarantees full and fair access to everyone, support and reinforcement mechanisms, as well as alternative pathways for everyone.

Education is also a pivotal sector that interacts with all the other sectors and public policies. In this chapter, such interactions were not covered because they would be detailed and addressed in a holistic approach in the next chapters.

From another perspective, it is worth noting that all the recommendations issued in this chapter are just examples of policies and instruments that can be deployed to move from an elitist education system to a middle-class nation education system. All the local specificities and constraints must be taken into account when drafting these public policies to ensure consistence and compliance to the overall context.

Finally, in the following chapters, there would be more recommendations to issue in order that the education system contributes to the achievement of the objectives of the different related public policies of the different sectors.

Table 3.8 Summary of the lifts and nets mechanisms as suggested for the education sector

Instrument	*Channel/Mechanism*	*Targeting/ Beneficiaries*	*Financing/Fiscal cost*	*Expected behavioral response*	*Risks/Challenges*
Government per child subsidy to private schools	Direct payment per enrolled student to private sector schools	All children, rich or poor	National education budget; cost depends on enrollment numbers	Encourages enrollment in quality schools; creates connection to public education	Over-subsidization, fiscal strain, inequity if cost differences across schools not managed
School classification system (3/4/5 stars)	Differentiates school funding and quality standards	All schools	Minimal administrative cost for classification; moderate oversight cost	Schools strive to improve performance to attract students	Gaming the system, inequities if low-rated schools underserved
National education mapping	Guides approval of private sector investment; balances school density	Government planners, private investors	Minimal mapping cost; avoids wasted investments	Private investment aligns with national needs	Poor data can misguide investment; implementation requires strong Education Management Information System-EMIS
Limiting foreign mission schools for locals	Taxation/regulation to restrict local enrollment	Local students seeking foreign curricula	Potential fiscal revenue from taxes; administrative enforcement cost	Families stay in national system; safeguards the national identity	Pushback from wealthy families; enforcement difficulties
Rural mobile schools	Schools physically rotate to reach multiple villages	Children in rural and remote areas	Medium infrastructure cost; operational cost for transport and staff	Increased rural enrollment, safer access	Maintenance, scheduling conflicts, partial attendance risk

Instrument	*Channel/Mechanism*	*Targeting/ Beneficiaries*	*Financing/Fiscal cost*	*Expected behavioral response*	*Risks/Challenges*
Digital learning platforms and home schooling bridges	Online content and blended learning	Students in rural or mobile school programs; homeschoolers	Cost of platform licenses, device distribution, internet	Enables self-paced learning, catch-up for absentees	Connectivity issues, digital literacy gaps
Attendance-linked subsidies (Blockchain/ impact tokens)	Subsidy payments triggered by verified attendance	Children at risk of dropping out; parents	Subsidy budget; minimal blockchain infrastructure cost	Parents keep children in school; incentivizes regular attendance	Technical adoption risks; digital divide; misuse of tokens
Holistic reinforcement: Differentiated minimum requirements	Tailoring learning based on student strengths	All students, especially those struggling in certain subjects	Minimal cost; mostly curriculum design and teacher training	Students focus on preferred areas, increased motivation	Potential gaps in essential skills if minimums too low
E-learning for catch up and path switching	Online courses for exploring new fields or upgrading skills	Students changing tracks or upgrading competencies	Platform costs, licensing, internet access	Students can catch up in subjects missed or switch specialization	Quality control, low engagement without supervision
Alternative pathways/ vocational and lifelong learning programs	Vocational schools, adult learning, recognition of prior learning	Youth entering labor market early; adults changing careers	Medium to high operational and curriculum cost	Enhances skills and employability; allows career mobility	Credential recognition, alignment with labor market, risk of underutilization

References

Amuakwa-Mensah, F., Boakye-Yiadom, L., & Baah-Boateng, W. (2016). Effect of education on migration decisions in Ghana: A rural-urban perspective. *Journal of Economic Studies, 43*(2), 336–356.

Anthony, C. J., DiPerna, J. C., & Amato, P. R. (2014). Divorce, approaches to learning, and children's academic achievement: A longitudinal analysis of mediated and moderated effects. *Journal of School Psychology, 52*(3), 249–261.

Astin, A. W. (1998). Higher education and civic responsibility. *NSEE Quarterly, 23*(4), 18–19.

Balsamo, F. (2000). *Education access: National Inquiry into rural and remote education*. Full text at web site: http://www.hreoc.gov.au/human_rights/rural/education/index.html

Doherty, C., & Pozzi, M. (2017). Elite and private education. In *Oxford Research Encyclopedia of Education*. Oxford University Press. https://doi.org/10.1093/acrefore/9780190264093.013.23

Heleta, S., & Bagus, T. (2021). Sustainable development goals and higher education: Leaving many behind. *Higher Education, 81*(1), 163–177.

John, P. J. (2017). Holistic approach in education-an overview. *International Journal of Research in Social Sciences, 7*(4), 346–353.

Jordan, K. F., Jordan, T., Lemons, R., Mattocks, T. C., Melver, T., & Orr, M., & Director, A. E. (2008). *Impact of the economic downturn on schools*. American Association of School Administrators.

McCowan, T. (2010). Reframing the universal right to education. *Comparative Education, 46*(4), 509–525.

Oluyomi, A. O., Lee, C., Nehme, E., Dowdy, D., Ory, M. G., & Hoelscher, D. M. (2014). Parental safety concerns and active school commute: Correlates across multiple domains in the home-to-school journey. *International Journal of Behavioral Nutrition and Physical Activity, 11*, 1–14.

Pharo, R. (2012). *Alternative education and pathways to success*. Colorado Children's Campaign.

Redecker, C., Leis, M., Leendertse, M., Punie, Y., Gijsbers, G., Kirschner, P., et al. (2010). *The future of learning: New ways to learn new skills for future jobs. Results from an online expert consultation*. Technical note JRC60869, JRC-IPTS, Seville.

Ritt, E. (2008). Redefining tradition: Adult learners and higher education. *Adult Learning, 19*(1–2), 12–16.

Speciale, B. (2007). *Are educational policies elitist*. Unpublished mimeo.

Van Zanten, A. (2009). The sociology of elite education. In *The Routledge international handbook of the sociology of education* (pp. 329–339). Routledge.

Vasconcellos, E. A. (1997). Rural transport and access to education in developing countries: Policy issues. *Journal of Transport Geography, 5*(2), 127–136.

Weedon, C. (2018). Learning difficulties and mathematics. In *Special educational needs policy in the 1990s* (pp. 140–156). Routledge.

CHAPTER 4

Lifts and Nets Mechanisms Applied to Housing and Transportation

Introduction of the Chapter

Throughout the human history, cities were designed and developed around their transportation networks and water supply (Cervero, 2001). Residential areas, economic zones (industries) and social institutions (education and health) were always deployed according to the transportation modes and networks targeting a highly smooth flow of goods and people (Abeysekara et al., 2021).

For people to survive, they need a shelter, a source of revenue to cover their expenses and a fair access to social institutions such as schools and hospitals. Therefore, people need to have appropriate healthy housing and to circulate smoothly to carry out their economic activity and to access healthcare and education. Obviously, the transportation networks have a significant impact on the sustainability of a city and the perspectives of its development (Kong & Wu, 2009).

For instance, people living in slums or people living in residential areas that are disconnected from the transportation networks and therefore from other parts of the city can easily fall under the poverty trap. Indeed, the poverty trap phenomenon is what explains why people prefer to stay jobless rather than having a job that does not cover the basic costs of transportation and clothing and does not improve their situation.

Improving housing and transportation can, in many cases, ease or even break poverty trap dynamics by giving households better access to jobs,

A. Tahiri Jouti, *Building Middle Class Nations*,
https://doi.org/10.1007/978-3-032-02134-2_4

education, and essential services. When these basic conditions improve, multiple other socio-economic indicators tend to follow. However, the opposite is also true: when public policies fail to provide adequate housing, mobility, and infrastructure, they can reinforce deprivation and generate broader negative effects—not only harming individuals, but also undermining national development as a whole.

This chapter addresses the issues related to housing and transportation that lead to create multiple and distinct clusters in a nation. Moreover, the chapter also explains how the multiplicity of classes and clusters can impact negatively the urbanization plans of the different cities. The analysis focuses mainly on the interactions between housing and transportation but is also extended to elements such as education, security, access to healthcare and economic zones.

Beyond diagnosing the issues and causes in housing and transportation, the chapter applies the "lifts and nets" framework to outline how these sectors can be strengthened to narrow gaps between social groups. It identifies practical mechanisms to improve housing quality, expand mobility, and ensure that benefits reach both vulnerable and middle-income populations. The chapter also highlights how well-designed housing and transportation policies generate positive impacts across other dimensions of people's lives, including employment opportunities, access to services, health outcomes, and overall social inclusion.

Finally, quality housing and effective transportation networks and modes are necessary to ensure a high level of happiness for the population that sees its mobility improving as well as its capacity to access to different opportunities in the city.

Housing and Transportation and Their Major Issues

The General Framework of Issues Related to Housing and Transportation

For Housing

In non-middle-class nations, housing conditions typically divide the population into three distinct clusters. The first group consists of people living in slums, often with no formal housing at all. They are frequently households that have experienced severe economic shocks and lost their assets, or rural migrants who moved to urban centers without the skills or opportunities needed to secure stable, well-paid jobs capable of covering housing acquisition or rental costs.

In many countries, housing policies focus on constructing low-standard but affordable units intended to relocate people from slums into more acceptable living conditions. While this approach helps lift households out of extreme poverty, it often places them just above the poverty line without truly integrating them into the middle class. As a result, the policy tends to preserve—and sometimes reinforce—the division of society into three distinct housing-based clusters.

Secondly, high-income households can afford expensive, high-standard housing. However, housing quality is not defined solely by the physical characteristics of the dwelling. It also depends on the overall quality of the surrounding neighborhood—including security, infrastructure, access to public facilities, such as hospitals and schools, and proximity to markets, transportation, and administrative services. These contextual factors play a major role in shaping the real living conditions of residents (Najafpour et al., 2014).

In this particular case, the quality of life in high-standard houses can be affected by the quality of the neighborhood itself. In modern urban plans and strategies, high-standard houses are built in isolated neighborhoods and zones. Such a public policy increases the value and the experience of high-standard houses but at the same time, it reinforces the gap between the different clusters of a nation (Thal, 2017).

Finally, the middle-income people are facing a dilemma where they are trying to join the rich people urban style by acquiring a house in these high-standard neighborhoods. When they cannot, they try to find a house isolated from low-standard building zones and areas with all the necessary requirements in terms of security and infrastructure which reduces the choices and the opportunities. In this case, the scarcity of the offer for middle-income people would lead to an increase in terms of prices and when it becomes unaffordable, middle-income people would turn into low-standard houses (Baqutaya et al., 2016).

Seen from this perspective, such public policies would just make gaps between the different clusters more visible and would reduce the middle-income cluster that would be divided into three sub-clusters: people who can afford buying houses in rich neighborhoods, those who can afford middle-class standard houses and those who would move to low-standard houses. Actually, low-standard houses would serve a cluster that is different from the one initially identified.

Indeed, low-standard houses would upgrade the quality of life of people living in slums if they have access to them but would downgrade the quality of life of middle-income people that would find their needs unmet.

From another perspective, it is worth noting that the policy of low-standard houses has almost achieved in many countries the zero slums target. It enabled people to live in better places with appropriate access to water, sanitation and energy. It improved the health situation in neighborhoods where schools are available and where security is under control.

The following table describes the housing public policies in middle-income countries such as Morocco,[1] Tunisia,[2] Algeria,[3] and Egypt[4] that adapt partially or fully the orientations as discussed below (Table 4.1):

Based on the previous elements, the following scheme presents the clusters and classes related to housing and the main underlying issues and challenges (Fig. 4.1):

Most of the housing public policies are focusing on numbers rather than on impact and quality. Indeed, public policies should not care exclusively about providing houses in adequate quantities and removing slums, they should create appropriate packages of services that enhance people's quality of life and horizons. Housing is a basic need for people to be safe and integrated in the society, to create families and contribute to the growth of the nation.

Moreover, these policies think that solving the housing issues for low-income class people is sufficient to achieve growth and prosperity since the other classes and clusters have the necessary resources and means to

[1] OECD. (2025). *National urban policy review of Morocco*. OECD Publishing. https://doi.org/10.1787/af7ee02f-en.

[2] Abdel-Razeq, M. (2010). Comparative assessment of social housing policy in the Maghreb: Algeria, Morocco, Tunisia. *L'espace politique*, (63). https://www.erudit.org/fr/revues/lsp/2010-n63-lsp3885/044149ar.pdf.

[3] Djafri, R., & Osman, M. M. (2024). *Housing crisis in Algeria: Challenges and perspectives*. *Planning Malaysia*, 19(1), Article 1073. https://doi.org/10.21837/pm.v19i19.1073.

[4] Architecture Department, Faculty of Fine Arts, Helwan University. (2021). Assessing the Egyptian public housing policies and governance modes (1952–2020): Towards achieving a sustainable integrated urban approach. *Journal of Architecture and Urban Planning*, 1(1). https://journals.ekb.eg/article_153759.html.

Table 4.1 A comparative analysis of the housing public policies in Morocco, Algeria, Tunisia, and Egypt

Country	*State role*	*Typical quality of social/ public Housing*	*achievements*	*Main problems/critiques*
Morocco (OECD, 2025)	Strong state involvement through Sovereign guarantee scheme for home loans, plus tax-/fiscal incentives for developers	Relatively standardized "affordable/social housing"—small/modest flats aimed at low-income; quality basic with limited access to services/ infrastructure (especially for mass housing on city peripheries)	Substantial reduction in informal housing/ slums; expanded housing supply; affordable entry for many low-income/ middle-income households	Spatial segregation: many projects on peripheries/new towns, away from services—risk of isolation; quality of neighborhood/ infrastructure may lag; pressure on middle-income to access decent housing
Algeria (Djafri & Osman, 2024)	State-led housing policy with multiple programs: subsidized/promotional housing, rental-to-own schemes (e.g. AADL), public housing construction—state as main promoter and regulator	Mixed—social/rental-sale housing units in suburbs/ suburban new areas; housing quality above slum standards (better sanitation, security, utilities) in many cases, but community design and social-cohesion aspects are uneven	Sharp reduction of informal settlements/ slums: many dwellings eradicated, low-income households rehoused into formal housing; improved living conditions relative to slums	Issues in design and social integration: housing blocks sometimes lack adequate community spaces, public services; social isolation, mismatch between housing and livelihoods; challenges in ensuring long-term sustainability and fair subsidy allocation

(continued)

Table 4.1 (continued)

Country	*State role*	*Typical quality of social/ public Housing*	*achievements*	*Main problems/critiques*
Tunisia (Abdel-Razeq, 2010)	State-led social housing and subsidized housing policies, often with public–private participation; housing bank for loans; social-housing targeted to low/modest incomes	Basic to modest housing—affordable priced units, smaller apartments; quality often meets minimum housing standards but may lack full infrastructure or urban amenities depending on project location	Made home-ownership more accessible for lower-income salary earners; provided subsidy-based housing for modest households; contributed to urban housing supply	Challenges: regulatory obstacles, rising housing prices making many ineligibles; risk of social polarization; inadequate integration with broader urban planning, limited supply relative to demand; sometimes mismatch between housing supply and real needs
Egypt (Architecture Department, Faculty of Fine Arts, Helwan University, 2021)	Historically heavy state involvement in public housing, shifting over decades—from direct provision under different governance modes to more liberalized or mixed-models over time	Public housing units often seen as minimal, with varying quality—many dwellings may not fully meet residents' needs in terms of infrastructure, accessibility, or integration	Social housing has provided many households with access to formal housing; provided a structural framework for affordable housing delivery	Significant shortcomings: insufficient supply relative to demand, growing affordability crisis, sometimes poor quality or poorly located housing, challenges in governance and matching housing supply to population needs. Recent reforms (e.g. changes in rental law) raise concerns about displacement and eviction risks for low-income tenants

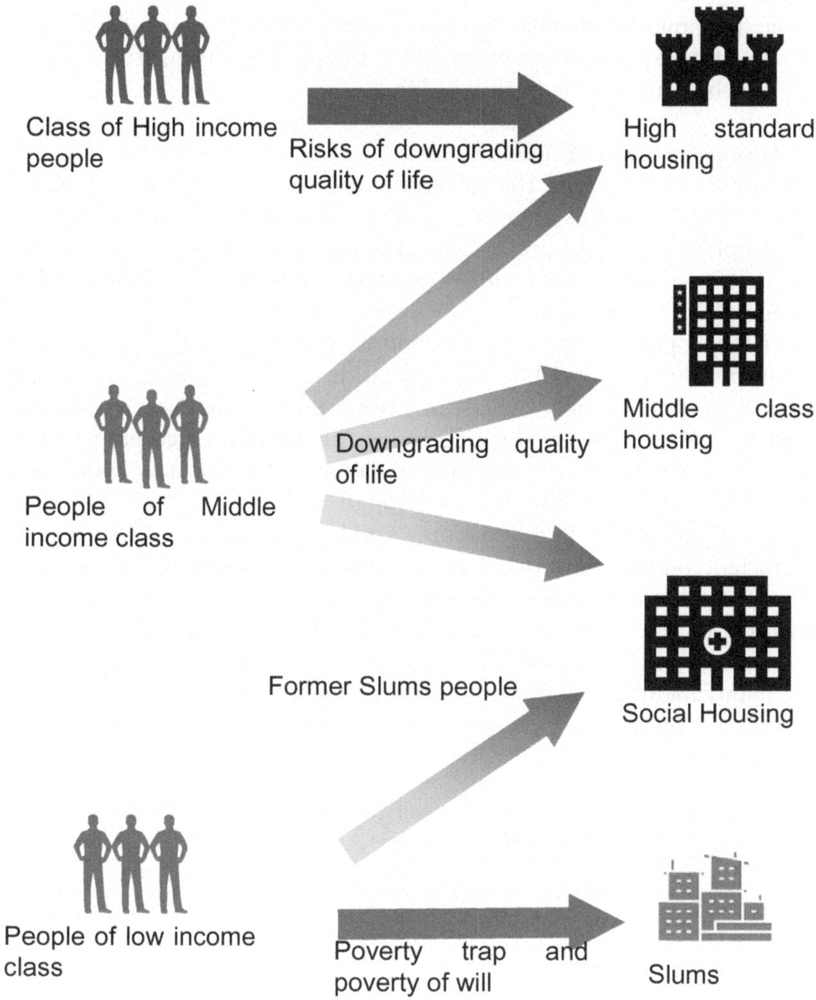

Fig. 4.1 The different classes and clusters and their housing standards

take in charge their needs. Nevertheless, ignoring the needs of other clusters can have negative consequences even for low-income families. For instance, people from middle-income class can turn into low-standard housing that was supposed to serve people from low-income class. Even people from middle-income class that could afford a high-standard house did so at the expense of so many other things (education, trips, leisure, etc.) which reduces their quality of life.

For Transportation and Mobility

In a middle-class nation, the government invests enough in the public transportation networks to make mobility accessible to everyone including rich people who would prefer using public transportation means rather than their own vehicles for more commodity (Weisbrod & Reno, 2009) (Table 4.2).

On the opposite side, in a non-middle-class nation, the government invests poorly in the public transportation networks making mobility accessible only for those who can afford buying their own cars and vehicles. Indeed, there are three classes or clusters when it comes to transportation. First, there are high-income families that can have more than one car and whose mobility is high enough.

Secondly, there are middle-income families who lack access to reliable or efficient public transportation. Because the existing networks often suffer from limited geographic coverage, low service frequency, safety concerns, or poor comfort, these households are frequently compelled to purchase their own vehicles. Without doing so, daily mobility for each family member—commuting to work, school, or essential services—would be extremely difficult. This forced reliance on private cars becomes

Table 4.2 Average share of urban population with convenient access to public transportation. (*Source* Our World in Data[5])

	Morocco	*Algeria*	*Egypt*	*Sweden (Stockholm)*	*Switzerland (Zurich)*
Average share of urban population with convenient access to open public spaces (%)	48,9%	40,6%	21,8%	87,1%	93%

[5] https://ourworldindata.org/grapher/share-with-convenient-access-to-public-transport?mapSelect=MAR~CHE.

a financial burden, especially when the cost of purchasing, maintaining, and fueling vehicles takes up a significant share of their income.

Thirdly, there are low-income families, who face the most severe mobility challenges in the absence of an adequate public transportation system. With limited financial resources and no access to private vehicles, they often rely on informal or less secure transportation modes, which can be unreliable, unsafe, or costly relative to their income. Importantly, the high cost and difficulty of daily mobility can reinforce the poverty trap: limited access to affordable transport restricts access to jobs, education, and essential services, which in turn constrains economic opportunity and perpetuates poverty.

Actually, whenever the government invests wisely and effectively in public transportation networks and means, it facilitates people's life and supports them in their daily activities. On the other hand, whenever the government invests poorly in public transportation networks and means, it makes people's life harder and everyone would bear the cost of the transportation public policy inefficiency.

The following scheme describes the clusters and classes related to transportation and the main underlying issues and challenges (Fig. 4.2):

The effects of public transportation availability extend far beyond the mobility of individuals; they shape the functioning and efficiency of other essential sectors such as education, health, and housing. When governments invest in reliable, affordable, and well-connected transportation networks, they reduce the need to multiply facilities across all neighborhoods simply to guarantee access. For example, instead of building small schools in every district to ensure proximity, a strong public transportation system enables students to reach larger, better equipped schools within reasonable travel times. This approach improves educational quality while reducing infrastructure duplication and public spending. The same logic applies to health services: efficient transport allows patients to access specialized hospitals or clinics without requiring each area to host costly, high-capacity facilities. In the housing sector, accessible transportation expands the geographical range within which households can live while still accessing jobs and services, reducing pressure on central urban areas and mitigating housing shortages. In short, investment in public transportation generates positive spillovers across multiple sectors, supporting more equitable access to essential services and contributing to better overall urban welfare.

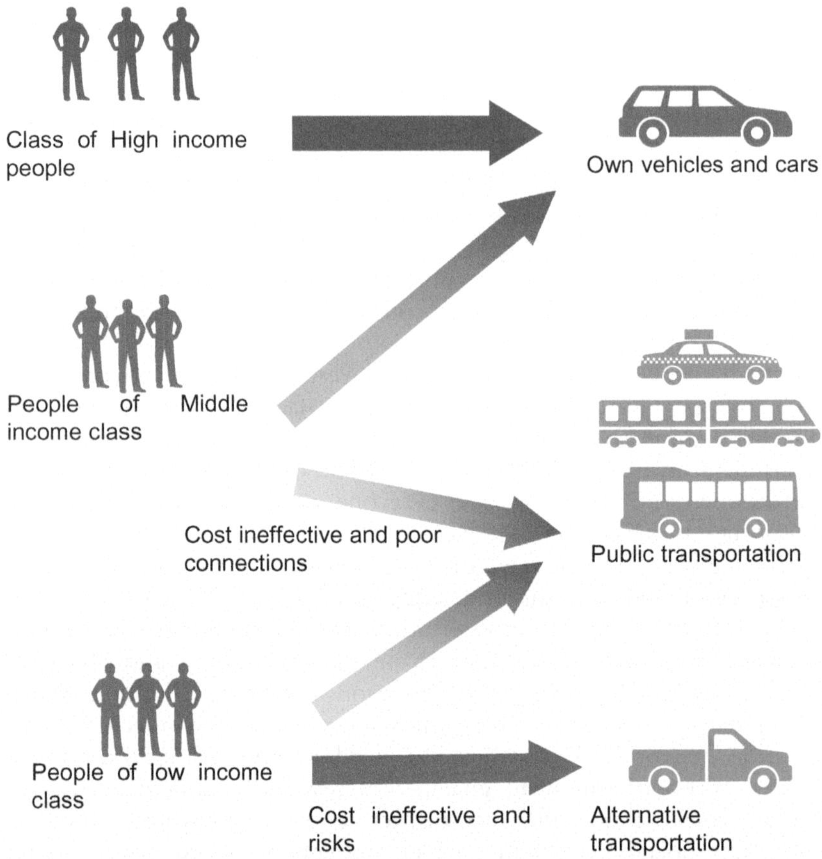

Fig. 4.2 The different classes and clusters and their transportation modes in a non-middle-class nation

The Major Issues Related to Housing and Transportation in a Non-Middle-Class Nation

The existence of different clusters and classes in the nation makes the elaboration of efficient and relevant housing and transportation policies hard to achieve. Every class has its own specificities and constraints. Nevertheless, the paradigm and the perspective of such policies need to be reviewed in order to reinforce the middle-class feature of a nation.

The Unbalanced Approach Toward Clusters and Downgrading Middle-Income Cluster

- *For High-Income People Cluster*: The high-income people cluster has no direct issue in terms of housing and transportation apart from the fact that they rely on themselves and on their own financial resources. Indeed, there are two scenarios. The first scenario consists of having special urban zones isolated from the other parts of the city to build neighborhoods for rich people. Transportation networks and modes are not an issue since people from high-income cluster have the necessary resources to have enough vehicles to serve all the members of the family. In this scenario, people from high-income cluster would have a pleasant experience in their own neighborhoods but not in the city where gaps become significantly visible to everyone.

  The second scenario consists of having urban zones where you can find people from all classes living in the same neighborhoods with different standards of buildings. In this scenario, people are living together but high-income people are having a downgraded experience and gaps are reduced but still visible. In terms of transportation, high-income people have their own transportation vehicles.
- *For Middle-Income People Cluster*: As mentioned earlier, middle-income people would try to live in neighborhoods of high-income people. Nevertheless, the cost of acquiring a house in these neighborhoods would be higher for two main reasons. First, to have exclusively rich people in the neighborhood, the luxury level will go up as well as the prices that would become unaffordable. Secondly, to live in such isolated neighborhoods, a middle-income cluster family needs to buy a car or two which increases the cost of living in high class neighborhoods.

  If people from middle-income cluster fail to have the necessary loans and mortgages to live in luxurious neighborhoods, they will try to get middle standard houses in highly secure and prosperous areas in the city. Nevertheless, the offer of such houses, if limited, would be more expensive especially if public transportation is not available. In this case, people would turn into social housing with lower standards in order to afford buying their own vehicles. In this case, the housing experience of middle-income cluster would be downgraded (Hegedüs & Tosics, 1983).

- *For Low-Income People Cluster:* Low-standard housing constitutes the new form of slums in cities. They regroup mainly people who were living before in slums. The low-standard of housing for low-income people is justified by the fact that the government would like to provide these people with buildings at a very low cost to make the transition from slums smoother and faster.

  When moving from slums to low-standard housing areas, people keep the same customs and habits in terms of cleanliness, good manners, and community life. Moreover, these neighborhoods are generally built in suburbs and lacking the access to the necessary infrastructure including public transportation and security (Gilbert, 2007).

  Such a situation reinforces the poverty trap. When families live in neighborhoods with limited opportunities, weak services, and little hope for upward mobility, the lack of prospects can shape the attitudes and expectations of both current and future generations. This environment can make it harder for young people to envision realistic pathways to education, employment, and personal development. As opportunities shrink, challenges such as higher unemployment, health problems, and exposure to unsafe conditions can become more common. Over time, these pressures can create cycles of disadvantage that are difficult to break, making some social housing areas particularly vulnerable and in need of targeted public investment.

  Finally, these conditions make social housing areas an unattractive choice for middle-income families, as living there could negatively affect their quality of life and limit their access to opportunities and services.

  In an alternative scenario, where middle-income families predominantly reside in these neighborhoods, the overall quality of life would generally be higher than in areas dominated by low-income households, due to better resources, upkeep, and social norms. Nevertheless, even in such cases, middle-income residents may still experience a decline in their living conditions compared to more affluent areas, as public services, infrastructure, and local opportunities may remain limited.

The Public Transportation Deficit

In practice, if housing prices rise to unaffordable levels, authorities can develop new urban zones on the outskirts of the city, equipped with necessary infrastructure and public services. This approach can be effective because it provides new, more affordable housing options for those who cannot afford the high prices of city centers and upscale neighborhoods, while also promoting more balanced urban development.

Nevertheless, the lack of accessible, affordable, and reliable public transportation—including adequate coverage, safety, and service frequency—would compel residents to rely on private vehicles for their mobility needs. As a result, the cost of living in these neighborhoods would increase, effectively excluding those who cannot afford private transport. Consequently, housing policies designed to provide more affordable housing while maintaining higher building standards could fail in practice, as the overall cost of living undermines their intended benefits (Dewita et al., 2018).

Moreover, residents who can afford one or two private vehicles may still face significant challenges over time. Daily life could require spending long hours driving, and in the event of a vehicle breakdown, there may be no viable alternative transportation options available, further limiting mobility and increasing stress and costs.

In an alternative scenario, where public transportation networks partially cover these new urban zones, access to transit would have a significant impact on the housing market. People would tend to prefer homes located near metro or bus stations, even as a backup option in case their private vehicle breaks down. Consequently, property prices in areas with good public transportation access would likely increase, while prices in areas without such access could stagnate or decline. Nevertheless, residents in zones without reliable transit would still need to rely on private vehicles, maintaining higher overall living costs.

This analysis is focused more on people's struggle in terms of access to affordable housing. How about the macroeconomic perspective?

First, it goes without saying that the connection of all the new urban zones to the different public transportation networks would reduce the impact of public transportation on the price of housing. In this case, people would be encouraged to move to new urban zones with bigger surfaces, better quality of life and lower prices. Such trends would also stabilize the prices in the city downtown and luxurious neighborhoods.

Secondly, if the authorities refuse to invest in public transportation networks, people would be obliged to fill the gap themselves by buying vehicles for their own needs. Over time, traffic jams would be more frequent and the authorities would be obliged to develop road infrastructure and to think seriously about alternatives including public transportation.

If authorities continue to prioritize road infrastructure while neglecting alternative transportation options, housing policies would become less effective, and the overall well-being and happiness of residents could be negatively affected (Cloutier et al., 2017). Longer daily commutes would result in multiple adverse outcomes, including a higher risk of traffic accidents, increased stress and mental health challenges, elevated CO_2 emissions, and broader environmental pollution.

At the opposite, when the authorities invest in public transportation networks and connect all the new urban areas while multiplying the alternatives for people, the housing public policy would be successful and efficient while their happiness level would be higher.

The Deficit in the Infrastructure of the New Urbane Zones

In practice, there are two major urbanist styles depending on the concept of proximity. Indeed, in the European style or urbanism, the prosperity of a neighborhood depends on the availability of the necessary infrastructure and shops. For instance, a family would prefer one house to another depending on its direct surroundings (a school, a drugstore, a bank branch, a coffee shop, a bakery, a hospital, etc.).

The American urbanist style is influenced by the merchant model based on malls where one can find all the necessary infrastructure including administration branches in some cases. Therefore, people do not require proximity. They just need fluid transport connections from their neighborhoods to these zones and malls.

Consequently, the deficit in terms of infrastructure in the new urban zones and whatever urbanist style adopted makes the situation even worse. Indeed, people would need to move to other neighborhoods to satisfy their basic needs and again they need to use their own vehicles. The development of the necessary infrastructure in the new urban zones takes time and when it occurs, the prices of the real estate assets go up.

Indeed, new urban zones can effectively address housing shortages only if they are equipped with essential infrastructure—such as schools, pharmacies, and public parks—or are well-connected to public transportation networks at an affordable cost. Otherwise, residents would face higher expenses for daily commuting and limited access to essential services, reducing the overall effectiveness of housing policies.

The Difference of Purposes Between Public PolicyMakers and People in Terms of Housing

A fair and relevant housing public policy aims at providing people with appropriate housing in terms of building standards, security, infrastructure, and connection to the other parts of the city. Appropriate housing also includes the affordability criterion.

Moreover, such public policy would need people to move to new urban areas with the most recent architectural designs and arrangements while having free spaces in the city center to develop new activities and areas such as business centers, museums, public spaces, etc. Such an approach would develop the city and make it attractive for tourists but also for people to move to the city.

Finally, public policymakers aim at stabilizing housing prices if not reducing them to make it affordable to all people.

From the people's perspective, a house constitutes a life project that includes a family and children. Obviously, owning a house constitutes in itself a kind of protection for families and individuals but people seem to expect more from the real estate world (O'Sullivan & Gibb, 2002).

First, when buying a house, people consider it as an investment with a rising value. Indeed, an individual would buy a house and would expect a capital gain on his investment to buy a bigger house in the future. Secondly, people would invest in secondary houses or in different real estate assets as a way to guarantee the value of their wealth and see it grow throughout time.

This growing enthusiasm for real estate drives up property prices and reinforces the perception that investing in housing is the best financial choice. Over time, the belief that real estate offers both high capital gains and a combination of social and financial security becomes widespread, until eventually, such speculation may lead to the formation of a market bubble that could burst.

Therefore, housing public policies when relevant have different intentions and purposes compared to people who would find in real estate a shelter from life's hazards. In some cases, housing public policies serve the interests of people. For instance, public investments in a particular area can enhance the real estate prices for a while. At the opposite, public policies can reduce the prices of housing by creating new urban areas with better infrastructure and connected with the public transportation networks.

Consequently, the differences in terms of purposes between public policymakers and people can have negative consequences for both. Indeed, rising the prices would make more pressure on public policymakers to provide subsidies or invest in new urban areas to suggest new alternatives for people. At the opposite, if the authorities adopt an expansionist housing policy, this would affect the value of the real estate assets that would decrease gradually.

In both cases, the gaps between the different classes and clusters would become more significant and visible.

Housing and Transportation: Lifts and Nets Mechanisms

The Consequences of Ineffective Housing and Transportation Policies

All the issues related to housing and transportation mentioned above are due to focusing on the wrong indicators and approaches. Indeed, elaborating public housing policies that focus exclusively on quantitative indicators and that prioritize low-income people to improve their situation would lead to neglect important qualitative aspects such as the quality of life of people and their happiness rate and other clusters (especially the middle-income class) that can see their situation downgraded in the absence of appropriate housing offer.

Such approaches would lead to reinforce the non-middle-class nation feature, create new urban zones that are inappropriate for housing and downgrade the quality of life of middle-income class.

Reinforcement of the Non-Middle-Class Nation Feature

It is important to note that the effectiveness of housing and transportation policies can be undermined by shortcomings in other public policies. For example, if national security policies fail to ensure safety in new urban zones, or if the government department responsible for education does not expand school coverage to these areas, housing policies alone will not achieve their intended outcomes.

Indeed, housing public policies should not focus exclusively on the standards of building and mobility, they need to integrate aspects such as security, access to education, availability of economic opportunities and many other aspects. This particular feature makes housing policies hard to elaborate without close coordination with other public policies and governmental departments.

From another perspective, the failure of a housing public policy reinforces the gaps between the different clusters. In some cases, it can even downgrade the quality of life of some clusters.

Therefore, housing public policies need to interact positively with other public policies to reduce the gaps between the different clusters and activate the upgrade mechanisms to make the standards of living more pleasant for all.

Inappropriateness of New Urban Zones

Creating new urban zones has always been beneficial to solve housing problems. First, they provide people with additional housing offers at lower prices. Secondly, they enable downtowns and city centers to reduce their demographic density and recreate themselves.

Nevertheless, without adequate connections to public transportation networks and essential infrastructure, even low-cost housing in new urban zones can result in higher overall living expenses for residents. In such cases, housing prices in city centers may continue to rise, while the benefits of the new urban zones may primarily accrue to higher-income groups rather than the intended target populations, as discussed earlier in this chapter.

To fully play their role, the new urban zones must offer approximately the same level of convenience to people than old neighborhoods in the city center. The only inconvenience that would justify the lower prices is the distance from the downtown that would require a strong and a well-connected transportation network.

Downgrading the Quality of Life of Middle-Income Class

Unfortunately, housing public policies focusing on low-income people try to upgrade their quality of life and reduce the gap with other clusters. Such an approach assumes that the other classes and clusters have the necessary resources and offers that match their needs and expectations.

Nevertheless, even if the assumption holds true, policies aimed at relocating people from slums to social housing may still perpetuate inequalities, even when gaps are somewhat reduced. On the other hand, if the assumption is false, middle-income households may face a limited supply of housing options and could be pushed into social housing to secure homes at affordable prices. In this scenario, rather than improving the conditions of low-income residents, the policy could inadvertently lower the living standards of middle-income families.

Moreover, such conditions may lead to widespread frustration, lowering the overall level of happiness among residents. This decline in well-being can contribute to reduced productivity, increased emigration, and the development of other negative social attitudes or mindsets.

All in all, at the individual level, living in a convenient home within a safe and well-equipped neighborhood, with a reasonable daily commute, is a major factor in personal satisfaction and a basic indicator of life success. When people are unable to achieve this standard, they may experience frustration, which, as discussed earlier, carries significant social and economic costs—a topic that will be explored further later in this book.

The Lifts and Nets Mechanisms for a Middle-Class Nation Housing System

Applying the Lifts and Nets Framework to the housing sector leads to several complementary mechanisms and policies. The lifts mechanism involves creating new urban zones with the necessary infrastructure at lower costs. The nets mechanisms focus on implementing various forms of social housing to support those in need. Finally, the upgrade mechanism aims to enhance the overall urban experience for all residents.

Clearly, improving the housing conditions of the population depends on the effectiveness of many other public policies, including education, health, transportation, tourism, and economic policies. The following section will explore the key interactions between housing policy and these other public policies.

New Urban Zones with the Necessary Infrastructure (The Lifts)

When prices go up or when the offer of housing becomes limited or does not meet the expectations of the population, creating new urban zones becomes necessary. In practice, creating new urban zones needs to solve many issues in order to achieve the expected goals and objectives.

- *The Balance in Terms of Offer and Demand*: New urban zones must strike a balance between housing supply and demand across different standards of living. In middle-income nations, the gaps between housing standards are often minimal, making the development of new urban areas to meet housing needs relatively straightforward. In contrast, in non–middle-class nations, new urban zones must accommodate a full spectrum of housing standards. In such cases, any mismatch between supply and demand for a particular housing standard can influence both prices and availability in the other standards, creating complex market dynamics.

  For example, consider a new urban zone that includes villas, luxurious residential apartments, middle-class housing, and social housing with lower standards. If the supply of villas is lower than the demand, households that can afford villas but cannot find suitable options may turn to luxurious residential apartments, increasing demand and driving up their prices. Subsequently, households that could previously afford these luxurious apartments may be pushed into middle-class residences, creating the same effect down the housing spectrum, including social housing. Ultimately, the demand for social housing would rise, and authorities might respond by simply building more social houses. In the end, this approach could unintentionally lower the overall quality of life across the entire population.

  At the opposite, in a middle-class nation, a new urban zone may have residential buildings with two main standards and the housing policy is providing different formulas to make it easier for people to access to appropriate housing.
- *The Different Formulas to Access Appropriate Housing* (Wilcox, 2000): Buying a house is not supposed to be the only way to access housing. Indeed, people can opt for a lease with purchase option or a state-subsidized lease or any other formula that can open the door to people to access appropriate housing.

  The aim of these approaches is to facilitate access to adequate housing for all, including low-income households. Consequently, social housing should be designed as a support mechanism rather than a fixed housing standard. This principle should extend beyond housing to other aspects of life, such as education and healthcare, as will be discussed in the following chapters.

Indeed, in non–middle-class nations, moving from one housing standard to a higher one requires additional financial resources to cover the costs associated with integrating into a new social class. For example, families may need to spend more on their children's education to meet the expectations of this higher class. Consequently, the cost of moving to a higher housing standard is not limited to the price of the house itself, but also includes the broader expenses required to participate fully in the lifestyle and obligations of that class.

- *The Necessary Infrastructure*: As discussed earlier, housing policies that create new urban zones aim to reduce house prices and improve affordability. However, relocating to these areas often entails additional hidden costs, arising from the lack of public transportation networks, insufficient basic infrastructure, limited public services, and other related factors.
- In such situations, people are forced to fill the gaps themselves. For example, if public transportation is lacking, people may need to purchase private vehicles to maintain mobility. Each of these self-imposed solutions represents an additional financial burden, making relocation to new urban areas less attractive. Furthermore, the development of these areas—including connections to public transport and the establishment of local infrastructure—can take years. By the time these amenities are in place, housing prices are likely to rise, keeping the areas unaffordable for many.

Indeed, the most effective approach would be to develop new urban zones that are connected to public transportation networks and equipped with basic infrastructure to minimize the cost of relocation. In practice, people may be willing to accept a daily commute of, for example, 40 minutes, if it allows them to access higher-quality housing at a lower overall cost.

This being said, it is important to recognize that new urban zones should not be connected to public transportation until the transit lines are viable and sustainable. The development of these zones depends on the availability of public transportation as a means to reduce relocation costs for residents seeking to improve their quality of life while minimizing expenses.

Other types of infrastructure can be developed gradually, taking financial feasibility into account; however, this is not the case for public transportation. Providing secure and affordable transit is essential, as it allows residents to access the city's public goods without requiring all of these services to be located within the new urban zone itself.

To monitor the effectiveness of these mechanisms, here is a list of indicators to measure (Table 4.3):

Implementing Different Formulas of Social Housing (Lifts and Nets)
From this book perspective, social housing is not a standard of housing but a package of formulas that can facilitate the access of people to affordable houses with an acceptable standard of living. Indeed, building new urban areas with the necessary infrastructure and an affordable pricing should be accompanied by a number of measures to ensure that all the population can get access to appropriate housing.

Therefore, subsidies can be handed to people and families who would like to own their homes as well as guarantee schemes to obtain mortgages at a lower cost. Moreover, people who have already mortgages need some support in case of economic downturns to cover their installments.

In fact, social housing financial packages can serve as lifts to provide people with opportunities to own their own homes but also as a net mechanism to support them in case of economic downturns or in the different hazards of life.

The objective of the public policy in terms of housing should be providing people with appropriate housing even during the darkest periods and situations of life. Consequently, the social housing scheme should integrate the following formulas:

- *Guarantee Scheme for Home Ownership Financing* (Lawson, 2013): This formula is more adapted to people having irregular or weak revenue but can afford having a mortgage to own their home. Nevertheless, due to their financial situation, they are not eligible to obtain appropriate loans. Guarantee schemes can be offered to people and families under certain conditions to be defined by the authorities. Such a formula reinforces the financial-inclusion mechanisms that connect people to appropriate housing opportunities.
- *Subsidies for Home Ownership Financing or Rental*: This formula consists of granting subsidies to people and families for their first property purchase. It could take the form of a tax cut or removal

Table 4.3 Main indicators to measure the effectiveness of the lifts mechanisms

Dimension	*Indicator*	*What it MEASURES*
Housing Supply and Standards	Housing price by standard	Assesses affordability relative to income levels
	Housing vacancy rate	Indicates balance between supply and demand and market efficiency
	Diversity of housing access mechanisms (purchase, lease-to-own, state-subsidized lease)	Evaluates inclusivity and accessibility for different income groups
Financial Accessibility and Social Mobility	Total cost of relocation including housing, commuting, education, and utilities	Measures the real economic burden of moving to a higher-standard zone
	Household disposable income vs. housing and transport costs	Indicates affordability and risk of exclusion
Infrastructure and Services	Public transport coverage (% of urban zone within walking distance to transit)	Measures accessibility to the city's public goods and overall connectivity
	Access to essential services (schools, healthcare, retail, parks) within 15–20 minutes	Measures adequacy of local infrastructure and service proximity
Urban Mobility and Commuting Costs	Average daily commute time per household	Measures efficiency and convenience of mobility
	Private vehicle dependency (% households owning cars due to lack of transit)	Measures how gaps in public transportation affect mobility costs
	Transportation costs as % of household income	Measures economic burden of commuting
Social Equity and Well-being	Socio-economic mix of residents (% low-, middle-, high-income residents)	Measures inclusivity and potential for social segregation
	Resident satisfaction/happiness index	Captures perceived quality of life and well-being
	Access to education and healthcare (% of population within reach)	Measures equity in essential public services

(continued)

Table 4.3 (continued)

Dimension	*Indicator*	*What it MEASURES*
Policy Implementation and Sustainability	Time from urban zone development to full connectivity with public transport	Measures efficiency and effectiveness of policy rollout
	Infrastructure investment per capita vs. utilization	Measures cost-effectiveness and sustainability of investment

on some operations or for a certain period of time. In some cases, subsidies can be granted to people who cannot afford paying the rental for a period of time by reducing the amounts of rentals and exempting the landlords from paying taxes.

In both cases, subsidies reinforce the economic inclusion of people to access appropriate housing according to their financial capabilities. These subsidies can be under conditions such as the location of the house (in new urban zones only, for example), the surface area of an apartment (not exceeding a certain surface), the percentage of the subsidies compared to the rental or the installment amount, etc.

– *Support Scheme for People in Financial Crisis* (Sihvo & Uusitalo, 1995): Some people can be excluded from the social housing packages when purchasing or signing a lease contract. Nevertheless, in case of economic or social downturn, these people may become eligible to subsidies or any other form of support. Therefore, the social housing package should include mechanisms that can fully support people in financial difficulty for a period of time until their situation improves even if these people were initially rich. Once this period is over, the social housing package should provide the minimum assistance and support according to the same conditions defined in the previous paragraph to accompany people under financial stress.

Consequently, subsidies are not only granted upfront to people when purchasing their first house. They are also provided when people are having financial troubles and issues. The aim is to constitute a net mechanism that can maintain people in their financial position.

To monitor the effectiveness of these mechanisms, here is a list of indicators to measure (Table 4.4):

Improving the Urban Experience (Upgrade Mechanisms)
Providing solutions to housing issues should not become a justification for lowering the overall quality of the urban experience. Any housing policy—whether aimed at affordability, densification, or territorial rebalancing—must ultimately enhance people's well-being regardless of their socio-economic status. To achieve this, several upgrade mechanisms must be integrated into the planning and development of new urban zones:

- *Upgrading the Building Standards of New Urban Zones:* In many cases, households consider moving to new urban zones for reasons that go beyond the price or the overall cost of living. For example, some families are attracted by the possibility of living in modern buildings that offer better construction quality and contemporary amenities. Others may seek larger dwelling surfaces at the same price range, or prefer settling in neighborhoods that provide more organized layouts, better-designed public spaces, and improved infrastructure. These expectations highlight the importance of ensuring that new urban zones do not solely respond to housing shortages, but also offer a clear upgrade in living standards that justifies the move for a wide range of households.

  Indeed, the new urban zones must offer such advantages to people and embody the latest architectural trends and urban planning at a lower price. These zones should not be downgrading the urban standard and experience with lower-standard buildings and poorly equipped neighborhoods. In the mid-term, these areas and zones would be perceived as black spots that would be even harder to remove than slums.

  From another perspective, people moving from the city center and downtowns would decrease the density of the population and would enable the authorities to recreate and modernize the city center while converting residential neighborhoods to business spots and knowledge centers.
- *Adopting an Appropriate Tax Regime* (Wood, 1990): Across the world, property taxation systems generally follow two main approaches. The first model imposes taxes at the moment of purchase, making the transaction itself the principal taxable event.

Table 4.4 Main indicators to measure the effectiveness of the Lifts and Nets Mechanisms

Dimension	*Indicator*	*What it Measures*
Access to Housing (Lifts)	Number of households benefiting from guarantee schemes	Measures how many people with irregular or low income are enabled to access home ownership
	Number of households benefiting from purchase or rental subsidies	Measures financial support provided to increase housing access for low- and middle-income families
	Average value of guarantees and subsidies per household	Measures the scale of financial assistance relative to household needs
	Percentage of first-time homebuyers assisted	Measures inclusivity and reach of social housing programs
Financial Inclusion and Risk Mitigation (Nets)	Number of households receiving temporary support during financial crises	Measures responsiveness of the system to unforeseen economic or social hardships
	Duration of support provided during economic downturns	Measures adequacy and sustainability of the net mechanism
	Average reduction in mortgage or rental payments during crises	Measures effectiveness of support in alleviating financial burden
Targeting and Equity	Distribution of assistance by income level	Measures whether support is reaching intended beneficiaries
	Compliance with eligibility conditions (location, surface area, income thresholds)	Measures efficiency of program targeting and alignment with policy goals
	Geographic coverage of supported households	Measures spatial equity and integration with new urban zones
Policy Effectiveness and Outcomes	Home ownership rate among supported households	Measures impact of lift mechanisms on increasing home ownership

(continued)

Table 4.4 (continued)

Dimension	*Indicator*	*What it Measures*
	Household satisfaction/perceived security	Measures the perceived success of housing packages in improving quality of life
	Default rate on mortgages for supported households	Measures financial sustainability and risk reduction of guarantee schemes

In this case, households pay a one-time fee when acquiring a property and are not required to make recurring annual payments based on ownership.

The second regime is more suitable in this context because it lowers the financial burden associated with moving to a new urban zone. By eliminating or minimizing upfront taxes on property purchases, households face fewer barriers when deciding to relocate, invest in new housing, or upgrade their living conditions. Over the medium term, this system also provides a more stable and predictable source of revenue for the government through annual property taxes.

Therefore, adopting the second tax regime would facilitate access to property ownership and support the broader upgrade mechanisms. However, transitioning from the current system to an annual property tax regime is particularly challenging. Households that have already paid a one-time transaction tax would understandably oppose being charged a new recurring annual fee on the same property.

To ensure a fair and smooth transition, the government could introduce a 20-year deductible period starting from the date of purchase. During this period, owners who have already paid the one-time tax would be exempt from the annual property tax. After the 20-year window, a reduced rate could apply for the first five years to avoid a sudden financial burden. Importantly, this preferential treatment should remain strictly linked to the original owner and should not be transferable to new buyers in the event of a sale.

In this case, the government should accept that during the first twenty years, the revenues collected would be reduced but at the same time, it would have a positive impact on housing and on the quality of life of people.

- *Exploring the Opportunities to Modernize the City Center*: Creating new urban zones should be an opportunity to provide people with affordable and modern housing as well as convenient neighborhoods. Nevertheless, it should be an opportunity to free old zones of the city centers and downtowns to recreate them and allocate them to new activities.

  For instance, the very old and authentic neighborhoods of the city can be transformed to host museums, hotels, cultural coffee shops and restaurants as well as malls to keep the spirit of the city alive while generating new streams of revenue for the population.

Apart from the preservation and revitalization of very old and authentic neighborhoods, urban planning can also redirect certain residential areas located in the city center toward new economic functions. For example, establishing an international financial district requires large, open plots of land that can accommodate office towers, green spaces, hotels, and shopping centers. Such facilities must be positioned close to—or ideally within—the city center to ensure accessibility, visibility, and integration with existing economic networks.

Indeed, such population flows toward new urban zones would generate multiple economic opportunities. In the short term, they would stimulate the construction sector through the development of new neighborhoods and the expansion of public transportation networks. In parallel, the relocation of residents from dense central districts would free up strategic land in the city center, enabling the creation of new economic zones capable of attracting investment and drawing additional residents and businesses into the city. Finally, these population movements would also enhance tourism, particularly in the historic and authentic areas of the city, by preserving their cultural value while allowing them to be converted into vibrant attractions for visitors.

To monitor the effectiveness of the policies, the following list of indicators needs to be considered (Table 4.5):

Finally, to measure the fair homogeneity of the nation in terms of housing and transportation policies and outputs, the following list of indicators is relevant (Table 4.6):

The Summary of Lifts and Nets Mechanisms for a Middle-Class Nation Housing and Transportation System (Table 4.7).

Conclusion of the Chapter

Efficiency in housing public policies depends on their active interaction with other key public policies such as taxation, public transportation, education, and healthcare. For example, the tax regime must be designed to make access to property easier and less costly, thereby encouraging homeownership. Similarly, the presence of high-quality education and healthcare infrastructure significantly enhances the attractiveness and livability of new urban zones and emerging neighborhoods.

Table 4.5 Main indicators to measure the effectiveness of the upgrade mechanisms for the housing sector

Dimension	*Indicator*	*What it measures*
Building Standards and Urban Quality	Resident satisfaction score with housing quality	Measures perceived quality of the built environment and functional living conditions
	Ratio of green/public spaces per inhabitant	Measures environmental and recreational quality of new urban zones
Urban Attractiveness and Population Redistribution	Share of households relocating from city centers to new urban zones	Measures the effectiveness of new zones in attracting middle-income households
	Change in population density in city centers	Measures the success of planned population redistribution and decongestion
Fiscal Policy (Property Tax Regime)	Annual property tax revenue under the new regime	Measures fiscal sustainability of the transition from transaction taxes to annual taxes
	Compliance rate with the new property tax system	Measures citizen acceptance and administrative feasibility
	Effective reduction in transaction costs for new homebuyers	Measures improvement in mobility and reduced switching costs for property ownership
Modernization of City Centers	Number of redevelopment projects initiated in old city centers	Measures progress in transforming central areas into cultural, economic, or tourism hubs
	Share of old housing stock converted into hotels, museums, riads, cafés, or cultural assets	Measures economic revitalization and cultural preservation
	Private investment volume in city-center renewal	Measures attractiveness of city-center redevelopment for investors

(continued)

Table 4.5 (continued)

Dimension	*Indicator*	*What it measures*
	Increase in tourist visits to restored historical areas	Measures the economic and cultural impact of urban heritage enhancement
Economic Opportunities and Urban Productivity	Job creation in construction, transport, and urban redevelopment sectors	Measures economic impact of population flows and infrastructure expansion
	Number of businesses relocated or created in redeveloped city-center zones	Measures attractiveness and economic diversification driven by urban upgrade
	Growth of commercial and service activities in modernized central districts	Measures urban vibrancy and improvement in economic density
Transportation and Connectivity Within Upgraded City Framework	Transit coverage of new urban zones compared to baseline	Measures integration of new zones into the metropolitan transport system
	Average commuting time of households moving to new urban zones	Measures efficiency of mobility improvements and quality of daily life
	Usage rate of public transportation among new-zone residents	Measures the success of mobility planning in supporting upgrade mechanisms
Social and Cultural Impact	Perceived improvement in quality of life (survey-based)	Measures whether residents feel the upgrade mechanism enhances their well-being
	Social mix index (income diversity in new and old zones)	Measures social balance and reduction of spatial segregation
	Preservation index of historical and cultural sites	Measures capacity to maintain the city's identity while modernizing it

Table 4.6 Summary of the homogeneity indicators in the housing and transportation sectors

Pillar	*Indicator*	*What It Measures*	*Why It Matters*
Housing Access and Distribution	Housing Availability Ratio (units per 1,000 inhabitants, by region)	Distribution of housing supply across territories	Shows whether all regions benefit from a comparable level of housing provision
	Homeownership Rate by Region	Percentage of households owning their home	Reflects regional disparities in access to property
	Average Waiting Time for Social Housing	Delays to access subsidized housing	Reveals whether some regions face structural shortages or discrimination
	Regional Coverage of Social Housing Programs	Presence and intensity of support schemes	Ensures that assistance is not overly concentrated in specific areas
Housing Quality and Living Standards	Average Housing Size per Capita	Square meters per person across regions	Helps detect overcrowded regions or unequal living standards
	Access to Basic Services (water, electricity, sanitation)	Share of households with reliable services	Essential for assessing territorial fairness in living conditions
	Presence of Urban Amenities per Capita	Schools, parks, clinics, commercial areas per inhabitant	Measures the urban experience and quality of life across regions
Affordability and Financial Inclusion	Housing Cost Burden Ratio	Share of income spent on housing (rent or mortgage)	Shows whether some populations are disproportionately strained

(continued)

Table 4.6 (continued)

Pillar	*Indicator*	*What It Measures*	*Why It Matters*
	Regional Mortgage Accessibility Index	Ease of obtaining home financing	Measures whether financial institutions serve all territories equally
	Price-to-Income Ratio (PIR)	Gap between housing prices and purchasing power	Detects areas where housing is structurally unaffordable
	Number of Subsidy Beneficiaries per Region	Distribution of financial support	Helps identify whether subsidies are equitably reaching populations
Transportation Coverage and Access	Public Transport Coverage Rate	Percentage of population living within 500–800 m of a public transport stop	Key for assessing mobility equity between regions
	Accessibility to Major Urban Services by Public Transport	Travel time to hospitals, universities, business centers	Measures whether essential services are equally reachable
	Transport Affordability Index	Cost of transport relative to income	Highlights inequalities in the financial burden of mobility
	Road Connectivity Index	Road density and quality by region	Evaluates geographic fairness in basic mobility infrastructure
Socio-Economic Outcomes Linked to Housing and Transport	Regional Employment Accessibility	Ability to reach jobs within a reasonable time	Shows whether infrastructure supports equal economic opportunity

Pillar	*Indicator*	*What It Measures*	*Why It Matters*
	Education Accessibility Indicator	Travel time to schools and universities	Reflects fairness in human capital development
	Health Accessibility Indicator	Availability of hospitals within acceptable distance	Measures territorial equity in basic welfare services

Table 4.7 Summary of the Lifts and Nets Mechanisms as suggested for the housing sector

Instrument	*Channel/mechanism*	*Targeting/ beneficiaries*	*Financing/fiscal Cost*	*Expected behavioral response*	*Risks/challenges*
Creation of New Urban Zones	Developing balanced housing supply across standards to meet demand and prevent spillover effects	All socio-economic groups, with emphasis on middle- and low-income households in non-middle-class nations	Government-led infrastructure investment; potential short-term fiscal strain from development costs	Increased relocation to affordable, diverse housing options; reduced pressure on existing urban areas	Mismatch in supply/demand leading to price inflation across standards; potential decline in overall quality of life if imbalances occur
Diverse Housing Access Formulas (e.g., lease-to-own, state-subsidized lease)	Alternative pathways to ownership beyond outright purchase	Low- and middle-income households seeking inclusive access	Subsidies or guarantees backed by public funds; low ongoing costs if tied to private sector partnerships	Broader participation in housing market; upward social mobility through flexible entry points	Limited uptake if awareness is low; administrative complexity in implementation
Integration of Public Transportation and Basic Infrastructure	Minimizing relocation costs via connectivity and services	All residents of new zones, particularly commuters from low- to middle-income backgrounds	High upfront public investment in transit and utilities; phased development to manage costs	Willingness to accept moderate commutes (e.g., 40 minutes) for cost savings; reduced private vehicle reliance	Delays in rollout causing price hikes before amenities arrive; unsustainable transit if not viable from inception
Guarantee Schemes for Home Ownership Financing	Financial inclusion for irregular/ low-income earners	Households with weak revenues ineligible for standard loans	Government guarantees on loans; fiscal exposure limited to defaults (e.g., via insurance pools)	Increased home ownership among vulnerable groups; reduced exclusion from credit markets	Moral hazard in lending; potential high default rates straining public guarantees

Instrument	*Channel/mechanism*	*Targeting/beneficiaries*	*Financing/fiscal Cost*	*Expected behavioral response*	*Risks/challenges*
Subsidies for Home Ownership or Rental	Direct financial aid for initial access	First-time buyers or renters, low- to middle-income families; conditional on location/size	Tax cuts, direct grants, or rental reductions; targeted to minimize broad fiscal impact	Accelerated entry into appropriate housing; economic inclusion and stability	Over-subsidization inflating demand; inequity if conditions exclude deserving groups
Support Schemes for Financial Crises	Temporary safety net during downturns	All households facing sudden economic/social hardships, regardless of prior status	Emergency subsidies or payment relief; short-term fiscal outlay with recovery clauses	Retention of housing during crises; quicker rebound to stability	Dependency on aid prolonging recovery; administrative burden in eligibility verification
Adoption of Annual Property Tax Regime	Reducing upfront barriers to relocation	Current and future property owners transitioning to new zones	Shift from transaction taxes to recurring revenue; short-term revenue dip (e.g., 20-year deductibles)	Easier mobility and investment in upgrades; stable government funding stream	Political opposition from existing owners; transitional revenue shortfalls impacting budgets
Modernization of City Centers	Repurposing freed land for economic/cultural uses	Broader urban population via tourism and investment; indirect benefits to relocating residents	Public–private partnerships for redevelopment; revenue from new economic activities	Population outflow enabling densification relief; influx of investment and tourism	Gentrification displacing remaining low-income residents; loss of authentic urban character if not preserved

In parallel, the expansion of a large, reliable public transportation network should accompany the development of new urban areas. This reduces the cost of mobility for households and supports the shift toward more inclusive, better-connected living environments. Additionally, basic public infrastructure—including schools, hospitals, and community services—must be planned and implemented early enough to stimulate local economic activity and make new districts desirable places to live.

A smart housing public policy must therefore operate within a broader, integrated urban strategy that aims to shape the city's future across social, economic, environmental, and technological dimensions. Cities need to reinvent themselves, modernize their infrastructure, and diversify their economic foundations while ensuring that all residents benefit from this transformation.

Creating new urban zones can generate benefits on multiple levels. First, it lowers the cost of homeownership for low- and middle-income households, widening access to adequate housing. Second, it provides residents with more generous living spaces and up-to-date building standards, offering modern architectural quality and better neighborhood amenities. Third, it frees up central urban land that can be converted into commercial or business areas, creating new opportunities for local populations and attracting talent into the city. Finally, population movements into these new zones give public authorities the opportunity to renew and rehabilitate very old neighborhoods while preserving their historical authenticity.

References

Abeysekara, B., Perera, P., Shrestha, G. K. C., Gunaruwan, L., Kumarage, A., Sadiq, R., & Hewage, K. (2021). Improving the capital deployment efficiency: An infrastructure investment planning process in transportation project. *Research in Transportation Economics, 88*, Article 101048.

Baqutaya, S., Ariffin, A. S., & Raji, F. (2016). Affordable housing policy: Issues and challenges among middle-income groups. *International Journal of Social Science and Humanity, 6*(6), 433.

Cervero, R. (2001). Integration of urban transport and urban planning. *The challenge of urban government: Policies and practices*, 407–427.

Cloutier, S., Karner, A., Breetz, H. L., Toufani, P., Onat, N., Patel, S., & Carlson, C. (2017). Measures of a sustainable commute as a predictor of happiness. *Sustainability, 9*(7), 1214.

Dewita, Y., Yen, B. T., & Burke, M. (2018). The effect of transport cost on housing affordability: Experiences from the Bandung Metropolitan Area, Indonesia. *Land Use Policy, 79*, 507–519.

Gilbert, A. (2007). The return of the slum: Does language matter? *International Journal of Urban and Regional Research, 31*(4), 697–713.

Hegedüs, J., & Tosics, I. (1983). Housing classes and housing policy: Some changes in the Budapest housing market. *International Journal of Urban and Regional Research, 7*(4), 467–494.

Kong, T., & Wu, X. (2009). Transportation and sustainable development. In *International Conference on Transportation Engineering 2009* (pp. 2638–2643).

Lawson, J. (2013). The use of guarantees in affordable housing investment-a selective international review.

Najafpour, H., Bigdeli Rad, V., Lamit, H., & Fitry, S. M. (2014). The systematic review on quality of life in urban neighborhoods. *Life Sciences Journal, 11*(7), 355–364.

O'Sullivan, A., & Gibb, K. (Eds.). (2002). *Housing economics and public policy*. Wiley.

Sihvo, T., & Uusitalo, H. (1995). Economic crises and support for the welfare state in Finland 1975–1993. *Acta Sociologica, 38*(3), 251–262.

Thal, A. (2017). Class isolation and affluent Americans' perception of social conditions. *Political Behavior, 39*, 401–424.

Weisbrod, G., & Reno, A. (2009). *Economic impact of public transportation investment* (pp. 1–7). American public transportation association.

Wilcox, S. (2000). *Housing finance review*. Joseph Rowntree Foundation.

Wood, G. A. (1990). The tax treatment of housing: Economic issues and reform measures. *Urban Studies, 27*(6), 809–830.

CHAPTER 5

Lifts and Nets Mechanisms Applied to Public Health

Introduction of the Chapter

Public health with all the threats it has to face such as pandemics, infectious diseases and other health crises can have a real impact on the stability of a nation including the different economic, social, and political dimensions (Price-Smith, 2001). Indeed, the COVID-19 crisis showed how vulnerable are the health systems (Haldane et al., 2021), and how they can expand easily the crisis to the different economic sectors.

According to the United Nations, the emergence of COVID-19 increased the number of individuals living in extreme poverty by almost 90 million over previous predictions. Such a finding demonstrates the vulnerability of both the health system itself—including the infrastructure and the capabilities—and the public policies related to economic inclusion and protection.

If the impact of poverty on the state of public health is obvious and does not require any additional explanations, the COVID-19 experience showed that Health public policies can have an impact on poverty (Pereira & Oliveira, 2020). Indeed, poor people do not have the access to appropriate health-care services and this has an impact on their productivity (Cole & Neumayer, 2006) and capacity to improve their situation. Therefore, it increases the gaps between the different clusters and segments of people.

A. Tahiri Jouti, *Building Middle Class Nations*,
https://doi.org/10.1007/978-3-032-02134-2_5

In the other way round, a vulnerable health system that cannot face different public health crises can impact negatively the economic activity of a nation and people who are most concerned are those who are already in a vulnerable situation and can be affected quickly and deeply. Indeed, the capacity of a health system to face a crisis should not be limited strictly to medical measures but should include policies to support people financially and economically during such situations.

From another perspective, public health is not supposed to be limited to physical health only. Indeed, it should take into account the mental health as well (Herman & Jane-Llopis, 2005). Both are interconnected in a way that a healthy mind necessarily requires a health body and vice versa.

This chapter addresses the issue of how health public policies can reinforce the non-middle-class feature of a nation as they can reduce the gaps between the different clusters if conceived properly and in line with the lifts and nets approach.

Health Public Policies Major Issues

The General Framework of Issues Related to Public Health

In a non-middle-class nation, the gaps in terms of public health between people would depend on many criteria such as the awareness toward the different threats and diseases, the lifestyle and hygiene and finally the ability to access to health-care services.

Moreover, a sound public health system is not limited to the health infrastructure, its bed capacity and the competencies of the medical staff. In fact, it is extended to prevention mechanisms and systems as well as public policies impacting people's lifestyle. Indeed, public health is also about the quality of food and diet (Wu et al, 2019), the quality of the air and water (Gupta et al., 2008), the practice of sport (Khan et al., 2012), and so many other elements that can reduce the spread of disease and require less health infrastructure.

The following table presents the main indicators related to good health and well-being in Morocco, Algeria, Tunisia, Egypt, Sweden, and Switzerland (African Exponent, 2022; Morocco World News, 2022; TheGlobalEconomy, 2022; IQAir, 2024; OECD & National Health Authority, n.d.) (Table 5.1):

Table 5.1 The major indicators related to good health and well-being in Morocco, Algeria, Tunisia, Egypt, Sweden, and Switzerland

Indicator/category	*Morocco*	*Algeria*	*Tunisia*	*Egypt*	*Sweden*	*Switzerland*
Local/Domestic Health Insurance Coverage	~78%	~70–90%	~70–80%+	~60–66%	~99%	~99%
Uninsured/Not Covered	~12–22%	~10–30%	<20%	~34–40%	~0–1%	<1%
Regular Sport/Physical Activity	>50%	~27%	~27%	~29%	~70%	~75.7%
Access to Safely Managed Drinking Water	~90.3% (urban)	~92% (overall)	~74% (overall)	Data not available	~99–100%	~97%
Air-Quality (PM2.5, annual avg.)	*Roughly moderate–high pollution;*	*Elevated PM2.5 exposure*	*Likely elevated PM2.5 exposure*	~42.4 µg/m^3 (2023 average, among more polluted countries)	*Relatively low PM2.5, generally good air quality by global standards*— part of few countries closer to WHO guidelines	*Low to moderate PM2.5*, better than many global regions, though not always meeting strict WHO guideline

Therefore, in this chapter, Public health would be addressed from a holistic approach that gathers all the instruments and policies that can improve the state of health and the prevention mechanisms (Woolf, 2008) as well the policies related to health infrastructure, its bed capacity, and the competencies of the medical staff. Therefore, public health must have both a preventive and a curative component.

When it comes to the preventive component, there are elements such as a friendly environment (Martuzzi et al., 2004) where there is less pollution in its various facets, where biodiversity is safeguarded for the interests of the nation and the next generations and where the connection with the nature is still preserved. In addition, this component also includes the connection of people with their bodies when it comes to practicing sport, adopting the right diet, carrying out regular health check-ups and feeding their mind and spirit (Mann & Ward, 2007). Finally, the preventive component also covers the connection of people with other people to preserve the strong relationships within the nation and hence its stability (Gurung et al., 1997).

For the curative component, it covers the health infrastructure, its bed capacity and the medical competencies. Indeed, it gives a priority to the sound governance of the health infrastructure to increase its performance and efficiency and to ensure that the sector is continuously supplied with a sufficient number of doctors and specialists.

Moreover, the curative component includes Research as a way to contribute to the global efforts of improving public health and to better understand the local context and constraints to adapt the instruments accordingly.

Indeed, Public health is expected to provide an appropriate framework where people can be productive and stable physically and mentally. Therefore, in a non-middle-class nation, health public policies can give rise to several clusters in terms of access to both the preventive and the curative components.

When it comes to the preventive mechanisms and instruments, there are three main clusters. The first cluster is composed of people that have access to pure water and air and a sound connection with the nature. In addition, they adopt a healthy lifestyle with a regular practice of sport and the policies take into account all the social and economic specificities of this cluster. The second cluster is composed of people that have access to pure water and air and the policies are adapted to their context but they do not have a healthy lifestyle that can maintain their mental and physical state.

Finally, the third cluster is composed of people that are excluded from the system. Hence, they do not have access to pure water, air, and sanitation systems. They cannot have a healthy lifestyle and the policies do not take into account their specificities.

In terms of ability to access to health-care services, there are also three clusters of people depending on their ability to access to health-care services. The first cluster has the necessary resources to travel abroad to benefit from the best health-care services. People belonging to that cluster have sufficient financial resources to undertake the expenses of the trip or to take out an international health insurance to cover all their needs.

The second cluster is composed of people who cannot afford traveling abroad but have local health insurance that can cover expenses in local hospitals and health institutions. These people may not be properly served for many reasons such as the low level of skills of local medical teams or the complete absence of certain specialists or the poor cover for certain illnesses under the insurance policy taken out.

The third cluster is composed of people who do not have any health insurance and should rely on their own financial resources and their families to undertake the various expenses. Sometimes, the access issue to health-care services is not related to financial resources only but is also linked to poor infrastructure and equipment as well as the level of skills and competencies of people.

Merging both clustering results can generate a very interesting scheme that identifies the different clusters based on their ability to access to the different preventive and curative mechanisms and instruments (Fig. 5.1).

By merging both components, there are mainly three main clusters in a non-middle-class nation. First, healthy people cluster that have access to pure water and air and are generally connected to nature, they have a healthy lifestyle and have international health insurance or at least they have the necessary financial resources to get world class health-care services.

The second cluster consists of people who generally enjoy good air and water quality and maintain some connection with nature. However, they tend to follow an unhealthy lifestyle—characterized by an unbalanced diet and limited access to sports infrastructure—although they do have access to local health insurance and basic health services.

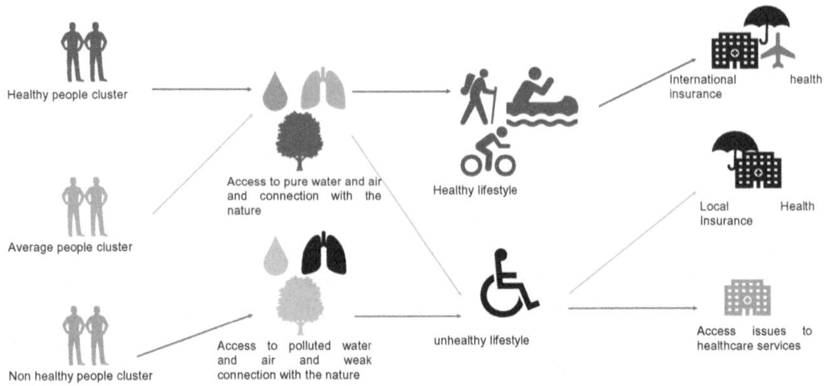

Fig. 5.1 The different classes and clusters related to health sector in a non-middle-class nation (*Source* Author's own)

The third cluster is composed of individuals exposed to polluted air and water and who have a weak connection to nature. They generally maintain an unhealthy lifestyle, marked by poor dietary habits and limited physical activity. In addition, they have restricted—or in some cases no—access to health-care services.

The Major Issues Related to Health in a Non-Middle-Class Nation

The health sector can lead to the creation of significant gaps between the different components of the population (O'Donnel et al., 2015). Indeed, unhealthy people cannot be productive enough and are unable to take optimal decisions. Moreover, public policies can reinforce the gaps between the different clusters in terms of health situation. From this perspective, the major issues related to the health sector in a non-middle-class nation can be summarized as follows:

The Absence of the Preventive Component in the Health Public Policies

In general, the approach adopted by governments and authorities in non-middle-class nations is limited. It focuses on the curative component covering aspects such as the health infrastructure capacity, the universal coverage, and insurance schemes as well as the fair access to health-care services among the population in different regions.

When it comes to the preventive component, it covers mainly and exclusively the policies and strategies to prevent disease or at least reduce their impact on the society. Meanwhile, people's lifestyle and the environment where they live are not directly monitored by the health sector authorities. Indeed, the access to clean water, pure air, sport equipments, and many other elements that can contribute to a healthy lifestyle are not part of the health public policies (Detels & Tan, 2015).

It goes without saying that an effective preventive public policy can improve the global state of health in a nation and would require less investment in the health infrastructure capacity. Consequently, ignoring the preventive component in health public policies can be costly.

From another perspective, investments oriented to projects that aim at improving the air quality or at providing clean water or at generalizing the practice of sport can be more effective than any other investments in the curative component.

Finally, the scope of the preventive component is not set in stone. It can be extended to other elements and aspects depending on the global context.

The Access Issues to the Preventive Mechanisms

As discussed earlier, many aspects of the preventive component are monitored by departments other than the authority supervising the health sector with considerations different from those of public health. In some cases, economic constraints and political considerations are given priority over public health matters (Tisdell, 2001).

In some cases, safeguarding public health would require strict decisions and clear orientations to suspend or at least limit certain industrial activities or products which will have a large economic impact that cannot be easily tackled and alternatives are not always available.

The preventive mechanisms should ensure a fair access for all to quality air, clean water, well-being, and sport as well as awareness campaigns. The access issues can be presented as follows:

- *Improving Air Quality*: According to the World Health Organization, 7 million deaths are recorded annually due to the exposure to polluted air. Moreover, due to Greenhouse gas emissions and climate change, heatwaves caused approximately 166,000 deaths globally between 1998 and 2017 (Kuehn, 2014).

In addition, poor air quality has so many health effects (Bingham, 2025) such as respiratory diseases (asthma, chronic obstructive pulmonary disease, acute respiratory infections), cardiovascular diseases, cancer, neurological disorders, child health issues (low birth weight, preterm birth, development issues), metabolic and other chronic diseases.

Therefore, improving air quality and contributing to the global efforts of climate action would reinforce the state of public health and would reduce the needs in terms of bed capacity and medical care services.

- *Providing Clean Water*: Clean water is fundamental to safeguard human health (Li & Wu, 2019). Some diseases such as cholera and typhoid are waterborne diseases and they can cause deaths all across the globe. According to the World Health Organization, the diarrheal diseases (waterborne diseases) cause annually around 485 000 deaths. In parallel, the access to clean water enables proper hygiene practices and reduce the spread of respiratory and gastrointestinal infections by up to 40%.

  From another perspective, long-term exposure to contaminated water can cause chronic conditions such as kidney disease and even cancers. In addition, with climate change, water is becoming a very scarce resource that would impact the food security of large populations.

  There are still many other connections between clean water and public health that are not covered in this paragraph. Nevertheless, providing clean water can prevent the population from so many diseases and health issues.
- *Encouraging the Practice of Sport*: Outdoors parks or Indoors gyms are both necessary to provide people with the necessary equipment to practice sport and improve their health conditions and well-being. For instance, public parks should be equipped with walking or jogging circuits, and with outdoors gyms adapted to all ages and for free. Moreover, gyms should be incentivized to reduce their prices and diversify their offers to target all the segments of the population.

  Obviously, when talking about the practice of sport as part of the preventive mechanisms and that it should be handled by the health department, it did not cover the professional sports. It is limited to the usual sports activities that benefit the health of everyone in the nation.

- *Raising Awareness*: Many of the health problems can be avoided if people adopt a healthy lifestyle with a strong spiritual connection, a life balance, and a link to nature (Lindley-French, 1986). People should contribute to the local, national and global efforts of safeguarding biodiversity, preventing themselves from different diseases and practicing sports regularly. As citizens, investors, consumers, and producers, people should take into account public interest and the balance of the planet.

  Such a targeted behavior requires huge efforts of education and awareness campaigns so that people can adhere to public policies. Moreover, people should be accompanied when taking decisions in order to be in line with the requirements and prerequisites for a healthy and balanced life as discussed in this chapter.

The Access Issues to the Curative Instruments and Infrastructure
When addressing the curative component, the main issues are related to accessibility that can take different forms such as the absence of sufficient infrastructure, the lack of financial means, and/or the limited competencies.

- *The Capacity Issues*: The fair and equitable access to health-care services requires an adequate and sufficient infrastructure size to host people and take care of them for an appropriate period of time (Baker et al., 2005). For this purpose, the public health departments are monitoring indicators such as the number of hospitals and clinics, the number of available hospital beds, the availability of essential medical equipment, the number of operating rooms and intensive care units, the number of doctors, nurses, and other healthcare professionals per capita, etc.

  Some indicators have thresholds and limits to be observed and monitored continuously to solve these capacity issues. For this purpose, the World Health Organization (WHO) defined a set of thresholds and recommendations that can serve as a foundation to guide public policies. For instance, the WHO recommends at least 5 beds per 1 000 inhabitants for advanced systems and at least 2 to 3 beds per 1 000 inhabitants for low- and middle-income countries.

Moreover, the WHO recommends at least 1 doctor per 1 000 inhabitants for low- and middle-income countries while it recommends 2,5 doctors in optimal systems (Tillman et al., 2010).

Other thresholds and limits need to be observed such as the healthcare coverage, emergency care availability, number of nurses and midwives per 1 000 inhabitants, the geographical distribution, etc (Table 5.2).

- *The Concentration Issues*: In most of the developing countries, the health infrastructure and the qualified human resources are all concentrated on the main cities and urban poles of the country. Moreover, some specialties can only be found in these large cities and people from other regions have to travel to access health-care services, putting pressure on the existing infrastructure, and reducing the quality of medical care (Yazbek, 2009).

  The United Nations Sustainable Development Goal n°3 related to good health and well-being aims at achieving universal health coverage including the access to quality essential health-care services and access to safe, effective, quality, and affordable essential medicines and vaccines for all.

  Therefore, all the regions need to be served and equipped with the necessary health infrastructure while taking into account their own specificities and features in terms of demography, most common diseases, and needed specialties and expertise (Table 5.3).

- *The Competence Issues*: To have a well-managed health sector, a variety of competencies is required starting from the medical staff to the management teams and experts in different fields such as strategic planning, governance, technology, and many other fields (Liang et al., 2018).

  Generally, developing countries have real issues to train the necessary resources in terms of medical staff to be in line with the World Health Organization standards and requirements. Moreover, due to the limited capacity of the sector, nurses and doctors leave the country to settle in other regions of the world with better life conditions. This brain drain worsen the situation in developing countries.

  From another perspective, developing countries only focus on medical expertise and ignore some specialties related to public health management in order to ensure the effectiveness and the efficiency of the sector (Table 5.4).

Table 5.2 Number of beds and doctors per 1000 people in Morocco, Algeria, Tunisia, Egypt, Sweden, and Switzerland.

Indicator	*Morocco*	*Algeria*	*Tunisia*	*Egypt*	*Sweden*	*Switzerland*
Physicians per 1,000 People (Year)	0.7 (2017)	1.0 (2019)	1.3 (2021)	0.7 (2020)	4.3 (2020)	4.4 (2021)
Hospital Beds per 1,000 People (Year)	0.7 (2020)	1.6 (2017)	2.4 (2021)	1.1 (2020)	2.0 (2020)	4.4 (2021)

Table 5.3 Medical Brain Drain[1] Rates by Country

MBD rate (2004)	*Morocco*	*Algeria*	*Tunisia*	*Egypt*	*Sweden*	*Switzerland*
Value	0.45	0.35	0.40	0.30	0.06	0.08

(*Source* Bhargava et al. (2011))

Table 5.4 Management of public health training programs and annual graduates per country

MBD rate (2004)	*Morocco*	*Algeria*	*Tunisia*	*Egypt*	*Sweden*	*Switzerland*
Value	0.45	0.35	0.40	0.30	0.06	0.08

(*Source* Nuwayhid et al. (2021))

- *The Lack of Financial Means*: In the three previous paragraphs, the access issues were focusing on the structure of the health sector. Nevertheless, the infrastructure may be available but people would not have the necessary financial means to afford the cost of healthcare services. Indeed, the development of the health infrastructure should be accompanied by the implementation of a universal health insurance coverage including all the segments of the population. Moreover, involving the private sector in the health infrastructure development and in resolving the various issues related to concentration would need the implementation of a universal health insurance coverage to ensure that people have the necessary financial means.

  From another perspective, a national health insurance scheme can be ineffective in several manners. First, it can exclude people who are jobless or who cannot afford the periodic contributions. Secondly, the scheme itself is limited and not covering all kinds of diseases or the coverage rate remains globally low or limited. Thirdly, the cost of the whole scheme can increase throughout time requiring the continuous contribution of the government to keep it ongoing. Such financial gaps can be due to the increasing number of people

[1] The Medical Brain Drain (MBD) rate is defined as the proportion of physicians trained in the source country who emigrate to OECD/high-income destinations, calculated as emigrants/(domestic physicians + emigrants).

who are supported by the government to access to the health insurance scheme or to the weakness and ineffectiveness of the operational model.

The Governance Issues of the Sector

In the COVID-19 crisis, the health sectors in different countries were strongly challenged in terms of their flexibility and capacity to adapt to the prerequisites and issues of the pandemic. Such a situation is not necessarily due to the lack of means or to the incompetence of people but rather to the governance systems that are running the health infrastructure and public policies (Barbazza & Tello, 2014).

Indeed, the main Governance issues of the health sector can be summarized as follows:

- *The Governance System Is Only Focused on the Curative Component*: The health departments in many countries are exclusively in charge of developing the health infrastructure and the necessary competencies. The interactions with the other policies and governmental departments are very limited and are not interested in providing healthy lifestyle conditions to reduce the need for the curative elements.
- *The Health Governance System Is Highly Centralized*: In many developing countries, the health system is monitored from the capital city without any interest in the specificities of each region of the country. Such an approach has generally two main impacts. First, in these countries, the health infrastructure is generally concentrated in the capital city and in the main center of the country. Secondly, policies are influenced by the needs of the capital city and its region. Such a situation would increase disparities between the country's different regions in terms of free and fair access to health-care services.
- *The Private Health Sector Supervision*: Opening the door to the private sector would generally reduce the necessary public investments in the sector. It would also increase the quality of services but most of the time, the lucrative approach can lead the investment decisions in terms of locations and implementations, new specialties to integrate and new technologies to adopt. Consequently, in most of the cases, there would be a conflict of interests and objectives

between the private sector approach and the government orientations. In this case, the principle of fair access to health-care services would be breached.

- *The Health Insurance Schemes Supervision*: Generally, as per all the other insurance products and instruments, the health insurance scheme is generally under the control and the supervision of the financial authorities. In some cases, the insurance schemes are guided by the pure financial perspective where the financial equilibrium of provident funds is more important than the impact on public health itself. It is worth noting that the financial equilibrium ensures the sustainability of the whole scheme but it is essential to integrate the impact management as part of the equation. In this case, if the health department is not involved in the supervision of the health insurance schemes, there would be a conflict of interest between the public health policy and the interests of the financial institutions.

Health Public Policies: Lifts and Nets Mechanisms

The Consequences of Ineffective Health Policies

In non-middle-class nations, Health public policies are neglecting two major aspects. First, they do not pay the necessary attention to the preventive component. Secondly, they focus more on quantitative indicators to fill the gaps at a national scale without taking into account the specificities or the different regions, clusters, and individuals.

The consequences of such an approach can be summarized as follows:

Increasing the Cost of Healthcare for the Underprivileged Population

In the absence of an efficient and effective lifts and nets approach applied to the housing, transportation, education, sports and environment sectors, unprivileged people would be forced to adopt an unhealthy lifestyle. For instance, if the neighborhood is located near an industrial zone, the quality of air and water would be deteriorating as will the health of people living in this neighborhood.

Moreover, if neighborhoods are not equipped with free and accessible sports' equipments, people may not have the financial means to join sport clubs and gyms and again the quality of life of people will be deteriorating.

Generally, privileged people (generally) would live in neighborhoods having better quality of air and water and would have the necessary financial resources to practice sport and have a healthy lifestyle.

Consequently, people with healthy lifestyle would be more productive and they would have less chance to have chronic illnesses unlike people with unhealthy lifestyle that would have bigger chances to suffer from different diseases. Therefore, the cost of the curative component would be higher for unprivileged people than for privileged people. Indeed, the less your lifestyle is healthy, the more you will have to spend on health-care services at later stages of your life.

From another perspective, the absence of the necessary health infrastructure and medical competencies would have two impacts on the cost of health-care services for unprivileged people. First, privileged people would prefer to travel abroad to get the necessary health-care services and for this, they will adhere to international insurance schemes. Hence, the number of adherents in the national health insurance scheme (if there is any) would be lower than it should be and it would reduce the soundness of the scheme itself. Moreover, the expenses of privileged people abroad for health-care services could constitute an additional revenue for local health institutions which would contribute to their financial balance and reinforce their capacity to reinvest. In this context, private health institutions would need to raise their prices in order to guarantee the sustainability of their business model.

Secondly, for example, the concentration of the health infrastructure in a particular region would require people to travel from a city to another to get the necessary health-care services. In this situation, people would have to bear the cost of transportation and accommodation in addition to the cost of health-care services. Moreover, the limited medical competencies may lead, in the best cases, to less efficient, longer care protocols and this may be more expensive.

Increasing the Gaps Between the Different Clusters

Having all the necessary ingredients to adopt a healthy lifestyle would improve people's performance and productivity as well as their capacity to improve their financial situation. At the opposite, having all the ingredients to impose an unhealthy lifestyle to people would deteriorate their performance and productivity and it would limit their financial situation. Indeed, instead of allocating their revenue to improve their financial situation, they would find themselves spending large amounts on their care.

From another perspective, it goes without saying that the more intellectual the nature of someone's work, the more money he will earn. The more physical the nature of someone's work, the less money he will earn. Moreover, health problems deteriorate people's physical capacity faster than their intellectual capacity. Therefore, unprivileged people with less revenue find their work capacity affected more quickly than the work capacity of people relying more on their intellectual competencies and abilities.

Consequently, there would be two major clusters, the healthy people cluster that are still productive and have sufficient resources to improve their situation and the unhealthy people cluster that are less productive and that are allocating their revenue (if there is any) on their health-care services.

Hence, inefficient and ineffective public health policies would increase the gaps between people in a given nation let alone the impact on the long-term growth perspectives of the whole economy.

The Lifts and Nets Mechanisms for a Middle-Class Nation Health System

As per the other public policies previously discussed in this book, the health-care system upgrade requires a variety of Lifts and Nets Mechanisms to better serve people and also to offset the negative impacts on the middle-class feature of the nation.

Applying the Lifts and Nets Framework to the health sector requires the following mechanisms and policies. The lifts mechanisms consist of improving the preventive component of the health sector by providing all the ingredients for a healthy lifestyle for people. Secondly, the nets mechanisms would implement better governance system for the sector to reinforce the curative component by increasing the sector's capacity and reduce its concentration on the main cities. Finally, the upgrade mechanisms consist of adopting new technologies and innovative solutions to improve the health situation at a national scale.

As discussed in this chapter, improving the global health conditions of the population relies on many other policies including housing, transportation, sports policy, education, etc.

Improving the Preventive Component (Lifts Mechanisms)

Many of the preventive component elements are linked to the environmental action that is meant to be global involving the whole international community. Indeed, we are all sharing the same planet and the massive GreenHouse Gaz (GHG) emissions in one country can have an impact on all the other countries even if they all have done their fair share of work. Nevertheless, efficient environmental action can have immediate impacts on people locally.

Therefore, the environmental action includes five major pillars that are mitigation measures (meant to reduce the GHG emissions), adaptation measures (meant to reduce the impact of climate change as per natural disasters, water scarcity, etc.), biodiversity (meant to safeguard the variety of species, ecosystems, and life on our planter), water (meant to provide clean water in sufficient quantities and reduce water wastage), and waste management (meant to minimize the environmental impact of waste, promote resource recovery, and protect human health).

In terms of mechanisms that need to be implemented, public policies can focus on the following aspects:

- *Reduce the GHG Emissions from Transportation*: Apart from the economic constraints of creating new urban zones and relying exclusively on personal vehicles as discussed in the previous chapter, creating public transportation infrastructure that runs on clean energy source is also beneficial to the environment since it will reduce the GHG emissions but also to public health. Moreover, to reduce the GHG emissions from transportation, the transportation public policy should accelerate the transition to electric vehicles with electricity provided from a clean energy source as well.
- *Accelerate the Transition to Clean Energy*: Renewable energy and nuclear energy can constitute both interesting alternatives to coal, gas and oil power stations. Nevertheless, they are not accessible by all the countries. For instance, some countries do not have the necessary expertise to build nuclear power stations or they are simply not allowed by international treaties to develop any form of nuclear power. Moreover, renewable energies depend on nature. For example, if the country does not receive large quantities of solar radiation, then, solar panels would be less productive. Indeed, the transition is not easy to put in place but it is necessary to find appropriate solutions.

- *Improve Urban Planning and Biodiversity*: An efficient urban planning would consist of green spaces to increase the urban vegetation and trees to act as natural filters. It would also consist of separating industrial zones from residential neighborhoods while reducing the GHG emissions of the different industries. In parallel, the urban planning needs to design compact cities promoting the proximity between homes, workplaces, and services.
- *Educate and Raise Awareness*: Education and public campaigns that aim at raising awareness within the community are necessary to accompany all the other efforts. Indeed, these campaigns involves people to adopt a responsible consumption lifestyle to reduce domestic waste, to improve the energy efficiency of their homes, to buy goods and items with an inferior carbon footprint. Another dimension related to education that needs to be undertaken is improving the average hourly volume of reading per person. Indeed, people who read can have a better perspective of life.
- *Adopt the Latest Innovations and Support Research and Development Projects*: Due to the sensitivity of the environmental issues, many of the research and development projects are trying to find adapted solutions to improve the air and water quality and to reduce the anthropogenic impacts. Therefore, public policies should encourage these projects by allocating the necessary funding, by adopting the latest innovations and by incentivizing the adoption by people.

It is worth noting that the preventive component is not exclusively linked to the environmental action but it includes other aspects such as assistance for mental health, preventive controls and health screening campaigns, and the regular practice of sports:

- *Implement Assistance for Mental Health*: It consists of mental support to people when they go through tough times. This assistance can be provided by different channels such as religious support—that can be one of the most efficient channel—psychologists and coaches with subsidized fees and associations that can assist people in finding their inner peace.
- *Organize Health Screening Campaigns*: These campaigns can be thematic. For instance, intensive cancer screening campaigns can detect cases in an early stage who may have a greater chance of

recovery with a lower cost as well. Nevertheless, artificial intelligence algorithms could improve the process and identify people who could develop a cancer months before.

- *Encourage the Practice of Sport*: Having a nation with a regular practice of sport can reduce the percentage of people with a chronic disease. Indeed, in partnership with the housing and urbanization departments, neighborhoods should be built in a way that provides free spaces to practice sport for all ages.

To monitor the effectiveness of these mechanisms, here is a list of indicators to measure (Table 5.5):

Implementing a Better Governance System for the Sector and Reinforcing the Curative Component (Nets Mechanisms)
To reinforce the efficiency of the health sector with his two components (the preventive and the curative), it is necessary to implement a comprehensive governance system that is objective oriented.

Indeed, governance systems should be made in a way that ensures their flexibility to detect new trends and threats in the health sector and to adopt the right approaches and solutions for a timely response. In addition, governance systems should ensure their independence from the influence of other stakeholders such as pharmaceutical laboratories and fund investments involved in the health sector.

Moreover, such governance systems should have the ability and the capacity to conceive and elaborate a strategic vision for the sector, to be in line with the needs and expectations of the different regions, to deploy the necessary control mechanisms and to have the right connections with other departments and sectors. Therefore, the Health Governance system should be composed of an internal component that takes in charge the health infrastructure and an external component that connects the sector to all the relevant departments and sectors.

- *The Internal Component of the Health Governance System*: This component is responsible for the elaboration of the strategic vision of the sector in order to upgrade its capacity and serve fairly all the people. The Governance system shall take into account the investment needs per location (region/city/or whatever other classification), the competencies required depending on the region

Table 5.5 Main indicators for lifts mechanisms in the health sector

Dimension	*Indicator*	*What it Measures*
Reduce GHG emissions from transportation	Percentage of public transportation running on clean energy sources	Extent of shift away from fossil fuel-dependent public transport,
	Adoption rate of electric vehicles powered by clean electricity	Progress in transitioning personal and fleet vehicles to low-emission alternatives
Accelerate the transition to clean energy	Share of renewable/nuclear energy in national power generation	Replacement of coal, gas, and oil with sustainable energy sources,
	Number of new clean energy installations per year	Pace of infrastructure development for renewables or nuclear
Improve urban planning and biodiversity	Proportion of urban area covered by green spaces/ vegetation	Integration of natural filtration systems in cities, assessing enhancements in air quality, biodiversity, and urban resilience to climate impacts
	Distance between industrial and residential zones	Effectiveness of zoning policies in minimizing pollution exposure for communities, reducing health risks from industrial emissions
	Compact city density index	Urban design promoting proximity between homes, workplaces, and services, quantifying reductions in travel-related emissions and support for sustainable lifestyles
Educate and raise awareness	Participation rate in public awareness campaigns	Community engagement in sustainability education,
	Average hourly reading volume per person	Broader societal literacy and perspective-building, indirectly supporting informed environmental and health decision-making
	Adoption rate of low-carbon footprint goods	Consumer behavior changes toward eco-friendly products

(continued)

Table 5.5 (continued)

Dimension	*Indicator*	*What it Measures*
Adopt the latest innovations and support research and development projects	Public funding allocated to environmental R&D projects	Investment in innovative solutions for pollution control
	Number of adopted innovations for air/water quality improvement	Integration and scaling of new technologies, quantifying enhancements in resource efficiency and anthropogenic impact mitigation
Implement assistance for mental health	Number of subsidized psychology/coaching sessions	Accessibility of professional mental health support
	Participation in religious/association support programs	Community-based mental health channels
Organize Health screening campaigns	Coverage rate of thematic screenings (e.g., cancer)	Reach of early detection campaigns, assessing preventive efficacy, cost savings, and recovery potential for targeted diseases
	AI algorithm accuracy in early detection predictions	Technological enhancements in screening processes
Encourage the practice of sport	Percentage of population engaging in regular physical activity	National adoption of active lifestyles, assessing reductions in chronic disease prevalence through sports participation
	Availability of free sports spaces in neighborhoods	Urban planning integration for exercise access across ages

requirements and the new technologies to integrate in the management processes and the health-care protocols. In the absence of such a governance system, gaps between the different regions would be higher and the inadequacy of the infrastructure to the needs of people would be more than visible.

- *The External Component of the Health Governance System*: This component is responsible for the coordination and collaboration with other departments to support the curative component of the system but also the preventive component. In real life, the sport

Table 5.6 Main indicators for nets mechanisms in the health sector

Dimension	*Indicator*	*What it measures*
Alignment with Regional Needs	Regional disparity index in health infrastructure investment	Equitable distribution of resources across regions,
	Percentage of regions with infrastructure matching local population health requirements	Adequacy of facilities and services to demographic and epidemiological needs
Internal Component: Competencies Matching	Proportion of health workforce competencies aligned with regional health profiles	Suitability of skilled personnel to local disease burdens and service needs
External Component: Coordination with Other Departments	Collaboration index with non-health sectors (e.g., sports, education) on preventive programs	Synergy in cross-sectoral efforts, such as joint campaigns for healthy lifestyles
External Component: Threat Integration	Incorporation rate of external threats (e.g., climate change, biodiversity loss) into health strategies	Resilience of the health system against non-medical risks,

management department is not dealing with the health department to encourage people to have a safe and healthy life style. Moreover, education and raising awareness toward particular aspects such as diets and life balance is conducted by the education department or the health department separately from each other. Therefore, such component of the Governance system would seem very important. Moreover, the health department should also take into account the threats on public health such as climate change, lack of biodiversity, and any other phenomenon that can impact the stability and the soundness of the whole system.

To monitor effectively the deployment of the lifts mechanisms, the following indicators are necessary to measure (Table 5.6):

Adopting Technologies and Innovative Solutions to Improve the General Health Situation (Upgrade Mechanisms)

To upgrade the heath situation of a nation, all the previous mechanisms need to be improved in a way that ensures efficiency and effectiveness.

From one side, threats on public health are increasing with all the environmental challenges such as climate change and the issue of invasive species such as mosquitoes that can move from equatorial and tropical regions to regions a little to the north spreading back Malaria. From the other side, advancement in technologies can provide us with very innovative solutions that would improve the public health situation.

Indeed, the main challenge of all nations is to exploit new technologies in order to offset the impact of all the threats that can deteriorate the public health situation. In this case, the main challenge consists of improving the preventive component in order to reduce the investments and reliance on the curative component.

Let us focus on the example of self-driving cars technologies replacing personal vehicles and let us explore the contribution to the improvement and the upgrade of the public health situation:

- *Self-Driving Cars and Reducing the GHG Emissions*: Many cities in the world started planning their transition to shared electronic transportation platforms especially with self-driving cars. Such a transition would reduce the number of cars circulating in the cities and it would reduce the consumption of natural resources and raw materials contributing to the protection of our planet. Moreover, there would be less pressure on roads and infrastructure. From people's perspective, driving cars would be safer and less expensive than owning a personal vehicle. Such an advancement would reduce the GHG emissions but also many other impacts on people's health such as rush hours and stress levels.
- *Self-Driving Cars and Urban Planning*: Giving up personal cars and replacing them with self-driving cars would also reduce the spaces required in cities for parking. Moreover, as mentioned in the previous paragraph, there would be less pressure on roads construction and enlargement. Such a transition would free up large areas for other uses, in particular green spaces and the enhancement of biodiversity, which will beautify our cities and make them healthier (Zakharenko, 2016).

From another perspective, artificial intelligence algorithms implemented in wristwatches can improve the health situation of people such advancement has so many impacts on people's health. These impacts can be summarized as follows:

- *Monitoring People's Mental Health*: Wristwatches can measure the stress level of people and when it is over the limits, they can recommend a few moments of meditation, breathing, and self-awareness to reduce it. With the technological advancements, wristwatches can do more than just detect high stress levels, it can measure blood sugar level, blood pressure, and many other indicators in order to make people aware of the situation and assist them in overcoming the situation.
- *Collecting and Analyzing Sata to Prevent Chronic Diseases*: Wristwatches collect a lot of health data for every individual, it monitors the evolution of heath rate, the cardiovascular fitness, the heart rate variability, the resting heart rate, the average heart rate, heart recovery, etc. The tracking of all these indicators and their evolution can help AI algorithms to predict chronic diseases and recommend the necessary elements to reduce the threats on people's health (Mujawar et al., 2023).
- *Adapting Insurance Schemes to People's Health Situation*: Based on the data collected, insurance schemes can be personalized to every individual. Therefore, the premium to be paid can constitute a reward for people who adopt a healthy lifestyle or a penalty for people who do not adopt a healthy lifestyle or who don't share their data to be assisted.

Finally, to measure the fair homogeneity of the nation in terms of health policies and outputs, the following list of indicators is relevant (Table 5.7):

The summary of Lifts and Nets Mechanisms for a Middle-Class Nation Health System (Table 5.8).

Conclusion of the Chapter

The chapter promotes three main ideas about the public health policies to contribute to the efforts of creating a middle-class nation. First, health is not exclusively about creating a performant health infrastructure and

Table 5.7 Summary of the homogeneity indicators in the health sector

Pillar/dimension	*Indicator*	*What it measures*	*Why it matters*
Regional Access and Infrastructure	Regional Health Infrastructure Disparity Index	Difference in number/quality of hospitals, clinics, equipment per region	Shows whether health infrastructure is evenly distributed across territories
	Share of Regions with Infrastructure Matching Local Needs	Adequacy of services to population size and disease patterns	Ensures all regions receive care aligned with their demographic and epidemiological profiles
	Density of Health Professionals per 1,000 (regional variation)	Availability of doctors, nurses, specialists	Detects territorial inequalities in access to medical personnel
Preventive Health Services (Regional)	Regional Screening Coverage Equity Index	Uniformity of screening campaigns across regions	Ensures early detection is not limited to privileged territories
	Participation in Awareness Campaigns (regional variation)	Engagement in health promotion	Shows whether preventive messaging reaches all regions
Environmental Exposure (Regional)	Air Quality Regional Disparity Index (PM2.5, NO_2)	Geographic distribution of pollution	Ensures no region is disproportionately exposed to unhealthy environments
	Green Space Coverage Equality Score	Access to parks and vegetation	Reflects equal access to natural health-supporting environments
	Industrial Risk Proximity Index (regional)	Pollution exposure from industrial sites	Identifies uneven territorial exposure to contamination
Lifestyle and Behavioral Equity (Regional)	Physical Activity Rate Variation Between Regions	Differences in sports participation	Shows if some regions are disadvantaged in promoting healthy lifestyles
	Distribution of Free Sports Infrastructure	Availability of public spaces for exercise	Reflects equal opportunities for physical activity

(continued)

Table 5.7 (continued)

Pillar/dimension	*Indicator*	*What it measures*	*Why it matters*
Individual Access and Financial Protection	Health Insurance Coverage Inequality Index	Insurance disparities across social groups	Shows whether financial protection covers all individuals equally
	Out-of-Pocket Health Expenditure Burden (by income group)	Financial difficulty accessing care	Ensures low-income individuals aren't disproportionately burdened
	Waiting Time Inequality	Differences in appointment delays between individuals	Reveals unequal access to timely care
Individual Health Outcomes	Life Expectancy Gap (income/education groups)	Differences in lifespan	Indicates deep structural inequality between individuals
	Infant Mortality Inequality (by mother's socio-economic status)	Differences in early-life health outcomes	Sensitive measure of societal health inequality
	Chronic Disease Prevalence Gap	Diabetes, hypertension, etc., across social groups	Shows unequal distribution of long-term illness burdens
	Mental Health Condition Inequality	Differences in depression/anxiety prevalence	Indicates uneven psychosocial well-being
Preventive Behavior Inequality (Individual)	Vaccination Rate Inequality	Immunization differences across age/income/education	Highlights uneven protection from infectious diseases
	Screening Participation Inequality	Likelihood of early detection by social class	Reveals behavioral or financial barriers
	Health Literacy Index Variation	Ability to understand health information	Shows educational or cognitive inequalities affecting health
Environmental Exposure (Individual)	PM2.5 Exposure by Income Group	Pollution exposure differences between individuals	Indicates environmental injustice not tied to geography only

Pillar/dimension	*Indicator*	*What it measures*	*Why it matters*
	Exposure to Industrial Risks by Social Group	Environment and income correlations	Shows whether disadvantaged individuals live nearer hazards
	Access to Clean Household Energy (income/education variation)	Clean cooking, heating, ventilation	Reflects inequalities in home air quality
Lifestyle and Behavior (Individual)	Physical Activity Rate Gap	Differences across age, gender, income	Indicates unequal adoption of healthy lifestyles
	Diet Quality Gap (healthy vs. ultra-processed foods)	Quality of individual nutrition	Shows socio-economic differences in diet
	Tobacco/Alcohol Consumption Inequality	Patterns of risky behavior by social class	Identifies groups disproportionately exposed to health-damaging habits
Mental Health Support Access (Individual)	Access to Subsidized Psychological Services (variation)	Affordability and availability for different social groups	Reflects equal opportunity to receive mental health support
	Participation in Community Support Programs	Differences in attendance to psychosocial support	Shows informal support inequities

Table 5.8 Fair homogeneity indicators in terms of the public health policies and outcomes

Instrument	*Channel/mechanism*	*Targeting/ beneficiaries*	*Financing/fiscal Cost*	*Expected behavioral response*	*Risks/challenges*
Clean Energy Public Transportation	Reducing GHG emissions from transportation via clean-powered infrastructure	Urban commuters and low- to middle-income residents reliant on public transit	Government investment in infrastructure upgrades; ongoing subsidies for clean energy operations	Shift to public over private vehicles; reduced commuting emissions and health risks from pollution	High initial capital outlay; dependency on reliable clean energy supply chains
Electric Vehicle Transition Incentives	Accelerating EV adoption with clean electricity	Middle-class vehicle owners and fleet operators	Subsidies, tax credits, and charging infrastructure funded publicly; moderate fiscal support	Increased EV purchases and usage; lower personal transport emissions and fuel costs	Uneven adoption in rural areas; battery production environmental impacts if not managed
Green Urban Planning Enhancements	Improving biodiversity through green spaces, zoning, and compact city design	All urban residents, emphasizing families and vulnerable groups exposed to pollution	Public planning budgets and land reallocation; phased development to control costs	Greater use of green areas for recreation; reduced urban heat and pollution exposure	Land acquisition disputes; potential gentrification displacing low-income communities
Public Awareness and Education Campaigns	Raising awareness on sustainable lifestyles, including reading promotion	General population, targeting youth and low-literacy groups	Low-cost media and community programs; partnerships with NGOs to minimize fiscal burden	Adoption of low-carbon habits and informed health decisions; higher engagement in preventive behaviors	Low participation if campaigns lack cultural relevance; measurement difficulties in long-term impact

Instrument	*Channel/mechanism*	*Targeting/ beneficiaries*	*Financing/fiscal Cost*	*Expected behavioral response*	*Risks/challenges*
R&D Funding for Environmental Innovations	Supporting adoption of air/water quality tech and pollution reduction	Researchers, innovators, and communities in high-pollution areas	Targeted public grants and incentives; high initial R&D investment with potential ROI via tech licensing	Faster integration of innovations; improved local environmental health metrics	Funding allocation biases; slow translation from research to scalable applications
Subsidized Mental Health Assistance	Providing accessible support via psychologists, coaches, religious channels	Individuals facing stress or crises, across socio-economic levels	Subsidies for sessions and programs; scalable through community partnerships to limit costs	Increased seeking of help; reduced mental health stigma and incidence of related issues	Over-reliance on informal channels; privacy concerns in support access
Thematic Health Screening Campaigns	Early detection via AI-enhanced screenings (e.g., cancer)	At-risk populations by age/ demographics; broad middle-class coverage	Public health budgets for campaigns and AI tools; cost savings from early interventions	Higher screening uptake; earlier disease detection and treatment success	False positives causing anxiety; equitable access challenges in remote areas

(continued)

Table 5.8 (continued)

Instrument	*Channel/mechanism*	*Targeting/ beneficiaries*	*Financing/fiscal Cost*	*Expected behavioral response*	*Risks/challenges*
Neighborhood Sports Infrastructure	Encouraging regular physical activity through free spaces	All ages in residential areas, focusing on inactive or chronic disease-prone groups	Integration into urban planning budgets; low ongoing maintenance via local management	Rise in population physical activity rates; decreased chronic disease prevalence	Underutilization if not promoted; space constraints in dense cities
Internal Health Governance Framework	Strategic planning for infrastructure, competencies, and tech integration	Regional health systems and providers; equitable beneficiary distribution	Administrative restructuring costs; ongoing monitoring with minimal fiscal escalation	Balanced regional investments; tailored competencies reducing service gaps	Bureaucratic inertia; resistance to tech adoption in legacy systems

providing the necessary services to people in need. It is about encouraging people to have a healthy lifestyle and to offer them a suitable environment where they can be more productive and less exposed to chronic diseases.

In theory, the setup of health insurance schemes at the national level would have a positive impact on the health of individuals while lowering the global cost. Nevertheless, the experience showed that health insurance schemes became throughout the years more costly and its due mainly to the curative approach and neglecting the preventive mechanisms.

Secondly, the public health governance systems should be reinforced to take into account the needs and specificities of the different regions and have regional—if not local—strategies to respond to the different issues in a more efficient manner. Moreover, the public health governance systems should include a preventive component that consists of involving other departments that run sectors or fields with a very close link with the health department. The aim of such approach is to reinforce the preventive mechanisms and rely less on the curative component.

Thirdly, the public health policies should take into account the technological advancements that are providing new perspectives to tackle the variety of health issues nations have to face. In practice, artificial intelligence algorithms can predict people who will develop chronic diseases or even cancers and submit them to preventive protocols which would reduce the cost of health-care services. Moreover, these algorithms can improve the accuracy of the different diagnoses in order to detect diseases at early stages which would save lives, money, and time for all.

Based on these three elements, the interactions between public health policies and other public policies is obvious. For instance, an urban planning that takes into account the requirements of a healthy lifestyle would have a positive impact on the global health situation. Moreover, education programs and awareness campaigns can encourage people to adopt the right behaviors and decisions for a healthy life.

References

African Exponent. (2022). *Top 10 African countries with the best water and sanitation systems in 2025*. https://www.africanexponent.com/top-10-african-countries-with-the-best-water-and-sanitation-systems-in-2025/

Baker, E. L., Jr., Potter, M. A., Jones, D. L., Mercer, S. L., Cioffi, J. P., Green, L. W., Maffetone, C. D., & Fleming, D. W. (2005). The public health infrastructure and our nation's health. *Annual Review of Public Health, 26*, 303–318. https://doi.org/10.1146/annurev.publhealth.26.021304.144647

Barbazza, E., & Tello, J. E. (2014). A review of health governance: Definitions, dimensions and tools to govern. *Health Policy, 116*(1), 1–11. https://doi.org/10.1016/j.healthpol.2014.01.007

Bhargava, A., Docquier, F., & Moullan, Y. (2011). Modeling the effects of physician emigration on human development. *Economics & Human Biology, 9*(2), 172–183. https://doi.org/10.1016/j.ehb.2010.12.004 (Dataset available via World Bank: https://datacatalogfiles.worldbank.org/ddh-published/0042054/1/DR0052583/mbddataset.xls)

Bingham, K. W. (2025). The health effects of poor air quality. *Nursing, 55*(1), 32–39. https://doi.org/10.1097/NSG.0000000000000112

Cole, M. A., & Neumayer, E. (2006). The impact of poor health on factor productivity: An empirical investigation. *Journal of Development Studies, 42*(6), 918–938. https://doi.org/10.1080/00220380600741962

Detels, R., & Tan, C. C. (2015). The scope and concerns of public health. In R. Detels, M. Gulliford, Q. Abdool Karim, & C. C. Tan (Eds.), *Oxford textbook of global public health* (6th ed., pp. 3–18). Oxford University Press. https://doi.org/10.1093/med/9780199661756.003.0001

Gupta, S. K., Gupta, R. C., Chhabra, S. K., Eskiocak, S., Gupta, A. B., & Gupta, R. (2008). Health issues related to N pollution in water and air. *Current Science, 94*(10), 1469–1477.

Gurung, R. A. R., Sarason, B. R., & Sarason, I. G. (1997). Close personal relationships and health outcomes: A key to the role of social support. In S. Duck (Ed.), *Handbook of personal relationships: Theory, research and interventions* (2nd ed., pp. 547–573). Wiley.

Haldane, V., De Foo, C., Abdalla, S. M., Jung, A. S., Tan, M., Wu, S., Chua, A., Verma, M., Shrestha, P., Singh, S., & Legido-Quigley, H. (2021). Health systems resilience in managing the COVID-19 pandemic: Lessons from 28 countries. *Nature Medicine, 27*(6), 964–980. https://doi.org/10.1038/s41591-021-01381-y

Herman, H., & Jané-Llopis, E. (2005). Mental health promotion in public health. *Promotion & Education, 12*(2_suppl), 42–47. https://doi.org/10.1177/10253823050120020111x

IQAir. (2024). 2024 World Air Quality Report: Morocco. https://www.iqair.com/world-air-quality-report

Khan, K. M., Thompson, A. M., Blair, S. N., Sallis, J. F., Powell, K. E., Bull, F. C., & Bauman, A. E. (2012). Sport and exercise as contributors to the health of nations. *The Lancet, 380*(9836), 59–64. https://doi.org/10.1016/S0140-6736(12)61078-4

Kuehn, B. M. (2014). WHO: More than 7 million air pollution deaths each year. *JAMA, 311*(15), 1486. https://doi.org/10.1001/jama.2014.3364

Li, P., & Wu, J. (2019). Drinking water quality and public health. *Exposure and Health, 11*(2), 73–79. https://doi.org/10.1007/s12403-018-0285-4

Liang, Z., Howard, P. F., Leggat, S., & Bartram, T. (2018). Development and validation of health service management competencies. *Journal of Health Organization and Management, 32*(2), 157–175. https://doi.org/10.1108/JHOM-09-2017-0218

Lindley-French, S. (1986). *Raising public awareness*. World Health, (Jan–Feb), 6–9.

Mann, T., & Ward, A. (2007). Attention, self-control, and health behaviors. *Current Directions in Psychological Science, 16*(5), 280–283. https://doi.org/10.1111/j.1467-8721.2007.00520.x

Martuzzi, M., Tickner, J. A., & World Health Organization, Regional Office for Europe. (2004). *The precautionary principle: Protecting public health, the environment and the future of our children*. World Health Organization. https://www.euro.who.int/__data/assets/pdf_file/0003/91009/E83077.pdf

Morocco World News. (2022, May 6). *Over 50% of Moroccans regularly practice sports*. https://www.moroccoworldnews.com/2022/05/46456/over-50-of-moroccans-regularly-practice-sports

Mujawar, M. S., Salunke, D., Mulani, D., Gajare, A., Deshmukh, P. M., Ranjan, N. M., & Tekade, P. (2023). Smart watch assisted multi-disease detection using machine learning: A comprehensive survey. In S. Muthu (Ed.), *Proceedings of the International Conference on Artificial Intelligence on Textile and Apparel* (pp. 381–394). Springer. https://doi.org/10.1007/978-981-19-9470-8_28

Nuwayhid, I., Krisht, G., Jabbour, S., DeJong, J., & Zurayk, H. (2021). Mapping university-based master of public health programs in the Arab world. *Annals of Global Health, 87*(1), Article 70. https://doi.org/10.5334/aogh.3297

O'Donnell, O., van Doorslaer, E., & van Ourti, T. (2015). Health and inequality. In A. B. Atkinson & F. Bourguignon (Eds.), *Handbook of income distribution* (Vol. 2, pp. 1419–1533). Elsevier. https://doi.org/10.1016/B978-0-444-59429-7.00011-3

Organisation for Economic Co-operation and Development. (n.d.). *Health coverage data for Morocco: Near-universal coverage*. https://www.oecd.org/health/

Pereira, M., & Oliveira, A. M. (2020). Poverty and food insecurity may increase as the threat of COVID-19 spreads. *Public Health Nutrition, 23*(17), 3236–3240. https://doi.org/10.1017/S1368980020003800

Price-Smith, A. T. (2001). *The health of nations: Infectious disease, environmental change, and their effects on national security and development*. MIT Press.

TheGlobalEconomy.com. (2022). *Urban population using safely managed drinking water services in Morocco*. https://www.theglobaleconomy.com/rankings/drinking_water_urban/MENA/

Tillmann, P. A., Tzortzopoulos, P., & Formoso, C. T. (2010). Redefining healthcare infrastructure: Moving toward integrated solutions. *Health Environments Research & Design Journal, 3*(2), 84–96. https://doi.org/10.1177/193758671000300209

Tisdell, C. (2001). Environmental constraints. *Asia Pacific Journal of Environment and Development, 8*(1), 15–33.

World Bank. (n.d.-a). *Hospital beds (per 1,000 people)*. https://data.worldbank.org/indicator/SH.MED.BEDS.ZS

World Bank. (n.d.-b). *Physicians (per 1,000 people)*. https://data.worldbank.org/indicator/SH.MED.PHYS.ZS

Woolf, S. H. (2008). The power of prevention and what it requires. *JAMA, 299*(20), 2437–2439. https://doi.org/10.1001/jama.299.20.2437

Wu, X. Y., Zhuang, L. H., Li, W., Guo, H. W., Zhang, J. H., Zhao, Y. K., Yang, Y. Y., Yang, X. Y., Han, L. X., Han, J. L., & Veugelers, P. J. (2019). The influence of diet quality and dietary behavior on health-related quality of life in the general population of children and adolescents: A systematic review and meta-analysis. *Quality of Life Research, 28*(8), 1989–2015. https://doi.org/10.1007/s11136-019-02173-5

Yazbeck, A. S. (2009). Attacking inequality in the health sector: A synthesis of evidence and tools. *World Bank Publications*. https://doi.org/10.1596/978-0-8213-7742-1

Zakharenko, R. (2016). Self-driving cars will change cities. *Regional Science and Urban Economics, 61*, 26–37. https://doi.org/10.1016/j.regsciurbeco.2016.07.002

PART III

The Lifts & Nets Based Public Policies in the Economic Sphere

CHAPTER 6

The Social Cost of Non-Middle-Class Nations on Economies

Introduction of the Chapter

When doing business in a particular country, investors are looking at the main economic, political, and social factors and indicators that can influence the business growth, its competitiveness and its profitability. Indeed, economic factors such as the Gross Domestic Product growth and stability, inflation, unemployment rate, currency stability, and exchange rates are very important to assess the dynamism of any country (Yasmin et al., 2003).

Moreover, regulations in terms of ease of starting a business, tax policies, and the flexibility of the labor laws are all factors and indicators that show the openness of a country (Wang, 2004) and its willingness to support the entrepreneurial mindset.

When it comes to political factors, the government stability and the consistency of the different regulations as well as the public sector efficiency are the main indicators that can encourage local entrepreneurs and attract foreign investors to start their business in the country. For social and market conditions, analysts are more focused on the availability of skilled workforce, the size of the consumer market and purchasing power as well as the cultural factors in general (Tam, 2023).

Indeed, all these indicators are visible and decisive when it comes to starting a business and investing in a particular country. Nevertheless,

A. Tahiri Jouti, *Building Middle Class Nations*,
https://doi.org/10.1007/978-3-032-02134-2_6

there are some invisible aspects that may not be identified by international indices and reports that may increase the cost of doing business in a particular country such as the efficiency of the public policies in the major social fields.

For instance, the absence of performant public schools and hospitals would force families to deal with the private sector institutions increasing their cost of living. Likewise, the underperformance of public policies in housing or transportation would mean that people would try to fill the gaps by themselves and hence this would increase their cost of living.

Therefore, these unhappy people with the outputs of public policies in the social sphere would require higher wages or would be unproductive or less performant since they are under pressure. If people are unable to get higher revenue, they will leave the country looking for better places to live. In this case, the country would lose its talented people.

In such a context, businesses and investors would be facing issues such as the lack of local talents (Muyia, 2018) and/or the increase of wages. Generally, countries promoting themselves as an ideal investment destination thanks to low labor costs would see this competitive advantage disappear throughout time.

This chapter addresses the issue of the underperformance of social public policies and its impact on the economic competitiveness of the country from different perspectives and indicators.

The Social Cost Major Issues

The General Framework of Issues Related to the Social Cost

The low level of wages and taxes has always been presented as a competitive advantage for certain countries to attract investors who want to reduce their production costs (Pfeffer, 1994). Nevertheless, in today's context, the sustainability of an investment is not limited to the ability of entrepreneurs to cut costs, but rather to innovate, invent, and maintain their customer bases.

Indeed, investors need to hire the most talented individuals and keep them focused in order to excel in achieving their objectives. To this end, they must offer a compensation package that provides the necessary resources to enhance their quality of life.

For investors, highly talented individuals may justify additional costs to retain them. In contrast, for less talented employees, investors are unlikely to increase wages until they demonstrate that such compensation is warranted.

Suppose, in a given context, that everyone's wages accurately reflect their true capabilities. If the cost of living rises, employees would naturally request higher wages, while investors would initially refuse to cover the additional expense unless productivity also increases. Such a response from investors may be acceptable in the short term. However, if inflation is widespread and employees continue requesting raises, investors will inevitably need to adjust wages in the medium term to accommodate the increased cost of living.

Now, consider an investor choosing between two countries. The first country offers a high-performing public education system and a robust public healthcare system. The second country relies entirely on private education and healthcare, with no public subsidies. In this scenario, the cost of living would be higher in the second country. Consequently, for the same level of productivity, employees in the second country would demand higher wages.

The following table presents the data related to the out-of-pocket health expenditure compared to the current Health expenditure in different countries (Morocco, Tunisia, Egypt, Sweden, and Switzerland) (ESCARDIO eAtlas, n.d.; Exaputra.com, 2025; Statista, 2024; The Global Economy, n.d.; World Bank & World Health Organization, 2025) (Table 6.1):

Table 6.1 The out-of-pocket health expenditure compared to the current Health expenditure in different countries

Country	*GDP per capita (PPP, international US$)*	*Out-of-pocket health expenditure (% of Current Health Expenditure)*	*Current health expenditure (CHE) as % of GDP*
Morocco	~ 9066 US$ (2024 est.)	~ 54.4% (2020)	~ 5.68% (2022)
Tunisia	~ 12,713 US$ (2024 est.)	~ 40.8% (2020)	~ 6.3% (2020)
Egypt	~ 15,091 US$ (2022)	~ 67.0% (2020)	~ 4.4% (2020)
Sweden	~ 74,900 US$ (2025 est.)	~ 14.1% (2020)	~ 11.3% (2021)
Switzerland	~ 83,598 US$ (2022)	21.6% (2022)	~ 11.8% (2020)

The data indicate that countries with weaker public health systems, such as Morocco, Tunisia, and Egypt, impose a heavy financial burden on their populations, with out-of-pocket health expenditures ranging from 40 to 67% of total health spending. This reflects gaps in public policy, where governments do not adequately fund or guarantee accessible health services, forcing households to cover a large share of essential medical costs. In contrast, Sweden and Switzerland invest heavily in public health, resulting in much lower out-of-pocket spending and stronger financial protection for citizens. When public policies underperform, people effectively pay twice: through taxes and private spending, increasing inequality, reducing purchasing power, and creating a high social cost that individuals must shoulder to access quality care, which ultimately constrains their socio-economic stability and well-being.

From another perspective, this additional cost of living, resulting from the absence of high-quality free public services, is referred to in this chapter as the social cost (Adachi, 1999). Linking this concept to the previous chapters, it is clear that when public policies fail, individuals are forced to rely on their finances to meet their needs, which increases their cost of life.

For this purpose, people would ask for higher wages and this extra cost is what businesses would pay to their employees to help them solve their own problems since the government is not able to do it for them.

In some contexts, a low level of taxation indicates government withdrawal from certain social services. As a result, investors may need to enhance their employees' quality of life by offering higher wages and additional benefits; otherwise, productivity could fall below expectations.

In a non-middle-class nation, local investors have their own strategies to handle this situation. For instance, they would pay less for people who are not essential to their activity and manage the turnover. They would try to pay less taxes to the government by different ways and means in order to make the business highly profitable and they would accept to produce goods and services of inferior quality especially if they are overprotected by local authorities and public policies.

The following table estimates the tax gap (% of GDP) due to the shadow economy in countries like Morocco, Algeria, Tunisia, Egypt from one side, and Sweden and Switzerland from the other side (Table 6.2):

Countries like Morocco and Tunisia, with shadow economies near 38–39% of GDP and relatively moderate tax-to-GDP ratios (25–26%), face a

Table 6.2 Shadow economy and estimated tax gap in different countries

Country	*Shadow Economy (% of GDP)*	*Average Tax-to-GDP Ratio (%)*	*Estimated Tax Gap (% of GDP)*	*Notes/Sources*
Morocco	38.7	26	10.1	Shadow economy 1985–2016; tax-to-GDP IMF/ OECD; Tax Gap = Shadow × Tax Ratio (ccsenet.org)
Algeria	24.2	24	5.8	Shadow economy 2023 estimate (ey. com)
Tunisia	38.5	25	9.6	Historical shadow economy (~38–39% of GDP); tax-to-GDP IMF/ OECD (iea.org.uk)
Egypt	21	19	4.0	Shadow economy estimate 2023 (sta tista.com)
Sweden	11.7	44	5.1	Shadow economy 2015; tax-to-GDP OECD (theglobaleco nomy.com)
Switzerland	7.2	28	2.0	Shadow economy 1991–2015 average; tax-to-GDP OECD (imf.org)

significant tax gap, meaning a large portion of potential revenue is effectively lost. This shortfall limits government capacity to provide public services, shifting social costs onto individuals and employers. In contrast, Sweden and Switzerland have smaller shadow economies (12% and 7%, respectively) and higher or moderate tax ratios, resulting in a much lower tax gap; this enables more comprehensive public services, reducing the need for individuals to bear private costs.

From the government's perspective, these investors and their business models should be protected, as they provide employment for many people, and any measures against them could result in significant job losses (Fellows & Kahng, 2013).

In this context, both the government and local investors are accomplices in maintaining the feature of a non-middle-class nation. Moreover, to solve the unemployment issue, the government can offer the same advantages to foreign investors by highlighting the low level of wages and taxes and hiding the social cost.

The social cost creates three main clusters in a particular nation. First, the cluster of investors who have higher earnings and takes advantage of the situation to increase their profitability. This cluster is not bothered by the social cost since they have the necessary resources to solve their own problems.

The second cluster of constituted of highly qualified people that accompany the investors in running their businesses. Generally, they have acceptable wages and they can handle their own social cost but if it increases, their quality of life is vulnerable and can be impacted easily.

The third cluster is composed of people who have a low level of wages and are highly vulnerable to the social cost. Both governments with their inefficient public policies and local investors with their attitude are reinforcing the feature of non-middle-class nations.

From another perspective, these nations would seem unattractive to foreign (Ben Malek, 2017)—and even to some local—investors who would find the local market highly limited and would need to manage the social cost (low productivity level). Therefore, if the local market is limited, increasing the productivity and the cost of production cannot be offset by increasing the sales.

The following figure summarizes the impact of the social cost on the non-middle-class feature of nations (Fig. 6.1):

If the social cost is eliminated from a particular nation, the gaps between the different clusters would be reduced (Avetisyan, 2020). First, many social services would be performant and undertaken for free or at least subsidized by the government. In this case, the cost of life would be reduced for everyone especially when it comes to education and health. The cluster of people with no qualifications would have a lower cost of life and can improve their skills and capabilities with the assistance of the government.

Second, investors would be attracted by the quality of life in the country and the qualifications of people to hire. In this case, the country would attract industries and investment with a much higher value which would generate more taxes and more income to the nation. This revenue

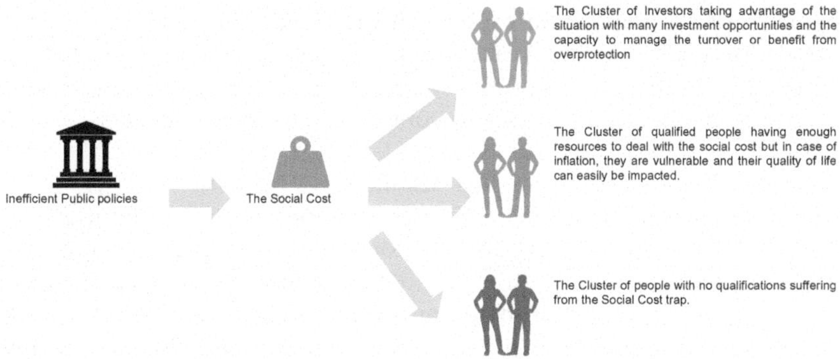

Fig. 6.1 The inefficiency of public policies and the social class in non-middle-class nations

can help the government to further reduce the social cost and make life better for everyone.

Third, vulnerability of people is reduced. Therefore, people's feeling of security from all the different clusters can be reinforced and this would encourage them to take risks and innovate while there are so many "nets" mechanisms that protect them from any source of vulnerability.

The Major Issues Related to the Social Cost in a Non-Middle-Class Nation

The social cost is mainly due to the inefficiency of public policies in the social and economic fields with people relying marginally and occasionally on public services. As explained throughout the book, the inefficiency of public policies may be due to the significant gaps between the different clusters of a nation (a non-middle-class nation) and vice versa, the gaps can be even greater due to inefficient public policies (Pampel, 1998).

In this context, public policy inefficiency arises from multiple, interacting factors. First, negative mindsets and behaviors influence economic decision-making, leading individuals and institutions to prioritize short-term gains or personal advantage over collective welfare (Tahiri, 2024). Second, resource insufficiency—often resulting from mismanagement, financial misconduct, or corruption—limits the ability of governments to implement effective programs. Finally, opportunistic behaviors by certain segments of the population exploit gaps in policy enforcement or institutional oversight, further weakening the system. Together, these factors reduce the effectiveness of public interventions, increase social costs, and force individuals and businesses to compensate for policy failures.

Negative Mindsets Governing Non-Middle-Class Nations

My book entitled "The Unlearning process of nations" (Tahiri, 2024) addresses the main mindsets and economic behaviors that can limit the growth potential of a nation. Such public policies could seem ineffective and totally inefficient if the dominant mindsets are hostile. The book identifies six main mindsets that can hinder economic development in any country:

- *The Comfort Zone and the Boomerang Effect*: Once individuals reach a particular degree of financial or social security, the comfort zone—which denotes a situation in which people and businesses operate with minimum effort—represents. This kind of mindset promotes complacency, therefore lowering output in the public and private sectors. This inefficiency over time causes inflation since the demand for better pay to keep the same degree of comfort results in price rises. Ironically, the boomerang effect results from people who profit from this cycle suffering from the identical inflation they help to create.
- *Under-Investment and the Customer Experience*: Under-investment results from investors giving cost-cutting first priority above improving customer experience, therefore reducing profits and causing market underperformance. In economies where risk aversion is strong, customer expectations are low, and a culture of excellence is weak this problem is especially common. Poor-quality standards, a reduced level of life, and an incapacity to fully investigate market potential—all of which compromise national competitiveness—are among the effects.
- *The "Business as Usual" Mindset (Traditionalism)*: The "Business as Usual" mindset describes the tendency to rely on conventional solutions rather than innovating for superior outcomes. This aversion to change perpetuates inefficiencies, reduces investment opportunities, and lowers living standards. At a macro level, it diminishes economic

dynamism and the nation's attractiveness to international investors, limiting long-term economic prospects.

- *The "No Decision" Mindset (The Ostrich Effect)*: Decision paralysis—whether intentional or unintentional—is a critical barrier to progress. Some decision-makers avoid making choices due to fear of failure, while others fail to recognize pressing threats. Weak accountability structures, short-term incentives, and incompetence reinforce this mindset. The consequences are severe, leading to stagnation in businesses, deterioration of socio-economic conditions, and a decline in national competitiveness.
- *Short-Termism and Its Impacts*: Short-termism prioritizes immediate gains over long-term sustainability. It manifests in two forms:
  - Political short-termism, where leaders focus on quick results to secure their positions rather than investing in long-term development projects.
  - Economic short-termism, where businesses and consumers seek immediate financial benefits at the expense of future stability and growth. This mindset erodes national vision, discourages ethical decision-making, and weakens the foundation for sustainable economic development.
- *The "Sky is the Limit" Mentality and Barriers to Growth*: While ambition is necessary for progress, a constrained vision of growth limits a nation's potential. Governments may impose artificial restrictions in the name of political stability, preventing necessary reforms in governance, wealth distribution, and economic transformation. This stagnation leads to reduced competitiveness, social and economic underperformance, and long-term decline in national prosperity.

Breaking free from these restrictive mindsets is crucial for any nation aspiring to sustainable economic and social development. Encouraging innovation, fostering a long-term vision, and reinforcing accountability are essential steps toward reversing these barriers and unlocking a nation's true potential.

Resource Shortages Due to Financial and Economic Misconduct

The inefficiency of public policies can be justified in some contexts by the insufficiency of financial resources. Indeed, the country is poor and does not have sufficient resources to elaborate and deploy effective and efficient public policies. Therefore, the authorities adopt public policies and solutions which relieve them of a number of obligations and commitments toward the citizens. Nevertheless, the insufficiency of financial resources is also an aspect that needs to be deeply analyzed.

First, the insufficiency of financial resources can be justified by the fact that the country is poor and has no leverage to mobilize additional resources to support the transformative policies. Nevertheless, if the authorities adopt the right policies with a clear vision, they would be able to attract foreign investors, to mobilize funds from international organizations, to restore confidence among local investors and to set a friendly environment for all.

Secondly, while the country possesses sufficient wealth to mobilize necessary financial resources, persistent governance challenges (Batley et al., 2012) and entrenched negative mindsets foster an adversarial climate for public policy implementation. These factors perpetuate resource wastage and policy inefficiencies in myriad ways. To address this, authorities must prioritize bolstering governance frameworks while launching targeted campaigns to dismantle pessimistic attitudes and cultivate a culture of constructive optimism.

Thirdly, the country is not poor and can mobilize financial resources, but fraud and economic misconduct (Farazmand et al., 2022) lead to significant waste. Although the negative mindsets discussed earlier may create conditions that allow such behavior to flourish, fraudulent transactions stem more directly from criminal intentions. In this sense, negative attitudes are blameworthy, whereas fraud is condemnable.

From another perspective, the social cost may also encourage fraud and economic misconduct. When individuals are left to face economic hardship without adequate support, the credibility and perceived usefulness of the government decline. As a result, people may be more inclined to evade taxes whenever the opportunity arises—particularly if they are self-employed or run their own businesses—or, in the case of public sector employees, to engage in embezzlement or misuse of public funds.

Such a position can be justified by the fact that people need more funds to find solutions to their housing, health, education, and other problems.

Indeed, the social cost can be the result of inefficient public policies due to the lack of financial resources but at the same time, the social cost can encourage fraud and economic misconduct in a way that would reduce and limit the financial resources of a specific country.

Certain Stakeholders Taking Advantage of the Situation

The inefficiency of public policies impact businesses and investors in different manners. First, governments and public sector policies that do not promote new growth factors as opening new markets and launching continuously impactful initiatives penalize businesses and investors and limit their growth. Indeed, governments and the public sector can guide private sector investments (including foreign investments) by creating new opportunities and incentives (Stiglitz, 1997).

Secondly, as customers—and in this specific context—public sector administrations and institutions operate at a very slow pace in terms of interaction and execution, with limited innovation and constrained budgets. Instead of supporting local businesses, the public sector often behaves as a poor-quality client, which can undermine firms' growth and, in some cases, threaten their survival (Checherita-Westphal et al., 2016). In addition, foreign investors are generally less attracted to frontier markets where the public sector is difficult to navigate and opportunities are limited, further reducing the share of foreign investment.

Thirdly, the public sector often delivers low-quality services in key areas such as education, health, security, and other essential functions. On one hand, low-skilled individuals—whose competencies do not match labor market needs—reduce the productivity of both businesses and public institutions when they enter the workforce. On the other hand, the poor quality of public services forces households and employees to seek alternatives in the private sector in order to obtain basic services that should normally be guaranteed by the state. This dynamic increases both the cost of production for firms and the cost of living for individuals.

In this context, for businesses to survive, they have to adopt special strategies and tactics such as lobbying to obtain monopolistic or oligopolistic positions (both leading to overprotection), tax evasion to pay less taxes in order to offset the cost of the inefficiency of public policies and/or hiring people at low wages to compensate for their limited productivity.

In all cases, such strategies and tactics undermine the effectiveness of public policies and create opportunities for certain actors to exploit institutional weaknesses. When some players are excessively protected, overall economic competitiveness declines, which in turn further reduces policy efficiency. Additionally, when businesses pay less in taxes than they are required to, the government faces resource shortages that limit its ability to design and implement effective public policies.

Finally, when people are under-qualified, it is expected that they will be underpaid; however, if businesses are excessively protected, this skills gap becomes less relevant for firms seeking to maintain competitiveness. In such contexts, companies may rely on large workforces not for productivity gains but as leverage in negotiations with the government. Their ability to claim that they provide significant employment can lead authorities to tolerate questionable tax practices, undue lobbying, and other forms of misconduct, allowing these firms to preserve their privileged position and benefits.

In this context, businesses and investors taking advantage of the situation, in collaboration with the public sector and the government, have no incentive to recreate the system or to upgrade it. Therefore, such a situation arranges everyone in the short term. However, the consequences can be significant in the long term and for all the stakeholders.

The Social Cost: Lifts and Nets Mechanisms

The Consequences of the Social Cost

The social cost on economies can be understood as a self-reinforcing trap: it is both a consequence of inefficient public policies and a factor that perpetuates this inefficiency. Furthermore, the exploitation of these weaknesses by actors in both the private and public sectors exacerbates the situation. As a result, the social cost further entrenches the characteristics of non-middle-class nations, limiting their economic development and societal advancement.

Increasing and Maintaining the Gaps Between the Different Clusters

As mentioned earlier, the social cost creates three different clusters with the first cluster constituted of all the people that are taking advantage of the situation such as:

- Overprotected investors who obtained advantages through lobbying strategies or any other type of strategies. This sub-cluster would try to maintain their advantage over the long term which would squeeze competitors, block new entrants and eliminate alternative products. Moreover, overprotected investors can stop innovation if it is not initiated by them.

- Tax avoidant investors who pay less taxes than they are expected to would justify their behavior by the fact that to maintain their businesses alive, they need to pay less taxes since they are incurring the limited size of the market due to overprotecting some players. In some cases, people from this sub-cluster would justify their behavior by the social cost concept and that there is no reason to pay taxes to a government/a public sector that do not provide any real services. Therefore, this sub-cluster would try to maintain their current behavior and not to reduce their income including taxes they should have paid to the government.
- Officials and public-sector executives and managers who do not want to conduct a deep reform in terms of public-sector services for many reasons such as the difficulty to change the culture and mindset of several million of public-sector employees in addition to the cost and time it requires. Moreover, a reform may require more transparency and accountability and both may not be interesting for those who will conceive and deploy the reform.

Overall, all the components of the first cluster would try their best to maintain the system as it is without any serious attempts to change the situation. Indeed, if the government keeps overprotecting some players and non-protected businesses keep refusing to pay taxes while the officials and public sector do not conduct the necessary reforms to improve the quality of the services and the efficiency of public policies, the social cost would even increase throughout time. In this situation, the gaps would keep increasing over time.

The second cluster is constituted of people who are exposed to the social cost but have the necessary financial resources to handle it without taking advantage of the situation. Generally, these are not entrepreneurs, investors or business people. This second cluster is constituted of senior and middle managers with incomes enabling them to cover the social cost in terms of health-care services, education, security, and housing. However, inflation or the increase of the social cost are felt more by this cluster than by the first, due to the absence of a relay to increase their income (apart from their employers) or reduce their spending.

Moreover, the more the social cost is increasing, the more people of this cluster move to the 3rd cluster. For instance, if the cost of the education of children (or the cost of the healthcare services) increases, the incomes would become insufficient, and people would be forced to compromise their quality of life or even make difficult choices to get by.

Over time, individuals within this cluster may follow three distinct paths. The first path involves migrating to another country with lower social costs and greater opportunities, thereby opening new prospects for themselves and their children. The second path entails becoming investors or entrepreneurs, seeking to capitalize on the existing situation whenever possible. The third path involves transitioning to the third cluster, accepting a lower quality of life as a means of survival. For example, families may choose to enroll their children in public schools or in lower-quality private institutions in order to balance their income with living expenses.

In all cases, the size of this second cluster would be decreasing throughout time. Indeed, as the social cost increases, the size of this cluster shrinks.

The third cluster is composed of people that are trapped in the social cost (Sachs et al., 2004). They are underpaid as well as underserved by public services and policies. From one perspective, the public services quality is lower than the expectations. Therefore, they are not fulfilling their basic needs such as the medical care, their children education or getting access to a healthy living environment.

From another perspective, public policies are not elaborated in a way to upgrade them and improve their quality of life and to bring them at least to the middle class. Instead, due to the social cost, more people are joining this cluster (especially from the second cluster).

Indeed, throughout time, the size of the second cluster (middle class) is decreasing through immigration outbound flows and the downgrade process to the third cluster is ongoing as explained earlier while the size of the third cluster is increasing. Meanwhile, the first cluster does not increase significantly due to overprotection of incumbents and the incapacity of the government to deal with tax avoidant people for the reason stated in this chapter.

Finally, from a research perspective, moderate inequality can promote productivity and stimulate economic growth, provided that income is not overly concentrated. In contrast, in contexts of high inequality, the wealthy capture a disproportionate share of resources, which can constrain overall growth. Low inequality supports stable increases in welfare without triggering social unrest, whereas high inequality can undermine social consensus and obstruct the implementation of pro-growth reforms.

All in all, there is a "inequality overhang" phenomenon between inequality and economic development. For instance, when net Gini is below 27%, inequality has a positive impact on development but if it is above 27%, inequality negatively affects economic development and the effect worsens as inequality rises.

Impacting the Happiness Levels of the Different Clusters
As per the "inequality overhang" phenomenon linking inequality and economic development, there may be also a link between inequality and the happiness and comfort level of the population. For instance, when the gaps are slightly visible, people who obtained better outcomes in terms of revenues and wealth will be happy and proud but when the gaps become significantly visible, this pride and happiness would transform to a discomfort feeling for meany reasons.

The following table establishes a connection between the Gini index, the GDP per capita and the happiness score in different countries (World Bank, 2011–2020; Helliwell et al., 2015–2023) (Table 6.3):

The data suggest that while economic prosperity strongly influences happiness, income inequality can significantly modulate this effect, particularly in lower- and middle-income nations, reinforcing the importance of both wealth and fair distribution in shaping life satisfaction.

For the first cluster, getting wealthier is a sign of success and economic performance and existing gaps serve to measure how successful an individual is, compared to others. Nevertheless, when these gaps become more visible, it would create a resentment between the different social clusters especially if the people from the other clusters (2 and 3) suffer

Table 6.3 Gini index, GDP per capita level and happiness score

Country	*Year*	*Gini (Income-based)*	*Happiness score (Cantril/Life evaluation)*	*GDP per capita (Nominal, US$)*
Morocco	2013	39.5	4.89	3049
Algeria	2011	27.6	5.37	5501
Tunisia	2015	32.8	4.74	3987
Egypt	2019	31.9	4.17	4138
Sweden	2020	28.9	7.29	52,654
Switzerland	2018	33.1	7.50	85,217

from the social cost which will create a discomfort for everyone including people from the first cluster.

Moreover, the shrinking of the second cluster—whether through emigration to other countries or through a deterioration of financial conditions—and the simultaneous expansion of the third cluster gradually reduce the consumer base available to businesses in the first cluster. Consequently, this erosion of demand will inevitably affect the first cluster as well, sooner or later.

For individuals in the second cluster, upward mobility toward the first cluster can be encouraging when it occurs, yet in non-middle-class nations such transitions are rare and do not represent a broader social pattern. Instead, members of the second cluster often experience a gradual decline in their living standards, largely due to the rising social cost and the expanding size of the third cluster. This dynamic generates frustration: moving into the first cluster becomes increasingly difficult, while over time the likelihood of falling into the third cluster becomes higher than the likelihood of moving upward. As a result, many people seek alternative solutions—such as emigrating—which further exacerbates the overall situation.

The following table tries to link the net migration rate with the Gini index and the GDP capita in different countries (World Bank, 2013–2020; CIA World Factbook, 2023) (Table 6.4):

The data suggest that both economic prosperity and income distribution influence population mobility: low wealth and high inequality tend to push people to emigrate, while high wealth and moderate inequality attract migrants.

Table 6.4 Gini index, GDP per capita, and the net migration rate (per 1000 pop)

Country	*Gini (Income-Based)*	*GDP per Capita (Nominal, US$)*	*Net Migration Rate (per 1000 pop, most recent)*
Morocco	39.5 (2013)	3049	−1.7 (2023 est.)
Tunisia	32.8 (2015)	3987	−1.3 (2023 est.)
Sweden	28.9 (2020)	52,654	+3.8 (2023 est.)
Switzerland	33.1 (2018)	85,217	+6.0 (2023 est.)

For the third cluster, collectively, people's situation is downgrading continuously with no appropriate lifts or nets mechanisms that can improve their situation or at least maintain them. Moreover, most of the immigration host countries (not all of them) have opted for selective immigration targeting mainly people from the first and the second clusters. Indeed, for people from this cluster, immigration is no longer an obvious solution.

In such an extreme context, resentment toward people in the first cluster is justified by the fact that people are overprotected or are getting rich illegally which reduces economic opportunities and has a direct impact on them. Then, resentment toward people in the second cluster is justified by the social cost trap and the impossibility of upgrading and improving their situation.

Reducing the Attractiveness of the Nation at the International Level

The Openness of a nation on the world is very important to reinforce its diversity and fill the gaps in terms of capabilities, commercial deficit, and investments. Therefore, creating an enabling environment, a fair and balanced community, and a clear vision to shape the future raises the attractiveness of any nation.

Indeed, such an approach is able to attract experts, investors, additional talented workforce and tourists to visit and enjoy the country. Nevertheless, if the environment is not enabling and if the community is suffering from disparities and if the vision is not clear, it will definitely not attract foreigners to migrate or at least to visit the country.

– Foreign Investors' Perspective

For foreign investors, a dominant third cluster offers access to a very low-cost workforce, though these workers tend to be less skilled compared to the global average. If production is aimed at the local market, the predominance of this cluster implies limited purchasing power, reducing domestic demand. Consequently, the most attractive scenario for foreign investors is when production requires minimal expertise and focuses on low-cost output. In such a context, investing in the country becomes appealing despite the workforce's lower skill level (Agosin & Machado, 2005).

This contributes to international specialization, so that developed countries specialize in heavy, high-skill industries, while less developed countries specialize in light, low-skill industries. Furthermore, this configuration will reinforce the non-middle-class feature of nations.

Furthermore, foreign investors may find issues investing in such countries because the authorities are overprotecting local players. This overprotection is applied to different sectors but also to substitute products.

Indeed, all these elements are different facets of the social cost concept as explained earlier in this chapter.

– Talented workforce and experts' perspective

From the perspective of talented workforce and experts, the country is not appealing at all because generally, non-middle-class nations end up exporting their workforce and local experts to countries with better perspectives and clearer horizons. Therefore, it is not conceivable to go the other way around and move to a non-middle-class nation unless it is in the context of a multinational relocation.

Moreover, international talented workforce and experts prefer contexts that provide them with the opportunity to lead or contribute to futuristic projects and not to be limited to basic projects and visions that consist of imitating what other did previously. Indeed, evolving in such contexts will classify them as second-rate experts.

In addition to this, when immigrating, people are looking for inclusive nations with invisible gaps between people in terms of social ranks, financial situation, and fairness from a political standpoint.

– Tourists' Perspective

A country may not be attractive for foreign investors and experts, but it can have a special vibe that attracts tourists from all over the world. Generally, tourists may appreciate the country and its beauty but would be bothered by the existence of significant gaps between the different clusters and segments of the community. Such gaps are easily noticeable to tourists through security levels, disparities between neighborhoods within the same city, the presence of beggars, and various other indicators.

Even if the country is unique and beautiful but the visible social and economic gaps may reduce the attractiveness of the country in the eyes of tourists that may decide not to return back again let alone the impressions they will share with family and friends about the experience, which may not always be positive. Indeed, no one loves to visit a country full of unhappy people.

The Lifts and Nets Mechanisms for a Middle-Class Nation to Tackle the Social Cost Phenomenon

As discussed earlier in this chapter, the "social cost" is the result of all the inefficient public policies combined together. Therefore, reducing—if not eliminating—the social cost would require the implementation of the different Lifts and Nets Mechanisms mentioned in the previous chapters. Nevertheless, implementing such mechanisms would be rewarding but not sufficient to obtain the expected results.

Indeed, eliminating gradually the social cost would also require a shift in the economic paradigm and the adoption of a different approach. It is worth noting that the Lifts and Nets Mechanisms in the different social fields would reinforce the credibility of the government to conduct the reforms in the economic sector as well and vice versa, the economic strength of the government would reinforce its ability to conceive and deploy efficient public policies in the different social sectors.

Applying the Lifts and Nets Framework to reduce—if not—eliminate the social cost requires the following mechanisms and policies. The lifts mechanisms consist of ensuring equal access to economic opportunities and tax fairness. Therefore, overprotection as an approach would be removed gradually and the government tax income would increase. Secondly, the nets mechanisms would consist of implementing efficient and effective public policies in the different social sectors. Finally, the upgrade mechanisms consist of improving continuously both the Lifts and Nets Mechanisms. This will set the country on a positive course and create a virtuous cycle.

Equal Access to Economic Opportunities and Tax Fairness (Lifts Mechanisms)

In the real world, there are two approaches related to the access to economic opportunities. First, there are highly liberal countries (generally from the global north) where anyone can launch his business ideas and innovations whenever his business model and case are relevant and fulfill all the legal and regulatory requirements even if the sector is deemed highly sensitive. For substitute and alternative products, legal, and regulatory frameworks are updated regularly to endorse innovations as fast as possible without missing the economic opportunity. Moreover, in these countries, regulations are also available to regulate other sectors and maintain competitiveness.

The second perspective is related to overprotecting countries (generally from the global south) where innovations take a longer time to be endorsed in sectors deemed highly sensitive and the legal process is complicated as well. Generally, in this context, what is not explicitly authorized by the law is therefore prohibited. Indeed, every new innovation in these highly sensitive countries needs to be regulated to make sure that it would not be destabilizing the incumbents and the market as a whole. In the opposite, in non-sensitive sectors, activities are not regulated which creates economic anarchy and undermines the level of competitiveness.

It is worth noting that an overprotective approach is often justified as a means to maintain market stability, but it can also serve to shield influential lobby groups within a particular sector. Consequently, in developing countries, some sectors are highly regulated and largely reserved for these lobby groups, while other sectors remain under-regulated. This dual structure restricts overall investment opportunities, limiting both domestic and foreign participation in the economy.

As discussed in my book "The Unlearning Process of Nations," lobbying practices and the sky is the limit paradigm led to privileging a minority of politically impactful people through lobbying maneuvers or any other means, and granting them exclusive access to lucrative economic sectors with overprotection mechanisms limiting investment and job opportunities for other members of the nation.

If this paradigm and approach change, combined with appropriate people empowerment policies and strategies, it will set free the economic sectors with fairness and equality among people from all the other clusters. Indeed, it will provide talented people with social lifts and promote competitiveness and eliminate gradually the comfort zone and exploitation.

This approach would create more jobs and opportunities and will contribute to lift people up from poverty and raising up the standards of living for all. Such a paradigm shift is not easy to achieve and requires a political willingness and capacity to dethrone the existing lobbying groups and gradually liberalize the various sectors. Indeed, the approach should be gradual and serious in order to achieve the expected outcomes.

Therefore, the public sector itself should be reformed and freed from the lobby groups before conducting a sectoral reform to downsize the overprotective approach. In my book "The Unlearning process of nations," there are many suggested pathways to improve the governance and the accountability frameworks in the public sector as well as the mindsets that are hindering development. Once, the public sector is totally reformed, the private sector reform would be much smoother.

In this context, the capacity to collect more taxes would increase because the credibility of the regime and the government would be enhanced. Indeed, as entrepreneur or investor, evolving in economic sectors with fairness, accompaniment, and visionary economic plans would justify the payment of taxes even higher ones because there is an obvious counterparty. Moreover, eliminating overprotection would give access to new players and would increase competition and competitiveness of the economy with local businesses exporting their expertise internationally reinforcing the national brand and increasing their revenue as well as the amounts of taxes to be paid to the government.

The following table illustrates indicators to monitor the deployment of lifts mechanisms (Table 6.5):

Efficient Public Policies in the Social Sector (Lifts and Nets Mechanisms)

As discussed earlier, eliminating the overprotective approach would lead to creating more investment opportunities and to fairness in terms of access to the different resources of production. To encourage new businesses and to maintain their productivity, the government needs to implement highly efficient public policies in the social sector (education, health, and many other fields) that would reduce the social cost.

Moreover, squeezing the social cost is necessary to reduce the economic gaps between the different segments and clusters composing the nation. For instance, the favorable impact of a certain public policy should not be offset by a negative impact generated by another public policy.

Indeed, public policies need to be drafted in a way that generates individually and collectively a positive impact on the population that would improve their quality of life, their purchasing power, and their welfare.

Table 6.5 Main indicators for lifts mechanisms to reduce the social cost

Dimension	*Indicator*	*What It Measures*
Sector Regulation	Degree of regulation in sensitive vs. non-sensitive sectors	Balance between overprotection and under-regulation, showing how sectors are controlled or open
Investment Opportunities	Number of sectors accessible to domestic and foreign investors	Availability of opportunities for investment and market entry
Competitiveness	Presence of fair competition/ market openness	How well the market rewards talent and innovation vs. maintaining comfort zones for incumbents
People Empowerment	Availability of social lifts/ access to training and education	Opportunities for individuals from all clusters to improve skills, productivity, and income
Tax Compliance/ Credibility	Willingness of entrepreneurs to pay taxes/perceived fairness of tax system	Level of voluntary compliance with taxation and government credibility
Economic Growth/Job Creation	Job creation rates/number of new business entrants	Overall growth, employment opportunities, and improvement of living standards
International Competitiveness	Export capacity/national brand recognition	Ability of local businesses to compete internationally and increase revenues for the economy

These efficient public policies, combined together, constitute at the same time Lifts and Nets Mechanisms. First, highly appreciated services provided to people by the public sector (for free) would make it easier to families to ensure a better future for their members. For instance, if the public education sector is highly performing, this means that families would keep enrolling their kids in public schools and reducing their social cost. For kids with better educational outcomes, they may improve their situation compared to their parents' situation and get better job opportunities.

Secondly, it can be considered as a net mechanism because people during the time of crisis would reduce automatically their spending on education and health and if these services are provided for free to people, this would constitute automatically a net mechanism.

In this book, the social sector comprises education, health, housing, and public transportation but can be extended to other sectors. The previous chapters identify solutions based on the Lifts and Nets Framework that can enhance the efficiency and the effectiveness of public policies in these sectors.

Continuous Improvement of the Framework (Upgrade Mechanisms)
The social cost can increase throughout time in different manners. For instance, a change in the age pyramid of a nation can put a lot of pressure on the health and medical coverage systems leading to an increase in the medical expenses. Therefore, such impacts should be anticipated and corrective measures should be taken in order to limit the impacts.

Now, in a favorable context where continuous improvement is made, the social cost is not only maintained but decreased. For instance, there are cities that offer free public transportation networks for both citizens and visitors such as Mulhouse in France, Hassels in Belgium, and many other cities.

Whenever the government achieves a decrease in the social cost, it would reinforce its credibility and people would be eager to pay more taxes since they all benefit from the system and it would help the government to increase the efficiency of public policies. There would be a virtuous cycle.

From another perspective, a decreasing social cost would have a positive impact on businesses and their competitiveness as well as on the attractiveness of the country to attract more people (investors and experts) to live in the country.

Therefore, it is important to monitor all the indicators that can anticipate any changes in the social cost and help the government in taking the right decisions at the right time for the interest of the different stakeholders.

Finally, it is important to remember that reducing the social cost means reducing the gaps between the different clusters and segments of a particular nation (Table 6.6).

Finally, to measure the fair homogeneity of the nation in terms of social cost policies, the following list of indicators is relevant (Table 6.7):

Table 6.6 Upgrade mechanisms main indicators

Dimension	*Indicator*	*What It Measures*
Social Cost	Total public expenditure on health, education, and essential services	Level of societal burden and cost of living on citizens
Public Service Accessibility	Availability and quality of services such as public transportation, healthcare, education	Degree to which citizens can access essential services affordably
Government Credibility	Citizen trust/willingness to pay taxes	Level of confidence in government effectiveness and fairness
Attractiveness for Investors and Talent	Inflow of skilled workers and foreign investment	Ability of the country to attract experts, investors, and talent
Gap Reduction Between Clusters	Equity indicators/income or opportunity distribution	Extent to which social disparities between population clusters are minimized
Monitoring and Anticipation	Tracking relevant indicators/early warning systems	Ability to foresee social cost changes and take timely corrective actions
Virtuous Cycle Effects	Correlation between reduced social cost, higher tax compliance, and improved services	Reinforcement loop where lower social cost strengthens public trust and economic performance

Table 6.7 Summary of the homogeneity indicators related to the social cost

Pillar/Dimension	*Indicator*	*What it measures*	*Why it matters*
Income and Wealth Distribution	Gini Index/Income quintile ratios	Degree of economic equality or inequality within the population	High inequality can create social tensions, reduce cohesion, and limit social mobility
Social Cost/Access to Services	Coverage and quality of health, education, and basic services	Extent to which all citizens have equal access to essential services	Unequal access increases disparities between clusters and reduces overall societal homogeneity
Employment and Skills	Employment rate/ Skill mismatch ratio	Distribution of employment opportunities and skill alignment across the population	Uneven employment or skill distribution weakens productivity and social cohesion
Economic Opportunity and Mobility	Ease of business creation/Regulatory barriers/Access to credit	Availability of opportunities for upward mobility and entrepreneurship	Unequal access to opportunities reinforces cluster stratification and reduces homogeneity
Public-Sector Governance	Transparency/ Lobbying influence/ Policy enforcement	Fairness and effectiveness of government in applying rules uniformly	Overprotection or favoritism distorts opportunities and creates inequality
Tax Fairness and Compliance	Effective tax-to-GDP ratio/Tax gap	Degree to which taxation is fair and evenly applied	Unequal taxation exacerbates economic gaps and erodes trust in institutions
Migration and Population Distribution	Net migration rate/ Regional mobility/ Demographic balance	Distribution of population and outflows/inflows across regions and clusters	Uneven migration or regional disparities can increase social fragmentation

(continued)

Table 6.7 (continued)

Pillar/Dimension	*Indicator*	*What it measures*	*Why it matters*
Access to Economic and Technological Opportunities	Adoption of innovation/Digital access/Investment distribution	Equity in access to technology, innovation, and investment opportunities	Ensures all clusters can participate in growth, reducing structural disparities
Social Mobility and Cluster Integration	Inter-cluster income mobility/ Opportunity ladders	Ability for individuals to move between social or economic clusters	High mobility strengthens national cohesion and reduces stratification

The Summary of Lifts and Nets Mechanisms for a Middle-Class Nation Social Cost

See (Table 6.8)

Conclusion of the Chapter

All the public policies' inefficiencies in the social sectors have an economic cost to be supported by businesses and individuals. For instance, education and health-care services are all necessary for the stability and the prosperity of the nation. If the cost is not undertaken by the government, someone should bear it instead, otherwise, the future of the nation will be compromised.

Indeed, when the government withdraws from the social sectors, it loses gradually its credibility and will be unable to impose its control over the various players and stakeholders which worsens the situation and increases the social cost.

The social cost creates a virtuous cycle that consists of people and businesses paying less taxes to the government deemed inefficient which reduces the efficiency of the public policies. The inefficiency of these public policies decreases the credibility of the government and people again would be eager to pay less taxes.

Therefore, for nations to get out this virtuous cycle, governments have to gradually raise the efficiency of the public policies and to reinforce their credibility in order to raise more taxes and funds. As long as the government initiatives and actions are reliable, efficient, and effective, people

Table 6.8 Summary of the lifts and nets mechanisms to tackle the social cost elements

Instrument	*Channel/Mechanism*	*Targeting/ Beneficiaries*	*Financing/Fiscal Cost*	*Expected Behavioral Response*	*Risks/Challenges*
Gradual Liberalization of Sensitive Sectors	Removing overprotection to allow innovation and competition in regulated sectors	Domestic and foreign investors, entrepreneurs from all socio-economic clusters; broad middle-class workforce	Initial regulatory reform costs; revenue gains from increased tax base and economic activity over time	Increased business entries and innovations; higher investment inflows and job creation across sectors	Resistance from entrenched lobby groups; potential short-term market disruptions or instability during transition
Public-Sector Governance Reform	Enhancing accountability and reducing lobbying influence to enable fair policy implementation	Government officials, public employees; indirect benefits to all citizens via improved service delivery	Training, oversight mechanisms, and anti-corruption investments; moderate fiscal outlay with long-term efficiency savings	Greater transparency leading to voluntary tax compliance; smoother private sector reforms post-reform	Political backlash from vested interests; implementation delays if lacking strong political will

(continued)

Table 6.8 (continued)

Instrument	*Channel/Mechanism*	*Targeting/ Beneficiaries*	*Financing/Fiscal Cost*	*Expected Behavioral Response*	*Risks/Challenges*
Tax System Reforms for Fairness	Improving perceived equity to boost compliance and revenue	Taxpayers, entrepreneurs, and investors valuing reciprocity	Administrative upgrades for fair enforcement; short-term revenue dip during transition, offset by higher voluntary payments	Willingness to pay higher taxes due to credible government; expanded tax base from new economic players	Evasion spikes if reforms seen as punitive; enforcement challenges in informal sectors
Continuous Monitoring and Early Warning Systems	Anticipating social cost changes (e.g., demographic shifts) via indicator tracking	Policymakers and government agencies; indirect benefits to entire population	Low-cost data collection and analytics tools; integrated into existing governance budgets	Timely corrective actions maintaining low social costs; proactive adjustments to policies	Data inaccuracies leading to misguided decisions; over-reliance on metrics ignoring qualitative factors

would be less relentless to contribute financially to the budget of the government.

From another perspective, the social cost can be easily tackled by high-income clusters compared to other clusters which will increase the gaps between the different components of the nation. Therefore, the existence of a social cost can reinforce the non-middle-class feature of nations.

It is worth noting that the efficiency of public policies in the social sectors and the soundness of the governance systems as well as the accountability frameworks are all necessary to reduce the social cost and the gaps between the different clusters. Nevertheless, such mechanisms are not sufficient to build a middle-class nation. Indeed, the modern financial systems, if not conceived properly, can contribute to the gaps between the different clusters composing a particular nation. Thus, the positive effect of all the instruments and mechanisms implemented in the social and economic sectors can be easily offset by the negative impact of the financial system based on risk transfer.

The next chapter would explain why it is relevant to adopt a different model in the financial system based on risk sharing instead of risk transfer.

References

Adachi, Y. (1999). Inefficiencies in public policies. *Journal of Comparative Policy Analysis: Research and Practice, 1*(2), 225–236.

Agosin, M. R., & Machado, R. (2005). Foreign investment in developing countries: Does it crowd in domestic investment? *Oxford Development Studies, 33*(2), 149–162.

Avetisyan, A. (2020). Country attractiveness: Analysis of the main factors. *Finance: Theory and Practice, 24*(4), 58–74.

Batley, R., McCourt, W., & Mcloughlin, C. (2012). The politics and governance of public services in developing countries. *Public Management Review, 14*(2), 131–144.

Ben Malek, H. (2017). *Risks and opportunities of investing in frontier markets*. [Master's thesis, High Institute of Management of Tunis]. Institutional Repository.

Checherita-Westphal, C., Klemm, A., & Viefers, P. (2016). Governments' payment discipline: The macroeconomic impact of public payment delays and arrears. *Journal of Macroeconomics, 47*, 147–165.

CIA World Factbook. (2023). *Country comparison: Net migration rate*. https://www.cia.gov/the-world-factbook/

Exaputra.com. (2025). *Healthcare expenditure per capita & % of GDP—Switzerland*. https://exaputra.com/healthcare/switzerland-2025

Farazmand, A., De Simone, E., Gaeta, G. L., & Capasso, S. (2022). Corruption, lack of transparency and the misuse of public funds in times of crisis: An introduction. *Public Organization Review, 22*(3), 497–503.

Fellows, M. L., & Kahng, L. (2013). Costly mistakes: Undertaxed business owners and overtaxed workers. *The George Washington Law Review, 81*, 329.

Helliwell, J. F., Layard, R., Sachs, J., & De Neve, J.-E. (Eds.). (2015–2023). *World Happiness Report*. Sustainable Development Solutions Network.

Muyia, M. H., Wekullo, C. S., & Nafukho, F. M. (2018). Talent development in emerging economies through learning and development capacity building. *Advances in Developing Human Resources, 20*(4), 498–516.

Pampel, F. C. (1998). *Aging, social inequality, and public policy* (Vol. 474). Pine Forge Press.

Pfeffer, J. (1994). *Competitive advantage through people*: Unleashing the power of the work force. Harvard Business School Press.

Sachs, J., McArthur, J. W., Schmidt-Traub, G., Kruk, M., Bahadur, C., Faye, M., & McCord, G. (2004). Ending Africa's poverty trap. *Brookings Papers on Economic Activity, 2004*(1), 117–240.

Statista. (2024). *Current health expenditure as share of GDP in North Africa (2022)*. by country. https://www.statista.com/statistics/1301284/healthexpenditure-as-share-of-gdp-in-north-africa-by-country/

Stiglitz, J. E. (1997, April). The role of government in economic development. In *Annual World Bank Conference on Development Economics* (Vol. 1996, pp. 11–23). World Bank, Washington DC.

Tahiri, A. J. (2024). *Unlocking economic development: The unlearning process of nations*. Taylor & Francis.

Tam, P. T. (2023). Determinants of foreign investment attraction contributed to social economic development: A case study in Vietnam. *Journal of Law and Sustainable Development, 11*(1), e405–e405.

Wang, C., Liu, X., & Wei, Y. (2004). Impact of openness on growth in different country groups. *The World Economy, 27*(4), 567–585.

World Bank. (2011–2020). *World development indicators: Gini index (income-based)*.https://databank.worldbank.org/source/world-development-indicators

World Bank. (2013–2020). *World development indicators: Gini index (income-based) and GDP per capita*. https://databank.worldbank.org/source/world-development-indicators

World Bank/World Health Organization. (2025). *Current health expenditure (CHE) as % of GDP and out-of-pocket (OOP) share of CHE*. WHO Global Health Expenditure Database.

Yasmin, B., Hussain, A., & Chaudhary, M. A. (2003). Analysis of factors affecting foreign direct investment in developing countries. *Pakistan Economic and Social Review 41(1/2)*, 59–75.

CHAPTER 7

Toward a Risk-Sharing Economy

Introduction of the Chapter

In today's global economy, financial systems are necessary to ensure a fluid circulation of funds between surplus agents (including individuals, businesses, and nations) and deficit agents that have projects. Indeed, financial systems mobilize as much as they can, depending on their maturity and their capabilities, the non-utilized financial resources to prevent hoarding and to contribute effectively to the economic growth and prosperity of individuals and nations.

Based on this analogy, money can be likened to blood, financial systems to the heart, and the nation to the body. The heart's primary function is to ensure that blood reaches every part of the body; without this circulation, those parts would wither and die. Similarly, financial systems must ensure that money flows throughout the nation, reaching all its sectors and citizens, thereby promoting financial, economic, and social inclusion.

Since the twentieth century, countries all over the world including developing ones started implementing their own financial systems as an economic tool to provide the necessary funding to the government projects and initiatives and to support businesses of all kinds as well as individuals. Such financial systems enable countries to get connected to the global economy (Rousseau & Sylla, 2003).

From this perspective, financial systems can be seen as an efficient means to reduce gaps between the different clusters of a nation since they

A. Tahiri Jouti, *Building Middle Class Nations*,
https://doi.org/10.1007/978-3-032-02134-2_7

can provide all the people with the financial support required to achieve their objectives and growth potential.

Nevertheless, from a micro-economic perspective, these financial systems that are supposed to include people economically and reduce the gaps can create them instead (Maldonado, 2017). Obviously, when a financial institution collects funds from an individual, it rewards him with two important elements that are an interest rate (which is a way to reward him for not hoarding) and the guarantee that his funds would be reimbursed. Then, the financial institution would use these funds to support a third party (an individual, a business, or the government) that would pay a higher interest rate to the bank with the necessary guarantees to get the funds back.

If this third party made a profit, everyone will be happy but if he failed to make a profit, the initial depositor and the financial institution would get their money back and the third party, beneficiary of the financing, would lose his assets that were given as guarantees to the loan or to the financing.

Indeed, the modern financial systems are all based on the principle of risk transfer and this would help rich people to maintain and develop their wealth without bearing any risk or threat while beneficiaries of loans are taking risks for the whole community (Culp, 2011).

From this perspective, risk is transferred from depositors to entrepreneurs and wealth is transferred from entrepreneurs to depositors which is acceptable when everything goes well but when there is an economic downturn, wealth will be accumulated between the hands of depositors.

Moreover, this risk transfer principle can contribute to the financial exclusion of the different clusters that do not have the necessary assets and guarantees to cover their financial commitments toward the financial institutions (Koku, 2015). In poorer countries with visible gaps between the different clusters, there are specialized institutions such as microfinance and nano-finance institutions to serve these clusters with less or no guarantees, smaller financing amounts but with much higher interest rates and fees.

This chapter will try to analyze the impact of the risk transfer principle on the efficiency and effectiveness of financial systems to include people economically and reduce the gaps. It will also try to understand the differences in terms of impacts of the risk transfer principle applied to middle-class nations and non-middle-class nations as well.

The Risk Transfer Major Issues

The General Framework of Issues Related to the Risk Transfer Principle

In theory, when discussing a financial system that channels funds from surplus agents to deficit agents, the natural image that comes to mind is one in which wealthy individuals support poorer individuals in their projects, fostering wealth creation. In practice, however, financial systems operate quite differently: they rarely support the poor, focusing instead—if not exclusively—on wealthy individuals who may lack liquid funds but are highly creditworthy.

Financial institutions cannot be entirely blamed for this orientation, as they are for-profit organizations obligated to provide guaranteed returns to depositors and investors. Within this context, three distinct clusters emerge.

The first cluster is composed of people who have funds and who are generally investors and depositors in financial institutions. They are expecting a guaranteed return from their investments and are generally diversifying their portfolio of financial instruments. This cluster can also easily raise funds from financial institutions because they are highly solvent and liquid and they can get the best rates. People belonging to this cluster benefit from the system that protects their wealth and develops it without any risk taken.

The second cluster is composed of people who own assets and for a particular project (personal or professional), they do not have the necessary funds. Thus, they need the support of the financial system institutions. People belonging to the second cluster can easily raise funds. If everything goes well, they can get richer while paying back the loan with extra fees. Otherwise, they can get poor and lose their assets and wealth in favor of people from the first cluster. Indeed, people from the second cluster can easily get the necessary funding and profit from the system if they do not fail achieving growth and profit.

The third cluster is composed of a variety of sub-clusters. First, there are people who do not have assets, but have little amounts of funds. They cannot raise funds because they are not solvent but they contribute through their deposits to the financing of other solvent people. Indeed, insolvent people support solvent people (Beck et al., 2007). Second, there are people who do not have assets, have no or very little amounts of funds but they have good business ideas while having the necessary talents, people from this sub-cluster cannot rely on risk transfer based financial institutions to get the necessary financial support. Finally, there are people who do not have assets, no funds and no ideas. They are totally excluded from the system, they need to get connected to economic opportunities to improve their situation (Fremstad, 2008).

Indeed, risk transfer based financial institutions do not contribute to reduce the gaps between the different clusters but instead, they protect people belonging to the first cluster and develop their wealth at the expense of people from other clusters (and sub-clusters) that fail to make profit.

In this context, there is a risk transfer from the first cluster to the second and third clusters and in parallel there is a wealth transfer from the third and second clusters to the first cluster. Such flows increase the gaps between the different clusters of a nation.

Obviously, a financial system that does not want to increase the gaps between the different clusters should replace the risk transfer principle with the risk-sharing principle in a way that all the clusters would share the losses and the profits. Moreover, if a financial system wants to reduce the gaps between the different clusters, it should invert the flows related to risk and wealth transfer. These elements would be detailed in the second section of this chapter.

The following table presents the main indicators regarding the banking sector in Morocco, Algeria, Tunisia, Sweden, and Switzerland (Data compiled from Bank Al-Maghrib (2025), Barlamane Today (2025), DZ Bank (2023), ECB (2024–2025), Wikipedia, and Reuters (2024), 2011–2025) Table 7.1:

Across these countries, the combination of banking-penetration, policy rates, and NPL levels highlights how the strength of the middle-class shapes financial system dynamics. Advanced economies with large, stable middle classes—such as Sweden and Switzerland—show near-universal banking penetration and very low NPL ratios, reflecting strong financial inclusion, predictable income flows, and low credit stress. Their moderate or low policy rates also indicate confidence in macroeconomic stability. In contrast, North African countries with weaker or more constrained middle classes show lower banking penetration and higher NPL ratios, signaling limited access to formal finance, higher household and business vulnerability, and greater credit-risk accumulation.

In developing countries, the negative impact of the financial systems relying on the risk transfer principle is not that visible because it is easily

Table 7.1 comparison of the main indicators related to the Banking sector in Morocco, Algeria, Tunisia, Sweden, and Switzerland

Country	*Banking penetration rate*	*Policy/Central Bank Key Rate (end of 2025)*	*NPL rate (2025)*
Morocco	~ 58%	2.25%	~ 8.6% (2024–25)
Algeria	~ 33% (older, ~2011)	— (no consistent recent published rate)	~ 19.9% (most recent available regional/reported)
Tunisia	34% (2022 data)	7,5%	14.7% (Q1 2025)
Sweden	~ 99.7% (2021 data)	1.75% (latest main policy rate)	~ 1.9%–2.2% (EU banking-system NPL including Sweden, 2024–25)
Switzerland	~ 99.5% (2021 data)	~ 0.5–0.75% (policy rate cut during 2024; see central-bank decisions)	*0.83% in 2023*

offset by all the efficient public policies in the social fields and the interest rates are very low. However, in non-middle-class nations, the financial system increases the gaps between the different clusters especially during economic downturns if not managed properly.

The following figure summarizes the different clusters in a risk transfer financial system Fig. 7.1:

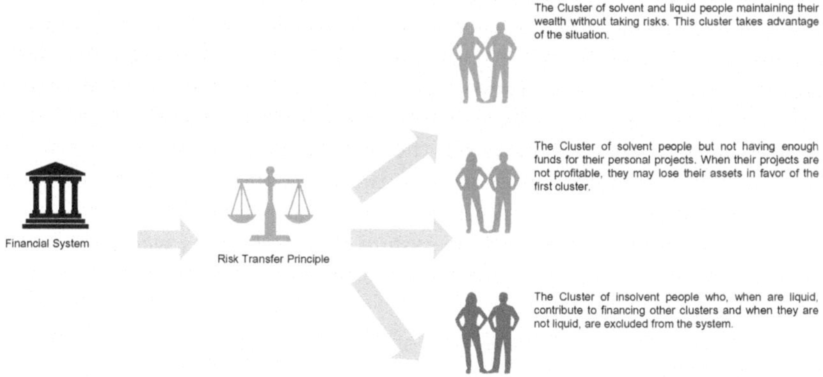

Fig. 7.1 The risk Transfer principle and the non-middle-class feature effect

The Major Issues Related to the Risk Transfer Principle in a Non-Middle-Class Nation

The Risk Transfer Principle Main Assumptions

A Risk transfer based financial system can reinforce the non-middle-class feature of a nation when the following assumptions are fulfilled:

Assumption 1.—The High banking penetration rate:

When most people have access to banking services, it means banks play a big role in how money flows through the economy (Kumar et al., 2014). So, when the central bank changes interest rates or other money-related policies, those changes are more likely to reach everyday people and businesses—affecting how they spend, save, or borrow. In short, the more connected people are to the banking system, the more powerful monetary policy becomes.

Indeed, the higher the banking penetration rate is, the more significant its impact is on the economy and the different classes of a nation (Wang, 2018). This is a key assumption since it defines how significant the risk transfer paradigm is in the economic activity. If the banking penetration rate is low, this means that a few people are concerned with the risk transfer principle.

Assumption 2.—The absence of alternative modes of financing:

Today's financial systems are open to new modes of financing based on different formulas such as equity, leasing, free interest loans, microfinance, and crowdfunding (with different formulas). Some of these formulas are not risk transfer based. Therefore, the impact of the financial system on the middle-class feature of a nation can be reduced if other non-risk transfer formulas are widely used.

At the opposite, if the banking system is dominant as well as the risk transfer formulas, then, the impact of the financial system can be visible.

Assumption 3.—The absence of support mechanisms and appropriate financial instruments to the unbanked people:

To enhance financial inclusion among countries with different clusters of people, the financial authorities deploy different mechanisms to facilitate the access of unbanked people to financial services and economic opportunities.

These support mechanisms can take the form of guarantee schemes provided by specialized governmental entities to different segments of the community to get home financing or business financing (Ayadi, 2023). They can also take the form of microfinance institutions specialized in providing micro-loans for unbanked people for their income-generating projects. They can also take the form of mobile payments and nano-finance institutions to enhance financial inclusion at a wider scale.

Moreover, a highly efficient financial system should integrate all the new innovative instruments that can improve the financial inclusion indicators especially those who are not based on the principle of risk transfer.

Assumption 4.—The high financing rates:

The high financing rates mean that the financial system investment instruments provide very competitive returns for investors especially that these rates are guaranteed. Therefore, the risk transfer mechanism is activated for investors who would prefer renouncing to all the investment opportunities in the real economy (with non-guaranteed returns) in return for a guaranteed interest rates.

Moreover, highly financing rates also mean that people raising funds from the financial system would need to make more profit to cover the financing cost or to deduct more from their salaries in order to pay the installments. In this case, the probability of failure would raise exposing these people to the risk of losing their own assets.

Another hidden impact exists in this case. For instance, a property developer who has built several real estate projects with a view to selling the properties at a given price. If the central bank decides to raise interest rates, fewer people will be able to buy real estate, forcing the developer to reduce prices in favor of financial institutions and depositors, who will earn more than before the interest rate increase.

In addition to this, the high-interest rates do not impact only the loan beneficiaries but also entrepreneurs and investments who may see their margins fall and, in some cases, their projects fail. Indeed, the risk transfer principle enables the financial system to take control over the prices in the different markets and sectors and take advantage of the whole situation.

Assumption 5.—The economic downturns and the absence of support mechanisms:

During medium size economic downturns, most of the projects would have difficulties and would not be able to honor their financial commitments toward financial institutions. In the absence of support mechanisms such as free rescheduling of debts, direct subsidies, or any similar mechanisms, again the risk transfer principle would be activated on a larger scale. In such conditions, all those who trusted the economic system would fail for those who did not and preferred to keep their funds within the Risk transfer financial instruments.

Indeed, investors who made the trade off to invest in term deposit instruments with a guaranteed return have in fact chosen to not trust the real economy and instead transfer all the risks to those who still trust it. Moreover, as discussed earlier, high financing rates can also impact those people who have chosen to trust the real economy.

The Issues Related to the Application of Risk Transfer Principle

The more assumptions are true, the more the principle of risk transfer is activated and vice versa, the less assumptions are true, the less the principle of risk transfer is activated. Now, to understand the major issues of the risk transfer principle applied in the financial system, let us draw the picture of an extreme scenario where all the five assumptions are true. In this context, there will be three main issues:

- Issue 1—The Financial system does not grant financing to insolvent people but uses their funds instead

In a risk transfer paradigm, the financial system supports exclusively people with profitable projects but also with valuable assets to submit as guarantees for the financing scheme. Therefore, anyone who does not have enough wealth and assets to provide as guarantees cannot be eligible to any kind of financing.

Moreover, non-eligible people for financing does not mean that their funds would not be used by the financial institution. Therefore, instead of allocating funds from Cluster 1 to Clusters 2 and 3, financial institutions use funds from non-eligible people belonging to Clusters 2 and 3 to solvent people.

Indeed, from this perspective, the financial system provides opportunities to solvent people who may get richer or lose their assets while making rich people even richer without any risk exposure.

- Issue 2—The financial system does not automatically take into account economic downturns

Economic downturns can be global, national, regional, sectoral, or related to a specific project or business. Generally, governments and financial authorities intervene to provide financial support when the economic downturn is regional or national. Otherwise, the financial system can deal with sectors and businesses suffering from the economic downturn based on what was convened in the loan contracts.

The intervention of the financial system in this case can increase the impact of the economic downturn on the different economic players and sectors. It can even destroy a whole industry and transfer wealth to the bank depositors and shareholders.

- Issue 3—The Financial system effect is multiplied when combined with failing public policies

The risk transfer paradigm increases the gaps between the different clusters. In non-middle-class nations, this impact is even greater since it is combined with a variety of failing public policies.

For instance, an entrepreneur can mortgage his own home to obtain financing for his new business idea. If his new project fails, he may lose his house and if the housing public policy does not provide subsidy packages for families in difficulty or support them, the entrepreneur would lose his assets and move to Cluster 3 without any net to save him and help him to maintain his financial situation.

Such a configuration would discourage entrepreneurs or people with new ideas to start their own businesses and take risks, it will encourage the status quo (Tahiri Jouti, 2024) in the economy. Indeed, the Risk transfer paradigm in the financial system amplifies the social cost effect on the economy.

Nevertheless, in advanced countries, this impact is reduced through different financial instruments and support mechanisms to ensure a wider financial inclusion. Moreover, the level of interest rates is very low compared to less advanced countries. Finally, the public policies in the social fields offset in an efficient way the gaps created by the financial system.

The Risk Transfer Principle: Lifts and Nets Mechanisms

The Consequences of the Risk Transfer Principle

In line with the social cost phenomenon, the risk transfer principle protects individuals in Cluster 1, often at the expense of those in Clusters 2 and 3. When one cluster benefits from privileged or even excessive protection, the disparities between clusters inevitably widen. This chapter therefore examines the mechanisms and outcomes that contribute to these growing gaps, highlighting how unequal protection reinforces structural divides within the population.

No Financing Opportunities to Improve the Quality of Life

As explained earlier, the risk transfer principle governing the financial systems means that the financing opportunities of people belonging to the third cluster are scarce. They are excluded from the system with no lifts to improve their quality of life.

Indeed, the financial system shall be conceived in a way that connects people to real economic opportunities to improve their quality of life and their advancement perspectives in different areas. Financial systems are double-edged sword. They can serve people and eliminate all the gaps or at the opposite increase them.

In practice, Clusters 1 and 2 can get a return from their deposits and investments in the financial system and can easily obtain loans and financing with very interesting financial conditions and rates to increase their wealth.

In this context, financing is very important to improve the quality of life and if it is limited to those who own assets and are solvent while others are excluded, it will definitely create gaps between people.

Losing his Assets to Honor the Financial Commitments toward People from Cluster 1

People from Cluster 2 who are trying to develop their wealth and improve their quality of life may lose their assets in order to set off a debt. When everything goes well, people from Cluster 2 share their profits with people from Cluster 1 and 2 but if they fail, they will lose their assets and become non eligible to financing.

Indeed, when things go wrong, people from Cluster 2 can easily see their situation downgraded and move to Cluster 3 with people who are excluded financially. Therefore, it will reinforce the gaps between people. Instead of reducing the gaps between clusters and improve the situation of people, the financial system can downgrade it and increase the gaps.

Less Initiatives and Entrepreneurial Courage (Miller & Le Breton-Miller, 2017)

When entrepreneurs and innovators are required to provide substantial guarantees to access financing, many talented individuals are effectively excluded from the formal financial system. Even those who possess enough assets to pledge as collateral may hesitate, as the frequent stories of people losing their homes or lifetime savings when projects fail create a strong deterrent. Faced with the possibility of severe personal loss, potential entrepreneurs become discouraged and often abandon their ideas, ultimately limiting economic dynamism and reducing the diversity of new initiatives.

As a consequence of the risk transfer principle applied in the financial system, people will be discouraged to launch initiatives and they will lose their passion for the entrepreneurial mindset. They will turn into the financial system to raise funds for home acquisition and basic needs but not for business opportunities especially when there are economic downturns.

Financial Systems Taking Control over the Whole Economies

It goes without saying that when interest rates increase, the general level of prices decreases and vice versa, when the interest rates decrease, the general level of prices increases. Moreover, in a country where the bank penetration rate is high, all the investment and consumption flows go through the financial institutions and systems. Therefore, the financial system takes control over the whole economy with the monetary policy impacting the inflation rates and the different economic indicators.

From a macroeconomic perspective, the survival and the sustainability of the financial system based on the risk transfer principle require that both investors and depositors keep trusting the different financial instruments and enjoy investing without any risk exposure. Thus, financial institutions can intervene as intermediaries between surplus agents and deficit agents.

Finally, it is essential to recognize that financial systems have a strong incentive to preserve their status as central actors within the economic landscape and to shape economic dynamics in ways that reinforce their influence. However, when this dominant position remains unchecked, it can contribute to widening the disparities between the different clusters. Without meaningful reforms aimed at improving inclusiveness, transparency, and fair access to finance, the financial system's structural advantages risk amplifying existing gaps rather than reducing them.

The Lifts and Nets Mechanisms for a Middle-Class Nation to Tackle the Risk Transfer Principle Applied to the Financial System

Before discussing the Lifts and Nets Mechanisms for a middle-class nation, to apply to the financial system, it is important to start by identifying the different financial systems and their risk exposure model.

The Classification of Financial Systems and Instruments Based on their Risk Exposure

In practice, there are three types of risk exposures for financial systems and instruments. First, there are financial systems that are based on the risk transfer principle. This class of financial systems has been discussed in detail in this chapter.

The second class of financial systems and instruments are those based on the risk-sharing principle. Indeed, this is a neutral class of financial systems where funds are allocated based on the principle of profit and loss sharing. The capital is not guaranteed unless the loss is due to a violation or a negligence from the beneficiary of the financing. Indeed, depositors are not protected from economic downturns as per beneficiaries from the financing. Therefore, the financial system is fairer and does not favor any part over the other. The instruments do not increase the gaps between the clusters during crises and downturns but may decrease them when everything goes well.

In this class of financial systems, generally, people got the financing because they are talented and have the necessary skills and vision to run properly the project. Moreover, such a financial system provides the necessary assistance and accompaniment to empower people to achieve growth and make profit.

The third class of financial systems and instruments are those based on the reverse risk transfer principle. Indeed, depositors and investors provide people with the necessary funds but if there is a loss, they will bear it by themselves. It is a system based on charity and free loans. Depositors want to achieve impact by supporting talented people with no guarantees and if there is a loss, these people would not be accountable or liable toward the fund providers. Such systems would decrease the gaps between the different clusters since the profit would be the exclusive ownership of beneficiaries of loans and financing and the loss would be borne by the fund providers.

The following table represents the main differences between the three classes of financial systems based on their risk exposure Table 7.2:

The Different Strategies to Adopt to Reduce the Impact of the Risk Transfer Principle in Financial Systems

Applying the Lifts and Nets Mechanisms framework to the financial systems in order to reduce their impact on the gaps between the different clusters and reinforce the middle-class feature of a particular nation, can be achieved through three different strategies:

- Strategy 1: Converting the whole system to a Risk-sharing-based financial system with components related to Reverse Risk Transfer based financial systems

Moving to a risk-sharing-based financial system means adopting new business models where depositors share profits and risks with the financial intermediaries that would share profits and risks as well with beneficiaries from financing and loans. Such formulas require well-structured economic sectors and activities and well-established laws and regulations to safeguard the rights of the finance providers. Moreover, information about people and businesses should be available on a timely and a transparent basis, so that financial institutions can assess the situation of all businesses easily.

Table 7.2 Comparison between the three classes of financial systems based on their risk exposure; Source: Author's own

Class of financial systems	*In case of profit*	*In case of loss*	*Impact on gaps between clusters*
Class 1: Risk Transfer principle based financial systems	Profit shared between fund providers and beneficiaries	Loss is borne solely by the beneficiaries	Reduces gaps when everything goes well. Increases gaps during economic downturn/business failures
Class 2: Risk-sharing principle based financial systems	Profit shared between fund providers and beneficiaries	Loss is borne by both the beneficiaries and the fund providers	Reduces gaps when everything goes well. Does not increase gaps during economic downturns/ business failures
Class 3: Reverse risk Transfer principle based financial systems	Profit is the sole ownership of the beneficiaries	Loss is borne solely by the fund providers	Reduces gaps when everything goes well and during economic downturns.

Indeed, converting the whole financial system to the risk-sharing principle could seem unrealistic. Indeed, profit sharing formulas cannot be adapted to all the financing needs such as home or car financing. Moreover, entrepreneurs may fear such formulas because they would change the governance requirements in terms of control and accountability. In addition to this, entrepreneurs would have to renounce to a more important share of the profits to finance providers since losses, if there are any, will be shared with them.

From another perspective, it is possible to add components related to the reverse risk transfer principle. For instance, it is possible to implement guarantee schemes where the government can support individuals from Cluster 3 to access housing or business opportunities while bearing entirely the losses if there are any.

- Strategy 2: Integrating the risk sharing and the reverse risk transfer models to the financial systems

The second strategy consists of keeping the risk transfer components while integrating the risk sharing and the reverse risk transfer principle to the financial systems. For instance, multiplying the venture capital funds and the business angels can support entrepreneurs in different steps of the entrepreneurial adventure.

The reverse risk transfer can be used in some particular cases to enhance the financial inclusion of people or to encourage businesses in some specific sectors. Such an approach can reduce the impacts of the risk transfer principle on economic gaps between the different clusters composing the nation.

Financial innovations in terms of risk-sharing financial instruments or reverse risk transfer financial instruments are unlimited. Indeed, new mechanisms achieving these objectives should be encouraged and deployed to improve the financial system situation.

- Strategy 3: Reforming the risk transfer based financial system to reduce its impact on the economic gaps

The third strategy consists of reforming the risk transfer based financial systems through the integration of new schemes in the current financial instruments. For instance, launching micro and nano-finance that facilitates the access to financing for people belonging to Cluster 3 or launching third party guarantee schemes for people who are not eligible.

Another element is to reduce financing rates to make financing accessible to everyone which will improve the quality of life of people. Nevertheless, relying exclusively on reforming the risk transfer based financial system cannot be sufficient to reduce the impact.

Indeed, strategy 2 seems to be the most relevant in order to reduce the impacts on the socio-economic gaps between the different clusters. Nevertheless, the combination of the different instruments and systems needs to be adapted to the local context depending on many factors.

The Lifts and Nets Mechanisms Applied to the Financial Systems

– The lifts mechanisms applied to risk transfer based financial systems

The lifts mechanisms to apply in order to improve the quality of life of people belonging to Cluster 3 are:

- Implementing new specialized institutions to serve unbanked people such as mobile payment institutions, crowdfunding platforms and microfinance institutions to serve unbanked people. These institutions can first connect people to real economic opportunities. Then, they can accompany them to improve their financial situation and then be eligible to banking products.

These institutions have shown strong performance in several regions of the world, yet their effectiveness remains limited in others. One common mistake made by financial authorities when such systems underperform is the decision to grant banks licenses to create their own subsidiaries—whether in mobile payments, microfinance, or other financial-inclusion activities. These subsidiaries often end up being managed with the same logic and culture as traditional banks, which prevents them from fulfilling their original mission effectively. Another frequent oversight is reducing the role of these institutions to the simple provision of funds. In reality, successful financial-inclusion models require more than financing: they involve empowering individuals, supporting their initiatives, and providing continuous guidance throughout their projects.

From another perspective, when these institutions work well, it is always when they are not under the control of a financial institution and when they have a business model that connects people to real economic opportunities such as M-PESA in partnership with M-KOPA.

Moreover, financial authorities need to pay a particular attention to new innovations and new schemes that can develop financial inclusion. Obviously, these specialized financial institutions cannot achieve a great impact in the absence of economic ecosystems and opportunities.

- Encouraging risk-sharing financial instruments and guarantee schemes such as equity financing through Islamic banking or capital venture funds or any other financial vehicles that can share risks with people. The implementation of such instruments is not easy in the context of unorganized economies with the lack of transparency. Indeed, all the reforms become easier to achieve in middle-class nations with structured economies.

Guarantee schemes can also facilitate the access to loans and financing in a particular context. Such instruments can achieve financial inclusion but their real impact would depend on the facilities provided. For instance, if the housing public policy is a failure, deploying such instruments would not make it a success.

- Lower financing rates can be achieved through different mechanisms such as special rates for specific financing purposes. For instance, the financial authorities can refinance social housing portfolios at lower rates compared to other portfolios. Moreover, the government can decide to deduct the installments from their income tax or to subsidize some categories of people that fulfill specific eligibility criteria.

The following table summarizes the indicators that monitor the nets mechanisms to deploy in the financial sector to be inclusive Table 7.3:

- The Nets mechanisms applied to risk transfer based financial systems

The lifts mechanisms consist of serving unbanked and underserved people to have access to financial instruments. If these people fail to honor their commitments, the net mechanisms serve to minimize the impacts on them.

Therefore, the nets mechanisms can be presented as follows:

- The implementation of risk-sharing instruments serves to transfer the losses to fund providers and not to bear the total loss. It is a way to protect people's assets in case of failure. Obviously, the risk-sharing feature is not activated if there is a negligence or violation.
- The Rescheduling Mechanisms: In case of difficulties or economic downturn, people can ask for a free rescheduling of their debts. Such a mechanism can protect people from losing their assets immediately. Indeed, they are provided with a second chance before they lose their assets.
- The Subsidies Mechanisms: The government can support people in difficulty with subsidies that can take many forms to reduce the impact of economic downturns such as monthly payments or free access to some public services. The subsidies can be paid to people in difficulty to honor their commitments toward the financial systems.

Table 7.3 The lifts mechanisms in the financial sector

Dimension	*Indicator*	*What It Measures*
Access to financial services	1–1 presence of specialized financial institutions (mobile payments, crowdfunding, microfinance)	The ability of unbanked populations (cluster 3) to access basic financial services and connect to economic opportunities.
	1–2 level of operational independence of financial-inclusion institutions	Whether inclusion-focused institutions operate with appropriate models rather than under traditional bank structures that limit their effectiveness.
	1–3 adoption of inclusive digital financial platforms (e.g., M-PESA)	The capacity of technological and partnership-based models to broaden financial access outside traditional banking.
Quality of support and empowerment	2–1 availability of non-financial support services (training, coaching, project accompaniment)	The extent to which institutions empower beneficiaries beyond funding, improving their financial and entrepreneurial capabilities.
	2–2 strength of local economic ecosystems	The degree to which real economic opportunities exist to support sustainable financial inclusion.
Risk-sharing and financing models	3–1 availability of risk-sharing instruments (equity financing, Islamic finance, venture capital)	How much financial systems share risks with low-income people instead of transferring risks entirely onto them.
	3–2 existence and design of public guarantee schemes	The extent to which guarantees support access to loans, and how effectively they reduce collateral constraints for vulnerable populations.
Cost of financing	4–1 access to subsidized or preferential interest rates for priority sectors (e.g., social housing)	The affordability of financing for low-income households and the government's willingness to reduce cost barriers.

(continued)

Table 7.3 (continued)

Dimension	*Indicator*	*What It Measures*
	4–2 tax incentives (e.g., deducting installments from income tax)	The degree to which the fiscal system supports households in managing borrowing costs.
Policy and regulatory environment	5–1 attention to innovations from financial authorities	The responsiveness of regulators to new financial-inclusion solutions and emerging schemes.
	5–2 alignment between public policies and financial instruments	The coherence between financial tools (e.g., guarantees) and sectoral policies (e.g., housing), ensuring reforms produce real impact.

Indeed, these mechanisms reduce the wealth-transfer flows from Clusters 3 and 2 to Cluster 1.

The following table introduces the necessary indicators to monitor the nets mechanisms to deploy in the financial sector Table 7.4:

- The Upgrade mechanisms applied to risk transfer based financial systems

These mechanisms would serve to reinforce the middle-class feature of a nation and create more opportunities for people. The upgrade mechanisms in the financial systems would consist of providing complementary instruments to public policies in different fields and economic sectors to enhance the expected impacts.

For instance, the upgrade mechanisms can aim at promoting innovation in sectors that would shape the future such as Artificial intelligence. Nevertheless, such a mechanism would not be that efficient if it is not deployed in line with public policies and incentives oriented to this particular sector.

Moreover, the upgrade mechanisms can aim at promoting investment in regions that are lagging behind to reduce the disparities between regions and again, if these mechanisms are not in line with public policies and incentives, the impact would not be maximized.

Table 7.4 The nets mechanisms indicators to monitor in the financial system

Dimension	*Indicator*	*What It Measures*
Risk protection for vulnerable groups	Availability of risk-sharing financial instruments	The extent to which financial losses are shared with fund providers rather than fully imposed on borrowers, reducing the likelihood of asset loss for cluster 3 and 2 households.
	Conditions for activating risk sharing (e.g., absence of negligence or violation)	The fairness and transparency of the mechanisms ensuring that protection applies only in legitimate hardship cases.
Debt Relief and stability	Access to free debt-rescheduling options	The financial system's ability to provide temporary relief in cases of economic downturn or personal difficulty, preventing immediate loss of assets.
	Frequency and effectiveness of rescheduling approvals	How often people receive a "second chance" before facing severe consequences such as asset seizure.
Government support and social safety nets	Availability of subsidies for vulnerable households	The extent of government intervention to support individuals facing financial stress and to reduce inequality during downturns.
	Types of subsidies (e.g., income support, reduced payments, free public services)	The breadth and depth of social protection tools used to reduce the burden on financially constrained people.
	Targeting efficiency of subsidies	How well subsidies reach the intended groups without leakage or exclusion.

(continued)

Table 7.4 (continued)

Dimension	*Indicator*	*What It Measures*
Reduction of wealth-transfer imbalances	Impact of nets mechanisms on wealth-transfer flows	The degree to which risk sharing, rescheduling, and subsidies reduce the structural transfer of wealth from clusters 3 and 2 toward cluster 1.
	Alignment between net mechanisms and financial system incentives	How effectively these mechanisms counterbalance risk transfer biases embedded in traditional financial systems.

It is worth noting that the combination of these mechanisms depends on the nation itself. If it is already a middle-class nation, policies should focus more on the nets and upgrade mechanisms. If it is a non-middle-class nation, policies should focus more on Lifts and Nets Mechanisms. Nowadays, financial systems have all known reforms to reduce their impacts on the gaps between clusters.

Finally, to measure the fair homogeneity of the nation in terms of financial inclusion, the following list of indicators is relevant Tables 7.5 and 7.6:

Conclusion of the Chapter

A financial system is a very important component of any economy. It is supposed to facilitate the different financial flows between the agents of the economy. It should be at least neutral—if it could not decrease the gaps between the clusters of a nation and enhance growth. Nevertheless, when financial systems adopt the risk transfer principle, it would have a negative impact on businesses and individuals whenever there is an economic downturn. Indeed, people who cannot honor their financial commitments have to pay with their assets. Risks are beard by entrepreneurs and beneficiaries of funding while profits are shared between them and fund providers.

As explained in this chapter, there are two opposite flows. The first flow is related to the wealth flow that is accumulated at the level of

Table 7.5 Summary of the homogeneity indicators related to the financial system

Pillar	*Indicator*	*What It Measures*	*Why It Matters*
Financial accessibility	Reduction in the share of unbanked population	The improvement in access to accounts, payment systems, and basic financial services.	Greater inclusion lowers structural exclusion and reduces gaps between clusters 1, 2, and 3.
Economic opportunity equality	Balanced regional financing flows	How evenly investments and financial products are distributed across regions.	Reduces territorial disparities and prevents geographic concentration of prosperity.
Affordability of financing	Access to preferential financing (housing, education, entrepreneurship)	The ability of middle- and low-income groups to access essential credit at reasonable costs.	Prevents financial polarization and supports upward mobility.
Risk mitigation/ financial stability	NPL rate among vulnerable borrowers	The proportion of loans in default or at risk in clusters 2 and 3.	Indicates whether financial reforms and risk-sharing mechanisms effectively protect vulnerable populations from losing assets and widening inequality between clusters.

funds providers and the second flow is related to risk transfer that is concentrated at the level of loan beneficiaries.

Throughout the years and without entering into details, financial systems try to reform themselves in order to continue existing. They tried to integrate new schemes and configurations in order to support people from Clusters 2 and 3, lower the financing rates and deploy specialized institutions and schemes.

These reforms are very interesting but the impacts would always depend on the combination between the financial instruments and the public policies. If the public policies are limited, the impact of the financial system would be limited and vice versa, the financial instruments can amplify the impacts of the public policies.

Table 7.6 Summary of the Lifts and Nets Mechanisms to reform the financial system

Instrument	*Channel/Mechanism*	*Targeting/ Beneficiaries*	*Financing/Fiscal Cost*	*Expected Behavioral Response*	*Risks/Challenges*
Financial-Inclusion institutions	Microfinance, mobile payments, crowdfunding	Unbanked/ underserved populations (cluster 3)	Operational costs; subsidies for institution setup	Increased access to financial services, initial integration into the financial system	Mismanagement if institutions operate like traditional banks; low adoption if economic opportunities are absent
Non-financial support	Training, coaching, project accompaniment	Unbanked/ underserved populations (cluster 3)	Program costs; capacity-building budgets	Improved project success, financial literacy, empowerment	Low participation; insufficient scaling; dependency without autonomy
Risk-sharing instruments	Equity financing, venture capital, Islamic finance	Borrowers/ small entrepreneurs	Shared-loss financial arrangements; potential contingent fiscal exposure	Encourages entrepreneurship, investment, risk-taking	Moral hazard; misuse of funds; complexity in unorganized economies
Debt-rescheduling mechanisms	Loan deferrals, flexible repayment plans	Borrowers facing temporary difficulties	Administrative cost of rescheduling; potential delayed repayment	Provides second chance; prevents immediate asset loss; stabilizes households	Abuse by negligent borrowers; fiscal impact if rescheduled loans fail

(continued)

Table 7.6 (continued)

Instrument	*Channel/Mechanism*	*Targeting/ Beneficiaries*	*Financing/Fiscal Cost*	*Expected Behavioral Response*	*Risks/Challenges*
Subsidies	Direct cash support, partial payment assistance, free access to services	Vulnerable households (clusters 2 and 3)	Government fiscal outlay; subsidy programs	Maintains repayment capacity; mitigates shock impact; encourages participation in financial system	Targeting inefficiency; fiscal burden; dependency risk
Guarantee schemes	Loan guarantees, collateral substitutes	Low-income borrowers, small enterprises	Government or fund-backed contingent liability	Facilitates access to credit, encourages risk-taking	Mispricing of risk; limited coverage; potential losses to guarantee provider
Lower-cost/targeted financing	Preferential interest rates, refinancing for social sectors	Households or businesses eligible for public-priority programs	Interest-rate subsidies; potential tax deductions	Increased uptake of financing; supports priority investments	Budgetary cost; risk of misuse; insufficient impact without public policy alignment
Connection to real economic opportunities	Integration with employment, income-generating projects, or business ecosystems	All beneficiaries of lifts and nets	Minimal fiscal cost if private sector-led; potential coordination cost	Converts access to financial instruments into real income	Lack of ecosystem reduces effectiveness; unequal access across regions

In parallel, a risk transfer based financial system without serious reforms can be very harmful to the economy with important exclusion effect and the reinforcement of a cluster at the expense of the other clusters. In advanced countries having efficient and effective public policies, the negative impacts of the financial system—without reform—can be offset by the positive impacts of these public policies.

References

Ayadi, R. (2023). The role of guarantee schemes in promoting financial inclusion: The impact of digital solutions.

Bank Al-Maghrib. (2025). Statistical releases and monetary policy indicators. https://www.bkam.ma

Barlamane Today. (2025). Financial sector indicators and banking performance reports. https://www.barlamane.com

Beck, T., Demirgüç-Kunt, A., & Levine, R. (2007). Finance, inequality and the poor. *Journal of Economic Growth, 12*, 27–49.

Culp, C. L. (2011). *Risk transfer: Derivatives in theory and practice*. John Wiley & Sons.

DZ Bank. (2023). Annual report 2023: Regional financial indicators. https://annualreport.dzbank.com

European Central Bank. (2024–2025). *Statistical Data Warehouse*. https://www.ecb.europa.eu

Fremstad, S. (2008). Measuring poverty and economic inclusion.

Koku, P. S. (2015). Financial exclusion of the poor: A literature review. *International Journal of Bank Marketing, 33*(5), 654–668.

Kumar, S., Parimal Sarkar, J., & Bonnerjee, S. (2014). Impact of banking penetration on economic growth: A state-wise comparative study. *Business Perspectives and Research, 2*(2), 47–64.

Maldonado, J. E. (2017). *Financial systems and income inequality*. College of Europe.

Miller, D., & Le Breton–Miller, I. (2017). Sources of entrepreneurial courage and imagination: Three perspectives, three contexts. Entrepreneurship Theory and Practice, 41(5), 667–675.

Reuters. (2024). *Swiss National Bank interest-rate decisions*. https://www.reuters.com

Rousseau, P. L., & Sylla, R. (2003). Financial systems, economic growth, and globalization. In *Globalization in historical perspective* (pp. 373–416). University of Chicago Press.

Tahiri Jouti, A. (2024). *Unlocking economic development: The unlearning process of nations*. Taylor & Francis.

Wang, O. (2018). Banks, low interest rates, and monetary policy transmission. *The. Journal of Finance*.

PART IV

The Lifts & Nets Based Public Policies in the Political Sphere

CHAPTER 8

The Individualistic Governance and Middle-Class Nations

Introduction of the Chapter

The political governance defines how political power is organized, exercised, and controlled in a specific country, organization, or system. It comprises the structures, the rules, the processes, and behaviors through which decisions are made and authority is exercised. To make it simple, political governance identifies who has the power, how they get it and use it, how accountable are they, and how citizens participate in the decision process.

Indeed, the effectiveness of public policies will depend on the nature of the governance system (Nachmias & Sened, 2001). Any deficiency in the governance system can have an impact on the performance of the public policies. For instance, a governance system that does not believe in diversity, or that promotes a hierarchical community where people are not treated equally, cannot conceive public policies, and sustainable strategies that would reinforce the middle-class feature of the nation.

Moreover, a governance system with no real accountability frameworks cannot produce highly performant public policies (Bayrakçı et al., 2012). Similarly, a governance system that relies on a rent-based political model can never strengthen the middle-class feature because granting advantages to a minority goes in the opposite direction of strengthening the middle-class feature of a nation, where resources are accessible to

A. Tahiri Jouti, *Building Middle Class Nations*,
https://doi.org/10.1007/978-3-032-02134-2_8

everyone depending on their ability to develop and grow them (Safdar et al., 2022).

A system of political rents drives beneficiaries to benefit from it without any additional efforts or investments and at the same cost. To this end, all energy is deployed to maintain these privileges, which directly undermines the economic model that is supposed to be optimal, inclusive, and effective.

Obviously, a sound governance system reinforces the middle-class feature of a nation and inversely, the dominance of the middle-class feature can maintain and reinforce the governance system of any country (Birdsall, 2016).

This chapter would discuss the contribution of the political governance system to the reinforcement of the middle-class feature of a nation. It would also identify the ingredients and the components of a highly effective governance system able to conceive and issue efficient public policies that reinforce the middle-class feature of a nation.

Indeed, the efficiency and the effectiveness of public policies can be hindered in the absence of strong and stable governance frameworks promoting inclusiveness and accountability at all levels.

The Individualistic Governance and the Middle-Class Feature Main Issues

The General Framework of Issues Related to the Individualistic Governance and the Middle-Class Feature

A sound governance system serves to safeguard and protect the interests of the different stakeholders. Indeed, it protects the minorities from the dominance of the majority and at the same time, it protects the majority from the misdeeds of the minority(ies). It aims at safeguarding the balance within the different components of a nation.

If there are any new trends (positive or negative), the governance system would implement the necessary mechanisms to discuss these trends and assess their impact on the nation and its different components. If the new trend is positive, the governance system should have the necessary mechanisms to encourage its adoption but if it is negative, it has to limit both its impact and its growth (Wilkes & Wu, 2018).

Governance systems are commonly categorized into those dominated by individual leaders and those anchored in formal institutions, a distinction central to the study of political regimes (Geddes, 1999; Levitsky & Way, 2010). Political sustainability and stability arise when power progressively shifts from personalist control to institutional authority, allowing rules and procedures rather than individual preferences to shape political life (Huntington, 1968; North, 1990). From this perspective, the consolidation of institutional hegemony over the different components of a political system is a key marker of durable and resilient governance (Jachtenfuchs et al., 2003).

Governance systems grounded in strong political, economic, and social institutions are widely regarded as more capable of delivering long-term stability, inclusive growth, and the expansion of a robust middle class (Acemoglu & Robinson, 2012; Evans, 1995; North, 1990). From another perspective, systems centered on individual leaders can also achieve developmental progress when authority is exercised by visionary, just, and capable figures who are able to mobilize resources and shape national priorities effectively (Geddes, 1999; Leftwich, 2009; Svolik, 2012). However, such personalist modes of governance carry significant risks, particularly during leadership transitions, as the succession of a less competent or less benevolent leader can undermine stability and reverse earlier gains (Brownlee, 2007; Bueno de Mesquita et al., 2003; Svolik, 2012).

A central indicator of weak governance is the widespread lack of interest displayed by citizens who are not directly involved in the political arena, a pattern closely associated with declining institutional legitimacy and civic disengagement (Dalton, 2004;Norris, 2011 ; Pharr & Putnam, 2000). Such disengagement often stems from the belief that political power is effectively concentrated in the hands of a small minority rather than distributed through truly representative institutions, reinforcing perceptions of elite dominance and limited citizen influence (Gilens, 2012; Gilens & Page, 2014; Winters, 2011). Another contributing factor is the perception that political parties offer no meaningful alternatives, as party convergence and organizational hollowing reduce citizens' incentives to participate (Dalton, 2009; Katz & Mair, 1995; Mair, 2013). Finally, disengagement is exacerbated when political debates fail to address the real problems and priorities of society, creating a growing disconnect between political elites and ordinary citizens (Hibbing & Theiss-Morse, 2002; Stoker, 2006). Together, these dynamics underscore how weak governance structures erode political interest by distancing citizens from the political system they are meant to shape.

Indeed, this lack of interest can also be explained by the perception that the political process is too complex or too constrained to produce meaningful change, reducing citizens' sense of political efficacy and discouraging their engagement (Norris, 2011; Pharr & Putnam, 2000). When individuals believe that political institutions are ineffective in addressing societal problems, they are less likely to participate, reinforcing patterns of disengagement (Dalton, 2004; Hibbing & Theiss-Morse, 2002). For this reason, one of the most important indicators of the soundness and legitimacy of a governance system is the level of citizen participation, particularly voter turnout, which reflects the degree to which citizens feel empowered and represented within the political system (Franklin, 2004; Lijphart, 1997). Below is a table summarizing voter turnout in various countries.

Generally, nations with a strong and sizable middle class are associated with stable and sustainable political regimes, whereas countries with a weak or small middle class tend to experience unstable regimes dominated either by individual leaders or by interest groups and lobbies (Acemoglu & Robinson, 2012; Haggard & Kaufman, 1995 ; Moene & Wallerstein, 2001).

In non-middle-class nations, society can often be divided into three main clusters. The first is the dominant cluster, which exercises power to advance its own interests, either directly or indirectly, and with or without the support of formal leaders (Acemoglu & Robinson, 2012; Svolik, 2012). In such contexts, the dominant cluster typically prioritizes the reinforcement of its own control rather than the stability or institutionalization of the regime. Weak institutions are generally unable to constrain the cluster's influence, allowing its hegemony to persist (North, 1990). Consequently, the distinction between regime stability and cluster dominance is often blurred: citizens may perceive opposing a cluster's dominance as equivalent to opposing the stability of the nation itself (Haggard & Kaufman, 1995; Moene & Wallerstein, 2001).

In the short term, the dominant cluster reinforces its hegemony by controlling the political scene, the major economic sectors and by supervising the social field. This strategy officially aims to stabilize the regime, but unofficially to reinforce the hegemony of a particular cluster and leads to a status quo from the economic and social dimensions.

Table 8.1 Comparison between the participation rates in different countries in elections between 2019 and 2024

Country	*Voter turnout (%)*	*Election type*	*Year*	*Source*	*URL*
Belgium	88.4	Legislative	2019	Federal Public Service Interior (IBZ)	https://elections2019.belgium.be/en
Sweden	84.2	Legislative	2022	Swedish election authority (Valmyndigheten)	https://val.se/servicelankar/servicelankar/other-languages/english-engelska/election-results/election-results-2022
Malta	85.6	Legislative	2022	Electoral Commission of Malta	https://electoral.gov.mt/
Germany	76.6	Federal	2021	Federal Returning Officer	https://www.bundeswahlleiterin.de/en/bundestagswahlen/2021/ergebnisse/bund-99.html
Indonesia	81.8	Presidential	2024	General elections commission (KPU)	https://www.kpu.go.id/
France	73.7	Presidential	2022	Ministry of the Interior (France)	https://www.interieur.gouv.fr/Elections/Les-resultats/Elu-ou-elue?type=PRE
Canada	69.5	Federal	2025	Elections Canada	https://www.elections.ca/content.aspx?section=med&dir=pre&document=apr2925&lang=e
Spain	66.2	General	2023	Ministry of the Interior (Spain)	https://www.infoelectoral.interior.es/
India	66.0	Parliamentary	2024	Election Commission of India	https://results.eci.gov.in/
United States	66.8	Presidential	2020	U.S. Census Bureau	https://www.census.gov/newsroom/press-releases/2021/2020-presidential-election-voting-and-registration-tables-now-available.html

(continued)

Table 8.1 (continued)

Country	*Voter turnout (%)*	*Election type*	*Year*	*Source*	*URL*
Italy	63.9	General	2022	Ministry of the Interior (Italy)	https://elezionistorico.interno.gov.it/index.php?tpel=A&dtel=25/09/2022&tpa=I&tpe=C&lev0= 0&levsut0=0&es0=S&ms=S
Guatemala (1st)	60.8	Presidential	2023	Supreme electoral tribunal (TSE)	https://www.tse.org.gt/
Japan	55.9	Legislative	2021	Ministry of Internal Affairs	https://www.soumu.go.jp/senkyo/senkyo_s/data/shugiin49/index.html
Algeria (Pres.)	46.1	Presidential	2024	Ministry of Interior (Algeria)	https://www.anienationale.dz/
Bosnia and Herzegovina	51.5	General	2022	Central election commission	https://www.izbori.ba/
Romania	31.8	Parliamentary	2020	Permanent electoral authority	https://www.roaep.ro/
Algeria (leg.)	23.0	Legislative	2021	Ministry of Interior (Algeria)	https://www.anienationale.dz/
Haiti	18.0	Presidential	2021	Provisional electoral council	https://www.cephaiti.gouv.ht/
Comoros	16.0	Presidential	2024	Independent National Electoral Commission	https://www.ceni-comores.km/
Tunisia	11.2	Legislative	2022	Independent high Authority for Elections (ISIE)	https://www.isie.tn/

The second cluster consists of individuals who are passive supporters of the dominant cluster. These citizens are partially satisfied with their material or political gains and are generally reluctant to challenge the dominant cluster due to the weakness of institutional mechanisms within the governance system (Acemoglu & Robinson, 2012; North, 1990). In such contexts, opposition is often perceived as futile: revolting against the current dominant cluster offers little assurance of improvement, since any alternative cluster would likely reproduce similar patterns of elite control and institutional weakness (Haggard & Kaufman, 1995; Svolik, 2012).

The third cluster consists of individuals primarily occupied with daily survival and who have little confidence in the political system or governance structures (Acemoglu & Robinson, 2012; North, 1990). While they may occasionally support the regime—if granted minor benefits or subject to effective indoctrination—their potential for revolt is significant, given their exclusion from the nation's economic and social opportunities (Haggard & Kaufman, 1995; Moene & Wallerstein, 2001). The accumulation of their frustration and resentment can generate instability that threatens both the regime and the broader society, as widespread discontent among economically and socially marginalized populations has historically been a catalyst for major political upheaval (Skocpol, 1979; Tilly, 1978).

In middle-class nations, governance regimes based on real institutions have the necessary mechanisms to avoid the hegemony of a specific cluster over the nation and to identify the frustrations and anger of people to take the right decisions in the right time.

The following figure presents the existing clusters in a non-middle-class nation:

The Major Issues Related to the Governance Regime in a Non-Middle-Class Nation

Obviously, a governance regime can have severe impacts on the middle-class feature of a nation. Moreover, the particular context of a nation can guide the governance regime to endorse specific values and principles. Indeed, the longer the regime exists, the more stable it has to be. The longevity of a regime means that it has been able to demonstrate its ability to adapt to new trends and circumstances, and to return to equilibrium and adjust accordingly.

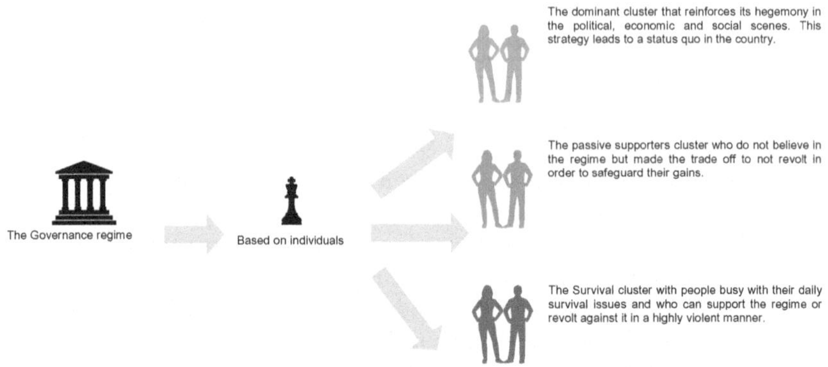

Fig. 8.1 The political clusters in a non-middle-class nation

In general, governance regimes can compromise the middle-class feature of their nations in many cases such as:

Seeking Legitimacy through Alliances
In the early stages of a regime, particularly when institutions are weak and popular support is uncertain, the short-term optimal strategy is often to form alliances with societal clusters capable of bolstering the new government (Acemoglu & Robinson, 2012; Svolik, 2012). Such alliances are rarely costless: regimes must provide incentives or rewards to secure the loyalty and active backing of these clusters, whether through political appointments, economic benefits, or other forms of patronage (Bueno de Mesquita et al., 2003; North, 1990). The careful management of these relationships is critical for regime survival until institutions are sufficiently consolidated to reduce dependence on elite or cluster support.

The rewards granted to supportive clusters can take multiple forms. Political rewards may include appointments to influential positions, granting members authority over key administrative or legislative functions, thereby extending their power within the regime (Bueno de Mesquita et al., 2003; Svolik, 2012). Economic rewards may involve preferential access to profitable sectors, regulatory advantages, or protective policies that enhance the wealth and influence of cluster members (Acemoglu & Robinson, 2012; North, 1990). By strategically allocating such rewards, regimes consolidate loyalty while maintaining control over the broader political and economic system.

In the medium term, these supportive clusters generally maintain their allegiance to the regime but progressively demand greater political, economic, and social rewards, which enables them to expand their influence across state institutions and strategic sectors (Acemoglu & Robinson, 2012; Bueno de Mesquita et al., 2003). Over the long term, such clusters may become sufficiently powerful to shape and preserve the existing governance model, ensuring the regime's continuity regardless of changes in individual leaders. At that stage, leadership turnover becomes secondary, as dominant clusters prioritize selecting individuals who best serve and reproduce the established system (Svolik, 2012; North, 1990).

In such a context, dominant clusters seek to reinforce their hegemony by obstructing or weakening any efforts toward institutionalization that might constrain their power. To preserve their position, these clusters can readily sacrifice individual leaders or members, as personal turnover poses little threat to their overall dominance. What ultimately matters is the continuity of the coalition's influence rather than the survival of specific individuals within it.

Finally, any individual leader—whether supported by specific clusters or not—faces two essential strategic orientations for long-term regime stability. The first is to cultivate active and broad popular support, which serves to reduce the influence and bargaining power of dominant clusters. Such support provides a critical buffer for the regime, ensuring societal backing during moments of political contestation or attempts to overthrow the leadership. The second orientation is to shift from a highly individualistic mode of governance toward a more institutionalized framework, in which robust and impartial institutions assume leadership across political, economic, and social domains, ensuring fair and equitable representation of diverse stakeholders. Institutionalization not only constrains excessive elite influence but also enhances the legitimacy and resilience of the regime.

Most of individualistic regimes prefer to back themselves with dominant clusters and the active popular support instead of strong institutions. Sometimes, having dominant clusters can make the regime unpopular.

Favoring Short-Term Balance (Political Stability) over Long-Term Stability (Middle-Class Feature)

Political, economic, and social stability is closely linked to the strength and resilience of a nation's middle class. In contexts where governance remains highly individualistic and institutions are weak, non–middle-class nations often maintain or even reinforce the gaps between societal clusters (Birdsall, 2010; Easterly, 2001). Yet governing elites are typically aware that the middle class bears a disproportionate burden: middle-class households contribute significantly to tax revenues, receive fewer direct benefits or favors from the state, and frequently compensate for deficiencies in public services through private spending or self-provision (López-Calva & Lustig, 2010; Milánovic, 2016). As discussed in the social cost chapter, these pressures erode the middle class's capacity to sustain national stability, making its reinforcement a central pillar of long-term governance and development.

In this context, the dominant cluster(s) believe(s) that the passive supporters are attached to their gains and positions and that in the absence of the existing regime, the survival cluster can be so violent and can lead the country into chaos.

The dominant cluster maintains political stability by investing small resources in the survival cluster to secure unconditional support, while avoiding significant improvements that would elevate them to the middle class—because the middle class is costlier to satisfy, harder to control, and more politically demanding.

Consequently, the dominant cluster faces no incentive to reform; it provides minimal subsidies to the survival cluster—enough to secure unconditional support—while offering little assistance to the passive supporters, who largely belong to the middle class. This arrangement preserves the existing political and institutional structure, avoids costly changes, and prevents the emergence of revolutionary pressures or demands for profound transformation.

Filling Labor Gaps without Real Integration

In some other contexts, the nation needs more workforce to improve its economic growth and power. Nevertheless, the country lacks sufficient resources to fill the gap either in terms of skills or numbers of people or both.

In this context, two major categories of countries can be distinguished. The first group consists of middle-class nations that actively encourage immigration and establish specific legal statuses for newcomers (OECD, 2020). These countries generally design clear eligibility conditions for acquiring citizenship, often based on structured criteria such as residency duration, language proficiency, and civic knowledge (Joppke, 2010). The immigrant-specific statuses outline the duties and responsibilities expected from newcomers while granting them an extensive package of rights that ensures adequate protection and access to essential services (Shachar, 2009).

Furthermore, once immigrants meet the requirements for naturalization, they become eligible to obtain citizenship (Goodman, 2014). However, the formal acquisition of citizenship does not necessarily guarantee full social integration. Research shows that naturalized individuals may still face various forms of exclusion or discrimination, limiting their sense of belonging and effectively positioning them as second-class citizens (Bloemraad, 2017). This phenomenon persists because symbolic and social boundaries often remain in place even after legal citizenship is obtained (Alba & Foner, 2015).

From another perspective, a real integration is not to force people from different countries or origins to endorse the country's principles, customs, and religion. This kind of integration would combat diversity under the pretext of preserving homogeneity but at the end, it would lead to heterogeneity instead.

Second, non–middle-class nations, even when they are economically prosperous due to abundant natural resources, often fail to provide fair and equitable legal statuses for immigrants when attempting to attract foreign labor (Rajan & Oommen, 2020). In many of these contexts, the acquisition of citizenship by immigrants is extremely rare, as naturalization policies are restrictive and designed to limit long-term settlement (Hertog, 2014). Moreover, two main categories of immigrants usually emerge: highly skilled experts who are recruited to manage complex projects aligned with national development strategies, and low-skilled workers who occupy basic or labor-intensive positions (Kapiszewski, 2006). Over time, a hierarchy forms within the immigrant population, shaped both by the level of expertise and by the workers' national or ethnic origins (Longva, 1999).

In both cases, immigrants are rewarded for their efforts and work with very interesting financial packages. Both Experts and basic workers earn much more in the host country than in their home country but can never obtain the citizenship and settle in for good.

If the country is also open to foreign investors, an additional layer is added to the existing hierarchy within the immigrant population (Cranston, Schouten, & Spicer, 2017). However, investors tend to choose a destination primarily when living conditions are attractive and the economic environment is favorable, making their presence highly sensitive to financial performance (Dunning & Lundan, 2008). As a result, investor mobility is characterized by high turnover, since countries often struggle to retain them over the long term (Saxenian, 2006). Ultimately, investors are generally motivated by two factors—financial returns and quality of life—and when profitability declines, they typically relocate to more favorable environments (Dustmann & Görlach, 2016).

All in all, non-middle-class nations will find themselves with a hierarchy of immigrants that further reinforces their non-middle-class nation feature. At the opposite side, middle-class nations would integrate immigrants in their systems and enrich their diversity while safeguarding the homogeneity of the different communities.

Minimizing the Involvement of the Government in the Social Field
One of the political orientations that can negatively affect the middle-class character of a nation is the extent to which the government intervenes in the social sphere. Broadly speaking, states tend to follow one of two approaches: a liberal model that emphasizes market mechanisms and limited state involvement, or a socialist model that prioritizes extensive public provision and state-led redistribution.

In a liberal orientation, public services are largely entrusted to the private sector, and individuals are expected to finance their own access to education, healthcare, and social protection; those who lack adequate resources receive limited or no state support (Hacker, 2004). In contrast, under a socialist orientation, the government assumes responsibility for ensuring that all citizens maintain a basic standard of living regardless of their income level, on the premise that taxation is justified only when the state provides meaningful social protection and universal services (Korpi & Palme, 1998).

In some contexts, with a socialist orientation, public policies end up concentrating primarily on the survival cluster, often as a result of political incentives and institutional arrangements that target assistance to the poorest groups while keeping them socially and economically isolated from the middle class (Mkandawire, 2005). These ecosystems maintain the survival cluster as a distinct segment of society, dependent on limited forms of support yet not fully integrated into broader welfare structures or middle-class pathways.

For non-middle-class nations, the social sectors can represent very interesting investment opportunities for dominant clusters especially if the public sector fails to provide social services properly. Therefore, the easiest way to tackle the deficiencies is to minimize the involvement of the government in the social fields, hand over to the private sector to invest in the social sector to supposedly reduce the gap and support the survival cluster when relevant. The middle class would find better services but they would need to pay larger amounts.

In many non-middle-class countries, national health insurance schemes generally cover only formally employed workers, leaving those with special statuses or limited financial means excluded from coverage.

To increase the proportion of people covered by national health insurance schemes, the government could extend coverage to those currently excluded by imposing higher contributions on high-income individuals while reducing reimbursement rates to maintain the scheme's balance. In the short term, this would raise the coverage indicator and could be presented as a political achievement. However, high-income contributors would effectively pay for comprehensive medical coverage while receiving relatively limited benefits, forcing middle-class individuals to purchase supplementary insurance to obtain adequate reimbursement. This pattern is consistent with OECD findings, which show that in many countries, even with broad public health coverage, middle-class populations often rely on private complementary or supplementary insurance to fill gaps in reimbursement and services (OECD, 2023).

Moreover, individuals newly integrated into the scheme would initially benefit, as they move from having no coverage to accessing a low-cost insurance plan. However, in the medium term, they would realize that the reimbursement rates are very low and provide limited real value.

From another perspective, extending such coverage could benefit the dominant cluster, particularly investors, by creating a larger customer base that may choose private healthcare services over public ones. Meanwhile, the middle class would effectively subsidize individuals from the survival cluster, indirectly supporting private investments by the dominant cluster in the health sector. This dynamic would raise the social cost for the nation. If this pattern holds true in the health sector, it could similarly apply to other social sectors that were traditionally public but have been privatized, such as education.

The Individualistic Governance and the Middle-Class Feature: Lifts and Nets Mechanisms

The Consequences of the Individualistic Approach in the Political Field

The individualistic approach emphasizes the dominance of individuals over institutions, prioritizing personal views and perspectives over formal or informal rules. Consequently, the stability of the nation can become heavily dependent on the inclinations and decisions of certain individuals, rather than on collective norms or established structures (Dwivedi, 2024; Mutlugün, 2025).

From another perspective, the individualistic approach means that decisions are taken by individuals in the absence of rules or with rules but with broader powers of derogation granted to individuals in the absence of any accountability framework.

Such a situation can have serious consequences on the future and the stability of a nation. This part would focus only on the impacts and consequences on the middle-class feature of a nation that can be summarized as follows:

The Lack of Visibility for Local and Foreign Investors Vs. the Insider Information for the Dominant Cluster

An individualistic approach to economic and social organization can constrain investors' visibility and planning horizons, thereby affecting their long-term projections (North, 1990). Even foreign investors who are aware of these limitations may deliberately restrict their exposure and investment levels. In this context, individualistic governance and market arrangements are often associated with medium- and long-term instability, regardless of how well-informed or rational individual decisions might be (Acemoglu & Robinson, 2012).

The individualistic approach does not provide a long-term visibility to economic players and does not inspire trust for local and foreign investors who are not going to commit to very long-term investment projects or to projects with high technological or scientific added value.

Indeed, the individualistic approach would reinforce the risks of instability for the different economic players who may see their investment and plans threatened if new instructions are issued.

Moreover, limited transparency and visibility in economic and regulatory systems tend to benefit members of the dominant cluster, who have privileged access to information and can leverage it to influence markets and investors (Shleifer & Vishny, 1994). Their close proximity to political power, combined with insider knowledge and networked practices, often allows them to serve as effective intermediaries or shortcuts for both foreign and domestic investors seeking to establish projects locally (Faccio, 2006).

At the end of the journey, the dominant cluster would reinforce even more its dominance over the whole economy and nation and as explained earlier in this chapter, it would impact negatively the middle-class feature of the nation.

The Contagion Effect and the Weakening of the Nation's Institutions

Planning a transition from an individualistic model of governance to an institutional approach involves more than simply establishing formal institutions with defined charters, powers, and visions (North, 1990). If the leadership at the top continues to operate according to individualistic principles and maintains weak accountability mechanisms, those appointed to manage these institutions are likely to adopt the same behaviors. Consequently, the individualistic approach can become embedded across all levels of the institutional structure, undermining efforts to implement a genuine institutional model and weakening the overall effectiveness of governance reforms (Acemoglu & Robinson, 2012).

However, it is important to distinguish between a head of state who has been elected through a formal electoral process, thereby operating under a well-defined program and policy direction endorsed by the electorate, and a head of state who governs without any meaningful interaction with or accountability to the popular will (Linz, 2000). The nature of the executive's legitimacy and its connection to citizens fundamentally shapes governance practices, policy implementation, and the responsiveness of institutions.

In the first case, when the head of state appoints people, he derives his power from the nation and the voters who have placed their trust in him to carry out the electoral program. Any deviation is detected and appropriately corrected.

In the second case, the head of state may draw his power from the trust the people have placed in his family and ancestors to lead the country (which is not necessarily a bad thing if accountability frameworks are clear and effective) and if the head of state is visionary, but the people appointed will be stronger than the institutions they lead. This in no way facilitates the transition to an institutional model.

Weak Institutions and Political Rent

In many contexts, institutions are emptied of their substance by the hegemony of individuals belonging to the dominant cluster (Infante & Smirnova, 2009). Even individuals within these institutions who do not formally belong to the dominant cluster often benefit indirectly from such proximity, gaining political rents that further erode the relevance and effectiveness of the institutions.

For example, membership in consultative or advisory bodies with limited formal power can still confer status, income, and opportunities to leverage connections, access privileged information, or pursue business opportunities. In such settings, political action becomes a vehicle for personal enrichment rather than public service. This represents the ultimate manifestation of an individualistic approach to political engagement, which significantly diminishes the prospects of strengthening a middle-class component within the nation (Infante & Smirnova, 2009).

By contrast, a middle-class nation requires institutions that are robust enough to prevail over individualistic pressures and resist attempts at hegemony by dominant clusters or political factions. Institutions must ensure that interactions among individuals serve collective interests, uphold ethical standards, and maintain governance accountability. Political office should be regarded as a professional, full-time responsibility, with defined compensation and close supervision, rather than as a source of opportunistic wealth accumulation (Infante & Smirnova, 2009).

Generally, an institutional approach reassures politicians, who can benefit from the stability and advantages of a middle-class nation even if they step back from active political roles. In contrast, an individualistic system creates uncertainty: politicians must secure their income by exploiting every available opportunity, and business actors are compelled to engage with or stay close to the political sphere to protect and expand their economic assets, as failure to do so allows competitors to gain an advantage (Infante & Smirnova, 2009).

The Prevalence of the Individualistic Approach over the General Interest

The weakness of institutions and the presence of political rent ensure that any public policy designed primarily serves the interests of those who conceived it, who seek to gain political or economic advantage from it. Each time, care is taken to present the public policy as aiming to reduce inequalities and disparities—at least on the surface—while in reality, it only serves the interests of a minority.

If we consider a profitability simulation comparing the construction of a mid-range real estate project with that of a social housing project in a country like Morocco, the estimated net margin for a mid-range project would be between 15% and 25%, while for social housing, it can reach up to 35% if all subsidies are obtained—even without questionable practices (such as buyers paying part of the amount unofficially, "under the table"), which could further increase the project's net margin.

Thus, although such measures aim to provide social housing for relocating people living in substandard conditions, in the end they tend to encourage developers who can become wealthier at the expense of the population, which ends up paying more for poor-quality housing.

What is striking in such nations is that people often criticize the individualistic approach to governance—as long as they are not benefiting from it. Once they gain access to its advantages, they stop criticizing it and, in some cases, take advantage of it without even realizing that they used to condemn this very system. In this regard, why would anyone want to change the approach or advocate for a different model of governance if they are benefiting fully from the current one?

The Lifts and Nets Mechanisms Applied to the Political Governance Approach

When addressing the Political Governance system, it is more about implementing the necessary systems and rules in order to facilitate the effective deployment of the Lifts and Nets Framework and philosophy at the level of public policies but also at the level of the different institutions and organizations.

For non-middle-class nations, the main element to consider when deploying the Lifts and Nets Framework is to ensure the smooth transition from the individualistic approach to the institutional framework. Then, it is about maintaining the supremacy of the institutions over people but also their flexibility, agility, and connection with the reality of the nation.

The Transition to the Institutional Approach (Acemoglu, 2015)
The transition to the institutional approach should respect the following process and milestones starting from the implementation of a relevant institutional framework, a clear vision, simple and relevant rules, a strong control environment, an objective-oriented nomination process, and finally a sound accountability framework.

A Relevant Institutional Framework
The transition to an institutional approach begins with establishing institutions that have clear and precise mandates, well-defined visions, and objectives that align with and contribute to the achievement of the national vision. Institutions are not merely functional entities; they are instruments for realizing visions and shaping the nation's future. Without an explicit duty to contribute to long-term development, an institution can inadvertently become an obstacle to national progress.

For instance, if a government seeks to leverage artificial intelligence (AI) as a driver of economic growth, the absence of a coordinated approach across all relevant institutions can result in bottlenecks. Agencies responsible for personal data protection, while fulfilling their regulatory mandates, may inadvertently block AI projects due to strict compliance requirements. Similarly, financial authorities that mandate physical procedures—such as in-person account opening interviews or company visits—may delay the adoption of AI applications in banking and finance.

This situation arises not because the agencies are failing in their core responsibilities, but because they are not integrated into the broader national vision. Consequently, ambitious national strategies may never reach full implementation if institutions operate in silos, without shared objectives or coordinated interaction.

A robust institutional framework therefore requires not only clearly defined mandates but also active involvement of institutions in formulating their own operational visions, which should be embedded within the national strategy. Institutions must be empowered to interact freely with all relevant stakeholders to ensure that their policies can be implemented effectively, without obstructing progress in other sectors (North, 1990; Ostrom, 2010). Even a single lagging institution can significantly undermine ambitious public policies, highlighting the critical need for inter-institutional coordination and vision alignment.

A Clear Vision for the Nation

As discussed previously, implementing institutions with their own mandates, powers, functions and visions while deploying an interaction framework between these institutions is a necessary milestone in the transition process. Nevertheless, the nation itself needs a clear vision to shape its future and the future of the next generations.

Therefore, adopting a clear vision for the nation with deadlines and key performance indicators have many advantages:

- First, the national vision can inspire the different institutions in building their own vision. Moreover, in this context, each institution would be required to conceive its own vision while knowing exactly what are the trends and orientations to be taken into account.
- Second, the existence of a national vision would reduce the probability of conflicts between the different institutions when conceiving their own visions or dealing with each other. Indeed, aligning with the national vision becomes a priority. It is worth noting that the national vision needs to have a 30 years or 50 years term with periodic review and updates based, among other things, on the different visions conceived by institutions.

At the opposite, the absence of a national vision can have negative impacts on the performance of institutions suchS as sticking to the mandates and rejecting changes or endorsing them slowly and generally when it is too late. Moreover, the absence of a national vision can create situations of conflicts of mandates and visions between different institutions and this would transform the interactions to a war of egos and powers and this is the main characteristic of individualistic governance approach.

Finally, it is important to understand that a national vision deployed at the level of institutions, governmental agencies and entities mean that the mandates can be easily enlarged to accompany the new trends if not to create them. For instance, an entity specialized in protecting personal data can see its mandates enlarged to cover the artificial intelligence regulations, policies, and applications in both the public and private sectors.

Simple and Relevant Rules
The best policies are those based on very simple and relevant rules for many reasons. They are easily understandable, thus, easily applicable. Moreover, they are easy to control and to make sure they are respected.

In non-middle-class nations, either the rules do not exist or they are so complicated as to be irrelevant. In this case, they are not easily understandable, not applicable and hard to control since they will require important resources to ensure highly effective controls.

During COVID-19, some countries required from the visitors to take a test 72 hours before the flight, and all passengers are checked without distinction. Those who exceed this time limit are not boarded, while those from countries known for their fraudulent practices are retested. On the other hand, some countries require passengers to take a test 48 hours before their flight, and to fill in 2 forms per passenger (making it difficult for large families traveling together). However, at the check-in point, the forms and tests are collected but due to the irrelevance of the checks, passengers are not actually checked.

A Strong Control Environment
The strength of a law or a rule is reflected in the performance of the control system, through three major indicators:

- Firstly, the control system must be complete and comprehensive, so as to detect any infringement, whatever its size or impact. Indeed, the control system should be deployed in all the different departments and entities of the public sector. Moreover, a central Audit office should be implemented to oversee all the entities on a regular basis while conceiving a general map of risks and a roadmap to mitigate them.
- Secondly, the control system must have the power to punish infringements, and the cost of fines must be higher than the gains made from infringements. Indeed, if the gains from infringements are greater than the costs of fines, infringements will remain more attractive. In addition to this, connections with the legal system need to be honed to react quickly to any form of fraud or negligence.
- Thirdly, the control system needs to enhance continuously its capabilities to keep up-to-date with new fraudulent and dubious practices in the various fields it supervises. Indeed, if the control system is not performant, relevant, and highly responsive, both its capacity to

detect anomalies and to issue relevant recommendations would be an issue.

From another perspective, it goes without saying that the control system should be independent and highly competent while having close interactions with both the executive and the legislative systems in order to upgrade the processes and the legislations to reduce the gaps in terms of external and internal control.

In many non-middle-class nations, rules are either absent or complicated to follow and to deploy. The absence of rules makes the whole control system irrelevant and can be contested while the complicated rules and laws make the controls totally ineffective.

Indeed, the control system is what makes the institutions able to exercise its powers and impose its respect. Institutional penalties and rewards should be no exception. Everyone is subject to the rules, with no immunity whatsoever.

An Objective-Oriented Nomination Process

Strengthening the primacy of institutions over individuals requires adopting a nomination approach in which leaders are selected not for their general reputations or personal standing, but for their alignment with the institution's strategic objectives at a specific moment in its development. This objective-oriented nomination process ensures that leadership decisions are rooted in institutional needs, enabling adaptive governance and preventing the personalization of authority (Peters & Pierre, 2016).

In this context, a clear governance framework is essential for shortlisting candidates and assessing their capacity to address the challenges and opportunities associated with the institution's current phase. Such frameworks allow institutions to match competencies with mission-critical needs, reducing arbitrariness and strengthening structural continuity (Christensen & Lægreid, 2011).

Equally important is the establishment of a formal, transparent revocation mechanism. Leaders must be removable at any time on the basis of predefined performance indicators that reflect the core purpose of the role. To avoid conflicts of interest and ensure procedural fairness, performance evaluations must be conducted independently and with methodological rigor (Bouckaert & Halligan, 2008). This approach reinforces accountability and discourages the entrenchment of ineffective or self-interested leadership.

Finally, institutions must systematically measure and document each leader's contribution to progress toward institutional excellence. This involves not only monitoring operational results but also assessing how leadership decisions advance long-term strategic objectives. Continuous performance tracking supports learning, institutional memory, and sustained improvement—key elements of mature governance systems (Pollitt & Bouckaert, 2017).

To ensure the strength of institutions and prevent the hegemony of individuals, two major principles must be taken into account. First, no one should be exempt from accountability. Every individual, regardless of rank or position, must be held responsible for their actions, decisions, errors, negligence, or violations of rules, a notion central to modern accountability theory (Bovens, 2007). Institutional and organizational frameworks must reflect this principle by embedding mechanisms that enforce transparency and responsibility at every level.

Second, everyone must take full responsibility for mistakes or misconduct under their purview. There should be no protective shields for anyone, no matter how influential or experienced. This culture of responsibility must be normalized rather than applied selectively, echoing the concept of accountability as an ethical obligation to own one's actions (Dubnick, 2005).

Moreover, this approach to accountability should be supported by the structural and procedural elements previously discussed. A robust and efficient control system is essential to monitor compliance and detect irregularities early. Equally important is a clear and objective process for both appointment and revocation of individuals in leadership positions, ensuring that responsibilities are assigned and removed based on performance and institutional needs rather than personal loyalties.

Finally, strong accountability requires rigorous management of key performance indicators (KPIs). These indicators must guide decision-making, track progress, and serve as objective references in evaluating both individual and organizational effectiveness, reinforcing a performance-driven culture essential to institutional integrity (Moynihan, 2008). When combined, these elements foster a resilient institutional environment in which accountability becomes a foundational value that supports long-term excellence and public trust.

A Sound Accountability Framework

The Agility and the Flexibility of the Institutions

One of the main pitfalls in the institutional approach is the risk of diluting individual power to the point where meaningful change becomes nearly impossible. While institutional frameworks are meant to prevent misconduct and ensure stability, they can paradoxically become obstacles to positive transformation when they grow excessively rigid, prioritizing procedural preservation over innovation (March & Olsen, 1989).

When institutions become overly focused on self-maintenance, they may resist necessary evolution. Therefore, institutionalization should not be about creating immovable systems but about instilling a lasting spirit and purpose that outlive individuals without suppressing the drive for adaptation. Institutions must endure beyond their leaders, yet remain flexible enough to respond to shifting challenges—an idea consistent with the view that institutions must evolve to maintain effectiveness within changing environments (North, 1990).

Giving institutions a coherent mission or "soul" means ensuring that their core values persist while still allowing adjustments and recalibrations over time. The objective is not to build structures impervious to change, but to develop frameworks that safeguard integrity while embracing renewal. This balance is essential for resilience without drifting into stagnation.

At the same time, individuals should be empowered to lead—but within clear temporal and contextual boundaries. Leadership authority must be limited in duration and scope to avoid entrenchment, reflecting the importance of preventing personal power from overriding institutional continuity (Burns, 1978). These leaders should possess the competencies needed to drive progress while also preparing to pass the organization to successors capable of advancing its mission. In this sense, leadership involves not only directing change but also creating the conditions for future leaders to succeed (Heifetz, 1994). Through this balance of visionary leadership and structured renewal, institutions gain both continuity and capacity for long-term evolution.

In this context, the following elements must be implemented and taken into account:

Clear Mandates and Powers

To support leaders in driving change, aligning institutions with national vision, and fostering ownership of their own strategic direction, it is essential to provide them with clear, well-defined mandates. These mandates should be designed to ensure institutional flexibility and to prevent leaders from becoming hostages to cumbersome processes and bureaucratic inertia.

A leader who is appointed should be seen as a trusted figure, and as such, their mandate must grant them the latitude needed to act decisively and effectively. However, this expanded authority must be balanced with appropriate control mechanisms—namely, the monitoring of key performance indicators, a strict accountability framework, and a swift, depersonalized revocation process. Such a system ensures that power is exercised responsibly and that leadership remains dynamic, accountable, and aligned with the broader mission of the institution.

An in-House Incubator for Young Leaders

To ensure both continuity and flexibility, an institution must adopt an internal policy for managing talent and leadership that serves to strengthen its present capabilities while safeguarding its future.

This policy should focus on developing a pool of skilled leaders from within, capable of sustaining the institution's mission and driving its evolution over time. Relying solely on external recruitment can be costly and may disrupt internal cohesion, while limiting leadership sourcing to internal candidates alone may lead to stagnation and a lack of fresh perspectives.

A balanced approach—nurturing internal talent while selectively integrating external expertise—is essential to build a resilient and adaptive leadership model that supports institutional excellence over the long term.

Conclusion of the Chapter

Beyond the internal dynamics of institutions, the overall governance model of a nation plays a decisive role in determining stability. Generally, middle-class nations are characterized by durable and balanced political regimes, founded on institutional strength rather than individual dominance.

In contrast, non-middle-class nations often fall into unstable systems driven by clusters of interest. One dominant cluster typically controls power, economy, and society—not to stabilize the regime, but to protect its own hegemony. A second, passive cluster tolerates the status quo due to lack of alternatives, while a third, marginalized cluster—excluded from all economic and social metrics—harbors deep frustration. This final group, when pushed to extremes, can unleash destabilizing revolt.

In middle-class nations, however, strong institutions detect and address such tensions proactively, ensuring that governance serves the people and not a dominant minority. This distinction underlines the critical importance of building institutions that are both strong and just—responsive to the needs of all, and immune to the monopolization of power.

In building strong and resilient institutions, a fundamental balance must be maintained between stability and adaptability. Institutions should be robust enough to endure beyond individual leadership while remaining flexible and responsive to evolving national priorities. Governance structures must not hinder change but rather facilitate positive transformation and long-term progress. The institutional framework must carry a purposeful identity—an "institutional soul"—that preserves continuity, encourages innovation, and transcends personal interests.

Leadership plays a central role in this system. Appointing leaders should be based on alignment with the institution's current phase and objectives, not abstract or static profiles. Leaders must be granted clear, flexible mandates that empower them to act and innovate, free from bureaucratic paralysis. At the same time, their authority must be governed by a strong accountability framework, a robust performance monitoring system, and a depersonalized and efficient revocation process. This ensures that trust in leadership is balanced with transparency and control, supporting responsible action without entrenching power.

Institutional accountability must also be embedded at all levels to ensure integrity and prevent the concentration of power. No one should be above the rules—everyone must answer for their decisions, especially in the face of negligence, fraud, or failure. Institutional strength lies in ensuring that checks and balances are effective and that governance mechanisms empower progress while safeguarding justice and fairness. Leaders should serve as enablers of change, with term-limited authority and a clear obligation to prepare successors who can build upon their work.

Furthermore, institutions must adopt a strategic approach to talent management, balancing internal leadership development with selective external recruitment. Relying solely on external figures can weaken institutional culture and cohesion, while promoting only from within may limit innovation. A hybrid strategy ensures that institutions remain dynamic, inclusive, and aligned with long-term objectives—capable of both honoring their traditions and evolving for the future.

Chapter References

Acemoglu, D. (2015). Why nations fail? *The Pakistan Development Review, 54*(4), 301–312.

Acemoglu, D., & Robinson, J. A. (2012). *Why nations fail: The origins of power, prosperity, and poverty*. Crown Business.

Alba, R., & Foner, N. (2015). *Strangers no more: Immigration and the challenges of integration in North America and Western Europe*. Princeton University Press.

Bayrakçı, E., Göküş, M., & Taşpınar, Y. (2012, June). Accountability in public policies: A comparative study. In *Proceedings of the Fifteenth International Conference of American Society of Business and Behavioural Sciences* (pp. 3–13).

Birdsall, N. (2010). The (indispensable) middle class in developing countries. Center for Global Development Working Paper No. 207.

Birdsall, N. (2016). Middle-class heroes: The best guarantee of good governance. *Foreign Affairs, 95*, 25.

Bloemraad, I. (2017). Understanding immigrant integration: Key insights from new research. *Journal of Ethnic and Migration Studies, 43*(1), 1–17. https://doi.org/10.1080/1369183X.2016.1248467

Bouckaert, G., & Halligan, J. (2008). *Managing performance: International comparisons*. Routledge.

Bovens, M. (2007). Analysing and assessing accountability: A conceptual framework. *European Law Journal, 13*(4), 447–468. https://doi.org/10.1111/j.1468-0386.2007.00378.x

Brownlee, J. (2007). *Authoritarianism in an age of democratization*. Cambridge University Press.

Bueno de Mesquita, B., Smith, A., Siverson, R. M., & Morrow, J. D. (2003). *The logic of political survival*. MIT Press.

Burns, J. M. (1978). *Leadership*. Harper & Row.

Christensen, T., & Lægreid, P. (2011). *The Ashgate research companion to new public management*. Ashgate.

Cranston, P., Schouten, C., & Spicer, N. (2017). *Sustainable development and the role of the private sector*. Routledge.

Dalton, R. J. (2004). *Democratic challenges, democratic choices: The erosion of political support in advanced industrial democracies*. Oxford University Press.

Dalton, R. J. (2009). The hollowing of political parties in advanced democracies. *International Journal of Public Opinion Research, 21*(2), 161–178. https://doi.org/10.1093/ijpor/edp002

Dubnick, M. (2005). Accountability and the promise of performance: In search of the mechanisms. *Public Administration Review, 65*(3), 404–417.

Dunning, J. H., & Lundan, S. M. (2008). Multinational enterprises and the global economy (2nd ed.). Edward Elgar Publishing.

Dustmann, C., & Görlach, J.-S. (2016). The economics of temporary migrations. *Journal of Economic Literature, 54*(1), 98–136. https://doi.org/10.1257/jel.54.1.98

Easterly, W. (2001). The middle class consensus and economic development. *Journal of Economic Growth, 6*(4), 317–335. https://doi.org/10.1023/A:1012786330095

Evans, P. (1995). *Embedded autonomy: States and industrial transformation.* Princeton University Press.

Faccio, M. (2006). Politically connected firms. *American Economic Review, 96*(1), 369–386. https://doi.org/10.1257/000282806776157704

Franklin, M. N. (2004). *Voter turnout and the dynamics of electoral competition in established democracies since 1945.* Cambridge University Press.

Geddes, B. (1999). What do we know about democratization after twenty years? *Annual Review of Political Science, 2*(1), 115–144. https://doi.org/10.1146/annurev.polisci.2.1.115

Gilens, M. (2012). *Affluence and influence: Economic inequality and political power in America.* Princeton University Press.

Gilens, M., & Page, B. I. (2014). Testing theories of American politics: Elites, interest groups, and average citizens. *Perspectives on Politics, 12*(3), 564–581. https://doi.org/10.1017/S1537592714001595

Goodman, S. W. (2014). *Immigration and membership politics in Western Europe.* Cambridge University Press.

Hacker, J. S. (2004). Privatizing risk without privatizing the welfare state: The hidden politics of social policy retrenchment in the United States. *American Political Science Review, 98*(2), 243–260. https://doi.org/10.1017/S0003055404001121

Haggard, S., & Kaufman, R. R. (1995). *The political economy of democratic transitions.* Princeton University Press.

Heifetz, R. A. (1994). *Leadership without easy answers.* Harvard University Press.

Hertog, S. (2014). Arab gulf states: Expanding citizenship but excluding foreigners. In Y. M. Haddad & N. S. Hopkins (Eds.), *Foreigner and state in the Middle East* (pp. 123–145). Routledge.

Hibbing, J. R., & Theiss-Morse, E. (2002). *Stealth democracy: Americans' beliefs about how government should work.* Cambridge University Press.

Huntington, S. P. (1968). *Political order in changing societies*. Yale University Press.

Infante, R., & Smirnova, J. (2009). *The role of institutions in economic development*. World Bank Publications.

Jachtenfuchs, M., Diez, T., & Jung, S. (2003). Which Europe? Conflicting models of a legitimate European political order. *European Journal of International Relations, 9*(4), 441–469. https://doi.org/10.1177/135406610394001

Joppke, C. (2010). *Citizenship and immigration*. Polity Press.

Kapiszewski, A. (2006). Arab versus Asian migrant workers in the GCC countries. In *United Nations expert group meeting on international migration and development in the Arab region*. United Nations.

Katz, R. S., & Mair, P. (1995). Changing models of party organization and party democracy: The emergence of the cartel party. *Party Politics, 1*(1), 5–28. https://doi.org/10.1177/1354068895001001001

Korpi, W., & Palme, J. (1998). The paradox of redistribution and strategies of equality: Welfare state institutions, inequality, and poverty in the Western countries. *American Sociological Review, 63*(5), 661–687. https://doi.org/10.2307/2657333

Leftwich, A. (2009). *Bringing agency back in: Politics and human agency in building institutions and states*. Synthesis Paper.

Levitsky, S., & Way, L. A. (2010). *Competitive authoritarianism: Hybrid regimes after the cold war*. Cambridge University Press.

Lijphart, A. (1997). Unequal participation: Democracy's unresolved dilemma. *American Political Science Review, 91*(1), 1–14. https://doi.org/10.2307/2952255

Linz, J. J. (2000). *Totalitarian and authoritarian regimes*. Lynne Rienner Publishers.

Longva, A. N. (1999). *Walls built on sand: Migration, exclusion, and society in Kuwait*. Westview Press.

López-Calva, L. F., & Lustig, N. (Eds.). (2010). *Declining inequality in Latin America: A decade of progress?* Brookings Institution Press.

Mair, P. (2013). *Ruling the void: The hollowing of Western democracy*. Verso.

March, J. G., & Olsen, J. P. (1989). *Rediscovering institutions: The organizational basis of politics*. Free Press.

Milánovic, B. (2016). *Global inequality: A new approach for the age of globalization*. Harvard University Press.

Mkandawire, T. (2005). *Social policy in a development context*. Palgrave Macmillan.

Moene, K. O., & Wallerstein, M. (2001). Inequality, social insurance, and redistribution. *American Political Science Review, 95*(4), 859–874. https://doi.org/10.1017/S0003055401004184

Moynihan, D. P. (2008). *The dynamics of performance management: Constructing information and reform*. Georgetown University Press.
Mutlugün, B. (2025). *Individualism*. Palgrave Macmillan.
Nachmias, D., & Sened, I. (2001). Governance and public policy. *Israel Affairs, 7*(4), 3–20.
Norris, P. (2011). *Democratic deficit: Critical citizens revisited*. Cambridge University Press.
North, D. C. (1990). *Institutions, institutional change and economic performance*. Cambridge University Press. https://doi.org/10.1017/CBO9780511808678
OECD. (2020). International migration outlook 2020. *OECD Publishing*.. https://doi.org/10.1787/ec98f531-en
OECD. (2023). *Government at a glance 2023*. OECD Publishing. https://doi.org/10.1787/3d5c5d31-en
Ostrom, E. (2010). Beyond markets and states: Polycentric governance of complex economic systems. *American Economic Review, 100*(3), 641–672. https://doi.org/10.1257/aer.100.3.641
Peters, B. G., & Pierre, J. (2016). *Governance and politics of the public sector*. Edward Elgar Publishing.
Pharr, S. J., & Putnam, R. D. (Eds.). (2000). *Disaffected democracies: What's wrong with democracy and what can be done?* Princeton University Press.
Pollitt, C., & Bouckaert, G. (2017). *Public management reform: A comparative analysis—Into the age of austerity* (4th ed.). Oxford University Press.
Rajan, S. I., & Oommen, A. (2020). *Migration, remittances, and development: Reassessing the Gulf model*. Springer.
Safdar, S., Khan, A., & Andlib, Z. (2022). Impact of good governance and natural resource rent on economic and environmental sustainability: An empirical analysis for south Asian economies. *Environmental Science and Pollution Research, 29*(55), 82948–82965.
Saxenian, A. (2006). *The new argonauts: Regional advantage in a global economy*. Harvard University Press.
Shachar, A. (2009). *The birthright lottery: Citizenship and global inequality*. Harvard University Press.
Shleifer, A., & Vishny, R. W. (1994). Politicians and firms. *Quarterly Journal of Economics, 109*(4), 995–1025. https://doi.org/10.2307/2118354
Skocpol, T. (1979). *States and social revolutions: A comparative analysis of France, Russia, and China*. Cambridge University Press.
Stoker, G. (2006). *Why politics matters: Making democracy work*. Palgrave Macmillan.
Svolik, M. W. (2012). *The politics of authoritarian rule*. Cambridge University Press.
Tilly, C. (1978). *From mobilization to revolution*. Addison-Wesley.

Wilkes, R., & Wu, C. (2018). Ethnicity, democracy, trust: A majority-minority approach. *Social Forces, 97*(1), 465–494.
Winters, J. A. (2011). *Oligarchy*. Cambridge University Press.

CHAPTER 9

The Impact of Middle-Class Nations on the Political Stability and Transition

Introduction of the Chapter

The institutional approach of political governance is the only way to ensure a sustainable middle-class nation. Indeed, institutions ensure a fair and just distribution of wealth among people and take into account the public interest over the individual interest (Acemoglu & Robinson, 2012). Moreover, institutions deploy their own adjustment mechanisms to improve their performance, their outcomes and outputs.

At the opposite, the individualistic approach of the political governance cannot reinforce the middle-class feature of a nation and make it sustainable. In such regimes, throughout time, alliances between individuals make it hard to break and the transition to the institutional approach becomes harder.

As per businesses that have formal and informal organizations, nations also can have hidden institutions or establishments under the control of individuals that can dominate the whole nation including all the formal institutions. From this book perspective, this configuration is also classified in the individualistic framework.

The previous chapter addresses the issue of how the political regimes can encourage the middle-class feature of a nation. Inversely, middle-class nations are generally aware of the importance of political regimes based on institutions and consider them as a privilege to defend and to reinforce regardless of the cost (Ahalya & Paul, 2024).

A. Tahiri Jouti, *Building Middle Class Nations*,
https://doi.org/10.1007/978-3-032-02134-2_9

This chapter would address two main ideas regarding the role and contribution of the middle-class feature of the nation to improve the performance and the stability of a political regime. First, public policies made to middle-class nations are easier to conceive and highly effective at the opposite of non-middle-class nations that need to conceive public policies that take into account each cluster's specific features and constraints. In the end, trade offs have to be made to optimize budgets and impacts. Generally, one cluster would be given priority over the others.

Second, middle-class nations enjoy their quality of life and the positive future prospects for themselves and for the next generations. Middle-class nations understand perfectly that their quality of life is due to the institutional approach of the political governance and it is something to safeguard and reinforce.

This chapter is a kind of synthesis of the various conclusions drawn in the previous chapters. This general synthesis refers to the various chapters to develop an overall understanding of public policies and their impact on strengthening the middle-class feature of a particular nation. More examples would be given to make the conclusions clearer for everyone.

Effectiveness of Public Policies Made to Middle-Class Nations

Comparison of Middle-Class and Non-Middle-Class Nations

In Chapter 2, middle-class nations were presented as being easier to serve and to upgrade while being politically stable. Indeed, the insignificant gaps between the different clusters make it easier to conceive homogeneous policies targeting the same needs and perspectives. At the opposite, the significant gaps between the different clusters in a non-middle-class nation make it harder to conceive policies targeting different needs and sometimes opposite ones.

Moreover, the development of a particular nation can be measured by its middle-class feature. In fact, a non-middle-class nation has two options. The first option would consist of leaving no one behind to the detriment of other clusters by reducing the gaps without paying attention to the upgrade efforts to be made. The second option would consist of focusing on the upgrade efforts without paying attention to the survival clusters to reduce the gaps and increase the homogeneity of the nation.

At the opposite, such trade offs do not exist in middle-class nations and all the policies are focusing on the upgrade efforts and how to maintain people in their position with all the necessary rights and nets mechanisms as discussed earlier in this book.

Finally, it is worth noting that being a middle-class nation does not mean that problems do not exist but they are less complex than those of non-middle-class nations.

In the Education Area

When comparing challenges faced by developed and developing countries, many issues stem from the middle-class feature. Examining the educational problems in Sweden (a predominantly middle-class society) versus Algeria (a country with a less developed middle class) can reveal the following elements:

The school dropout rate, grade repetition rate, and transition rate between educational cycles are all critical indicators. In Algeria, these rates are alarmingly high, suggesting that many young Algerians may grow up without the necessary qualifications or skills to be productive members of society. This situation risks creating isolated social clusters. In contrast, these rates remain low in Sweden, reflecting a more effective educational progression and inclusion.

Moreover, in Sweden 62% of swedes still trust public education institutions. In Algeria, public trust in the education system is low due to a weak curriculum and poor governance. As a result, many families turn to the private sector, which exacerbates inequalities between social groups. Those with sufficient financial means can afford a better educational environment for their children, while families with limited resources often face early school dropout among their children.

Finally, in terms of academic performance, Sweden is doing better than the OECD average while in Algeria, national exam results show high failure rates and large regional disparities in student achievement.

Based on this comparison, the Algerian education system tends to reinforce the non-middle-class feature, with many individuals dropping out-of-school. Additionally, regional and financial disparities further deepen inequalities by giving an advantage to the private education sector.

From another perspective, Sweden has also its own challenges such as maintaining the reduced gaps between regions and families and improving the academic performances but obviously, the future is clearly brighter

Table 9.1 Comparison between Sweden and Algeria in terms of Education issues

Indicator	*Sweden*	*Algeria*
School dropout/early leavers	7.4% of youth aged 18–24 (2023). Foreign-born: 11.1%, native-born: 6.4% (European Commission, 2024).	Exact national dropout rate unavailable. UNICEF estimates show high risk of dropout, especially in middle school: ~26.6% boys, 13.7% girls (MICS 2019) (UNICEF Algeria, 2019).
Grade repetition rate	Very low; only ~0.1% of lower-secondary students are two or more years older than expected (OECD, 2025).	No comprehensive data; historical evidence indicates high repetition rates contribute to dropout risk (UNICEF Algeria, 2019).
Transition between education cycles	Smooth progression from primary to secondary and higher education; student-centered policies support continuity (OECD, 2025).	Low progression, especially from middle to high school, due to dropout, poor performance, and lack of support structures (UNICEF Algeria, 2019).
Trust in Public Education	Generally high; OECD surveys report strong satisfaction with public services, including education. (OECD, 2024).	Trust declining due to outdated curricula, overcrowding, teacher strikes, and reliance on private tutoring (UNICEF Algeria, 2024).
Academic Performance (PISA 2022)	Participates in PISA: Math 482, Reading 487, Science 494; scores above OECD average but declining (OECD, 2023).	Algeria does not participate in PISA. National exams (BEM, BAC) show low completion rates and high regional disparities (~50% secondary completion) (UNICEF Algeria, 2019).

which will reinforce the economic but also the political stability of the nation.

In Housing and Transportation

Transportation and housing are highly connected and together, they can impact positively or negatively the middle-class feature of any nation. When comparing Switzerland, Tunisia, and Morocco in terms of transportation and housing, the following elements were revealed:

Table 9.2 Comparison between Switzerland, Tunisia, and Morocco in terms of Transportation and Housing policies

Aspect	*Switzerland*	*Tunisia*	*Morocco*
Public transport usage	~30–40% of urban trips (Swiss federal statistical office, 2024)	Moderate, mostly urban areas (APIA, nd)	Moderate to low, varies by city (HCP, nd)
Rail network	Dense, modern, punctual (Swiss Federal Railways, 2023)	Limited, connects major cities with variable punctuality (World Bank, 2017)	Developing, major routes like Casablanca–Rabat, less dense (HCP, nd)
Urban transport modes	Trams, buses, metro (Zurich), funiculars (Swiss federal statistical office, 2024)	Buses, light metro (Tunis), shared taxis (APIA, nd)	Buses, trams (Casablanca, Rabat), taxis (HCP, nd)
Quality and reliability	Very high (punctuality, comfort, frequency) (Swiss federal statistical office, 2024)	Variable (crowded buses, aging infrastructure) (World Bank, 2017)	Moderate, buses often crowded, improving infrastructure (HCP, nd)
Road infrastructure	Extensive, well-maintained highways and roads (Swiss federal statistical office, 2024)	Developing, main roads well-maintained but congested in cities (World Bank, 2017)	Improving network, highways connecting major cities (HCP, nd)
Active mobility	Highly developed (bike lanes, pedestrian zones) (Swiss federal statistical office, 2024)	Limited infrastructure for cycling and walking (APIA, nd)	Limited cycling and walking infrastructure (HCP, nd)
Fare system	Relatively high, integrated passes and subsidies (Swiss federal statistical office, 2024)	Generally affordable, service quality varies (APIA, nd)	Affordable but service quality varies (HCP, nd)
Residential accessibility	Efficient transport allows wide dispersion of housing, including suburbs (ARE, 2023)	Limited transport infrastructure concentrates housing near city centers (World Bank, 2017)	Limited transport options led to dense urban centers (HCP, nd)

(continued)

Table 9.2 (continued)

Aspect	*Switzerland*	*Tunisia*	*Morocco*
Urban development	Balanced urban and suburban growth, controls urban sprawl (ARE, 2023)	Denser, sometimes informal urban growth due to poor transport access (World Bank, 2017)	Urban sprawl around major cities, with limited planning (HCP, nd)
Social and spatial equity	Wide public transport coverage ensures equitable access to housing and services (ARE, 2023)	Transport inequalities reinforce residential segregation by income (World Bank, 2017)	Economic disparities reflected in transport access and housing locations (HCP, nd)
Property values	High in well-connected areas (ARE, 2023)	Concentrated value in central and well-connected areas (World Bank, 2017)	Higher values in well-connected urban areas (HCP, nd)

When comparing Switzerland, Tunisia, and Morocco in terms of Transport infrastructure, it becomes evident that less attention is given to transport networks in Tunisia and Morocco. While Switzerland has heavily invested in integrated, multimodal transportation systems that support both urban and rural connectivity, Morocco and Tunisia continue to face challenges related to planning, investment, and maintenance of transport infrastructure. This disparity significantly affects mobility, accessibility, and urban development in both North African countries.

Although transport costs in Morocco and Tunisia remain relatively affordable, the quality of service is often poor. Public transport systems suffer from irregular schedules, overcrowding, and outdated equipment. This gap between cost and quality results in a lack of reliability and efficiency, which discourages widespread use and contributes to increased reliance on private vehicles, worsening traffic congestion and urban stress.

The concentration of transport infrastructure in city centers prevents balanced urban development. As a result, property prices in central areas and neighborhoods well-served by public transport are significantly higher. Conversely, peripheral zones—which lack sufficient transit options—develop more slowly and often fail to attract sustained investment. In both Morocco and Tunisia, the creation of new urban zones does not necessarily lead to lower real estate prices. And when it does, it often comes at the expense of user experience, accessibility, and quality of life.

In terms of social housing and subsidies granted to people with low income in the three countries (Switzerland,[1] Morocco,[2] Tunisia[3]), the following table summarizes the main elements:

In Morocco and Tunisia, public housing policies have primarily benefited real estate developers through tax incentives, access to subsidized land, and public–private partnership mechanisms. This supply-driven approach has often led to the mass production of low-cost housing, but with limited attention to construction quality, infrastructure, and urban integration. As a result, low-income households—despite being the intended beneficiaries—frequently end up in poorly built, inadequately serviced, and poorly located housing that fails to meet their actual needs.

In contrast, Switzerland adopts a more inclusive and cooperative housing policy, where local authorities and housing cooperatives play a leading role. The focus is not on volume but on equitable access to high-quality housing, even for economically vulnerable populations. This system not only curbs real estate speculation but also helps reduce social inequality by ensuring dignified living conditions and strong urban integration, even in areas with high housing demand.

Obviously, Switzerland has more financial resources than Morocco and Tunisia but the effectiveness of the Swiss Housing public policy and its contribution to reinforce the middle-class feature of the nation is not limited to the abundance of financial resources, it is mainly due to the relevance of the strategic orientations.

In Public Health

When it comes to the public health sector, the comparison between Norway and Egypt reveals the following elements:

Norway, a middle-class country, relies heavily on the public sector and a public insurance scheme funded by taxes that covers all citizens. In this model, the private sector plays only a minimal role in the provision of

[1] https://www.bfs.admin.ch/bfs/en/home/statistics/cross-sectional-topics/housing-switzerland.html?utm_source=chatgpt.com

[2] https://housingfinanceafrica.org/countries/morocco/

[3] https://unhabitat.org/sites/default/files/documents/2019-07/tunisia_urban_housing_sector_profile.pdf

Table 9.3 Comparison between Switzerland, Tunisia, and Morocco in terms of social housing policies

Criteria	*Switzerland*	*Morocco*	*Tunisia*
Main objective	Provide affordable and sustainable housing through cooperative models and local initiatives (Swiss Federal Office for Housing, 2022).	Reduce housing deficit and eliminate slums by promoting affordable housing for low-income households (UN-Habitat, 2022).	Improve living conditions and reduce urban poverty through public housing programs and neighborhood upgrading (World Bank, 2018).
Key stakeholders	Municipalities, housing cooperatives, and cantonal authorities (Hartmann, 2021).	Government, private developers, and public–private partnerships.	Government agencies (e.g., SNIT, AFH), local authorities, and international donors.
Subsidies and incentives	Indirect subsidies such as land provision, tax incentives, and low-interest loans to cooperatives (Swiss Federal Office for Housing, 2024).	Direct subsidies to developers, tax exemptions, and subsidized land for affordable housing projects (CRI, nd).	State-funded programs offering subsidized housing units and infrastructure improvements in underserved areas AFD, 2018).
Access criteria	Income-based eligibility, with priority given to residents with limited means; varies by canton (Swiss Federal Office for Housing, 2024).	Targeted at low- to middle-income households, with specific programs for first-time homeowners.	Focused on low-income families, with eligibility based on income thresholds and housing conditions (Oxford Business Group, 2018).
Average cost of social housing	Rents are typically set below market rates, often 20–30% less, depending on the region and cooperative (Swiss Federal Office for Housing, 2024).	Approximately 140,000 MAD (~13,000 USD) for a 50 m^2 unit under social housing schemes (Oxford Business Group, 2013).	Around 40,000 TND (~12,000 USD) for basic housing units provided through national programs (UN-Habitat, 2023).
Quality and standards	High construction standards with emphasis on energy efficiency and sustainability (Swiss Federal Office of Energy, 2024).	Variable quality; some projects face criticism over construction standards and lack of amenities (Oxford Business Group, 2013).	Generally modest quality; ongoing efforts to improve infrastructure and service delivery in housing projects (UN-Habitat, 2023).

(continued)

Table 9.3 (continued)

Criteria	*Switzerland*	*Morocco*	*Tunisia*
Current challenges	Limited availability in high-demand urban areas; reliance on local initiatives leads to regional disparities (Swiss Federal Statistical Office, 2024).	Persistent housing shortages, especially in urban centers; challenges in ensuring quality and timely delivery of projects (Oxford Business Group, 2013).	Slow pace of housing delivery; issues with maintenance and integration of housing projects into urban planning frameworks (UN-Habitat, 2023).
Dominant housing model	Cooperative housing with community involvement and non-profit orientation (Swiss Federation of Housing Cooperatives, 2023).	Public–private partnerships focusing on ownership-based affordable housing units (Oxford Business Group, 2013).	State-led housing initiatives aimed at providing rental and ownership options for low-income populations (Oxford Business Group, 2018).

Table 9.4 Comparison between Norway and Egypt in terms of public health policies

Criteria	*Norway*	*Egypt*
Hospital bed capacity	3.35 beds per 1000 people (2022) (source: Trading economics)	1.2 beds per 1000 people (~121,617 total, 2020) (source: Wikipedia)
Access to universal health insurance	Universal healthcare via National Insurance Scheme (NIS), tax-funded (source: Commonwealth Fund)	Progressive implementation of universal health coverage, ~66% covered (target: 2032) (source: Arab finance)
Health system structure	Public, tax-funded system with services delivered mainly by public hospitals (source: Wikipedia)	Mixed system with dominant private sector alongside public subsidized services (source: Wikipedia)
Private sector share	Private sector < 5% of total healthcare services (source: Commonwealth Fund)	Private sector accounts for ~60% of services and growing (source: Enterprise press)

healthcare services. The strength of this system lies in its universal nature, ensuring equal access to care regardless of income level.

In contrast, Egypt has taken a different path. Instead of generalizing medical coverage through a publicly funded system supported by taxes, the state leans heavily on the private sector, which accounts for more than 65% of healthcare provision. The national insurance scheme is primarily financed by direct contributions from citizens, in addition to the taxes they already pay—taxes that are not effectively redirected to fund public healthcare infrastructure.

This imbalance between public and private healthcare is not unique to Egypt. Similar patterns can be observed in several other countries, where reliance on citizen contributions and underfunded public systems hinder the establishment of equitable and universal healthcare coverage.

Relevance of Public Policies in Middle-Class Nations

Social Cost and Risk Transfer in Middle-Class and Non-Middle-Class Nations

Combining the impacts of the different policies in the social sphere on the social cost as defined in the 6th chapter identifies the following results and conclusions:

Even if developing countries had adequate budgets, effective social service delivery would not necessarily follow—underperformance in the public sector often stems from structural and governance challenges rather than merely financial scarcity. Weak administrative capacity, lack of coherent policy orientation, and incentive problems within public institutions are major barriers to delivering quality social services, leading to higher social costs despite available funding (ODI, 2016).

In middle-class nations, banking penetration rates are close to 100%, accompanied by relatively low interest rates and a wide range of highly performant public policies in sectors such as education and healthcare (Birdsall, 2010; OECD, 2020). These policies contribute significantly to lowering the cost of living and narrowing the gaps between different social clusters (Easterly, 2001). It is important to note that high-interest rates tend to favor wealthy depositors, effectively circulating wealth within the upper economic class. In contrast, lower interest rates have the opposite effect, enabling broader access to credit and fostering economic inclusion (North, 1990). Even when risk transfer mechanisms are in place, low interest rates combined with strong social policies play a key

Table 9.5 Comparison between middle-class and non-middle-class nations in terms of social cost

	Middle-class nation	*Non-Middle-Class nation*
Education	People trust public education institutions + low school dropout + high academic performance = no additional cost for education + equal and equality of opportunity	High school dropout + low academic performance + people do not trust public education = additional cost for education + reinforcing gaps between clusters
Health	Free health insurance scheme + highly performant public health institutions = no additional cost for health	Underperforming public health institutions + dominance of the private sector with extra cost + universal insurance scheme based on people's contributions = additional cost for health
Housing and transportation	Affordable, high-standard and accessible housing = no additional cost for housing while there is a possibility to receive subsidies	High cost of housing in accessible zones, low standard of housing for social housing = additional cost for transportation/housing for high-standard houses
Social cost	Almost nil	Creates the horizontal inflation with additional cost to be beard by households moving people to the poverty trap in some cases

Table 9.6 Comparison between middle-class and non-middle-class nations in terms of interest rates and banking penetration rates

Country	*Central Bank Interest Rate (2024)*	*Banking Penetration Rate (15+ years old—2024)*	*Source*
Norway	4.50%	~100%	Norges Bank
Sweden	2.50%	~99%	Riksbank
Switzerland	0.50%	~99%	Swiss national bank
Morocco	2.50%	~44%	Bank Al-maghrib
Algeria	3.00% (Est.)	~43%	Bank of Algeria
Tunisia	8.00%	~48%	Banque Centrale de Tunisie
Egypt	27.25%	74.8%	Central Bank of Egypt

role in mitigating wealth concentration and promoting a more equitable distribution of resources (Birdsall, 2016).

Effectiveness of Reforms in Middle-Class Vs. Non-Middle-Class Nations

In middle-class nations, all the public policies seem to be effective and achieve the objectives and targets for many obvious reasons. In non-middle-class nations, public policies reinforce the non-middle-class feature of the nation as demonstrated previously. Therefore, conducting reforms is not as effective and rewarding as it should be because of the orientation itself and not only because of the lack of financial resources.

The effectiveness of public policies increases the happiness and the satisfaction of people and opens new horizons to the new generations of the nation. Thus, people in middle-class nations are satisfied with their political regimes and governance and are ready to support them and defend them.

At the opposite, public policies reinforcing the non-middle-class feature of the nation make them ineffective and people from all clusters would be frustrated from the government action and from the whole regime if the situation keeps worsening. Therefore, people in non-middle-class nations are less satisfied with their political regimes and governance and can initiate at any time actions against them.

Most of political regimes in non-middle-class nations, instead of adopting public policies that focus on reinforcing the middle-class feature, do the opposite and establish the heterogeneity of the nation through policies that rely on poor public-sector performance and on private sector hegemony to fill the gaps.

In middle-class nations, all reforms can be successful because of the high degree of awareness and education of people, their level of income, the democratic process of involvement and adherence to draft and conceive the policies.

In contrast, in countries without a strong middle class, reforms often struggle to succeed due to limited public awareness and education, low-income levels, and a lack of understanding of the rationale behind various public policy decisions. When such policies further entrench the middle-class feature, they risk deepening public frustration and discontent. In this context, the political regime and governance can be contested by the survival cluster and the passive supporters cluster.

Toward Middle-Class Nations

General Scheme for Public Policies

General Scheme for Non-Middle-Class Vs. Middle-Class Nations
Based on the theoretical frameworks explored in the previous chapters, the withdrawal of the government from the social sector has enabled the private sector to impose its dominance, thereby driving up the cost of living for households. This upward pressure on household expenses fuels inflation, which in turn hinders the overall economic performance. The deepening economic pressure on households not only threatens social cohesion but also poses risks to political stability. Ultimately, this withdrawal reflects a poorly calibrated policy decision—one that intensifies social disparities instead of addressing them.

The following scheme summarizes the factors that increase or decrease the disparities between the different clusters:

General Scheme toward a Middle-Class Nation
Based on the previous chapters and the outputs of the different analysis, the milestones to be taken into account in order to build a middle-class nation can be summarized as follows:

The Milestones toward a Middle-Class Nation

The Political Willingness to Build a Middle-Class Nation
Building a middle class nation requires strong political will to shift from the individualistic to the institutional governance. This transition involves empowering institutions to lead development while ensuring their flexibility, effectiveness, and alignment with national aspirations.

The foundation lies in building relevant institutions—entities with clear mandates and visions that actively contribute to a long-term national strategy. Isolated institutional visions risk undermining national objectives, as misaligned agencies can unintentionally hinder innovation or reform.

A clear, long-term national vision (30 to 50 years) is essential to coordinate institutional efforts, reduce inter-institutional conflicts, and enable the adaptation of mandates over time to address emerging challenges, such as the regulation of artificial intelligence.

Simple and relevant rules ensure policy effectiveness by making regulations understandable, enforceable, and scalable. Complex or absent

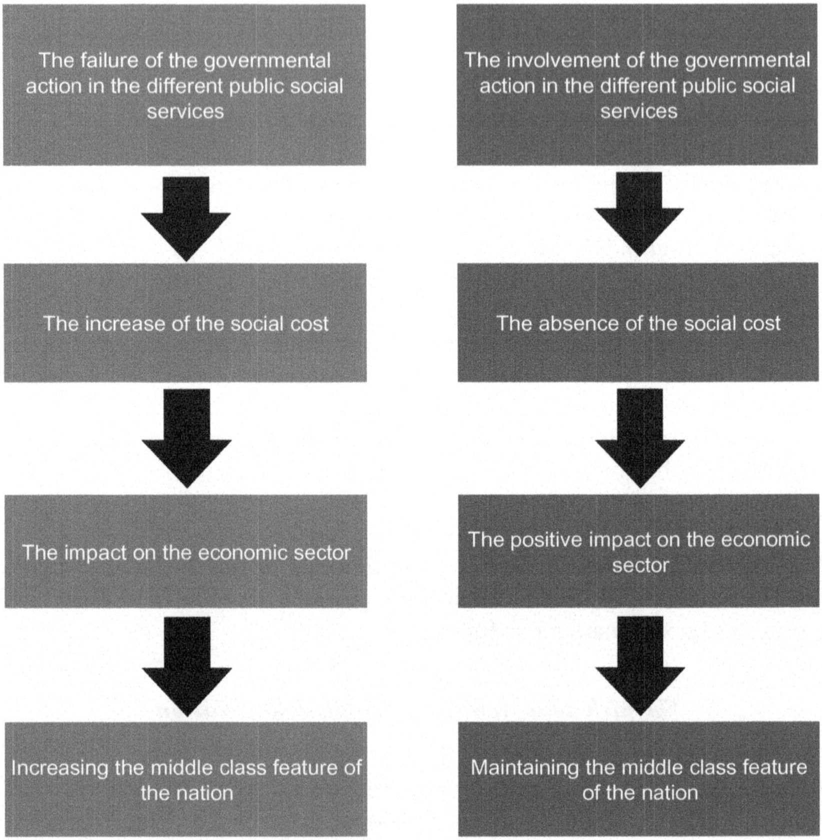

Fig. 9.1 The global scheme leading to the reinforcement of a non-middle-class vs. middle-class feature of the nation

rules, typical of non-middle-class nations, undermine implementation and oversight.

A strong control environment is essential to maintaining institutional authority. This includes a comprehensive audit system, proportionate sanctions, and dynamic capabilities to respond to evolving risks. Without rigorous oversight, laws lack impact.

Objective-driven leadership appointments align institutional direction with the specific objectives of each development phase. Transparent

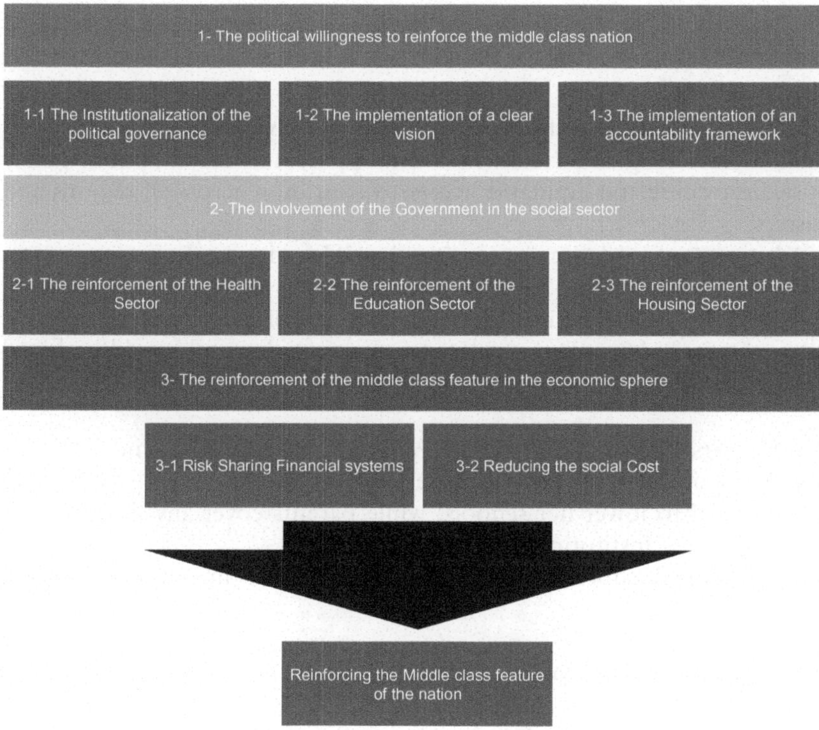

Fig. 9.2 The milestones toward a middle-class nation

recall and performance evaluation mechanisms preserve integrity and adaptability.

A sound accountability framework ensures that no individual is beyond scrutiny. Institutional cultures must normalize responsibility and transparency, guided by measurable performance indicators.

Finally, institutions must remain agile and flexible, balancing structure with responsiveness. Leaders should have defined mandates with built-in checks and be supported by internal leadership pipelines, ensuring continuity and innovation.

In sum, political will must manifest not only in declarations but in building resilient, visionary, and accountable institutions capable of shaping a sustainable and inclusive national future.

The Involvement of the Government in the Social Sector

- Reinforcing the Role of the Government in the Education Sector

Education has the transformative power to change lives and ensure a stable future. To guarantee fairness and opportunity for all, public policy must ensure free and equitable access to education across all regions and clusters.

A key recommendation is to externalize education to the private sector, given the inefficiencies of public education, such as rigid unions, centralized staff, and lack of competition. The new governance model would see the government become a regulator, not a provider, and would be based on three pillars:

- Universal public aid per child, regardless of family income;
- A classification of schools based on performance, with public aid indexed to lower-tier schools, while parents cover any difference in higher-tier institutions;
- A national education map, directing private investment to local needs.

Special attention must be paid to rural areas, where traditional school models are unsustainable. Solutions include mobile schools with rotation between villages, blended learning via digital platforms, and blockchain-based attendance tracking to link subsidies to actual school attendance. These innovations close access gaps and reduce inequalities between urban and rural populations.

For students who are struggling or falling behind, reinforcement and support mechanisms should ensure that no one is left behind. A holistic educational approach must consider physical, emotional, and social development, promoting practical skills and personalized learning pathways. Students should be able to focus on their strengths, with minimal requirements in other subjects and flexible catch-up options.

Finally, alternative pathways must be integrated into the system. These include:

- Recognizing the dignity of all professions through vocational training;

- Enabling individuals to start working early and then return to school to improve their skills;
- Offering conversion pathways that allow for career changes, even years later.

This model integrates lifelong learning, making education more inclusive, responsive, and empowering, and enabling the transition from an elitist system to one focused on the middle class, valuing potential rather than rigid trajectories.

– Improving Housing and Transportation Policies

When real estate prices rise or supply is insufficient, particularly in countries with a marginal middle class and diverse incomes, the strategic creation of new urban areas becomes essential. These areas must meet different housing standards—luxury, middle-class, and social housing—to avoid a cascade effect where shortages in one segment push wealthy groups to lower housing standards, ultimately overburdening the social housing segment and degrading the overall quality of life.

However, housing construction alone is not enough. New urban areas must be supported by essential infrastructure, including public transportation, to ensure housing affordability and sustainability. If this infrastructure is delayed or absent, hidden costs (such as the need for private vehicles) make relocation less attractive. Conversely, if well-connected and well-planned, these areas can attract residents by offering more spacious and modern living spaces at a lower cost.

Rather than being a specific standard of housing, social housing under this framework is defined by flexible financial tools that ensure inclusive access. These include:

- Guarantee schemes for individuals with low or irregular income, enabling them to obtain mortgages they wouldn't otherwise qualify for.
- Targeted subsidies, which can support both homeowners and renters through tax relief or direct financial assistance, often linked to conditions like house size or location.

- Crisis response schemes, allowing temporarily distressed individuals—even previously wealthy ones—to receive short-term support and rejoin the housing market when their situation stabilizes.

These mechanisms act both as lifts, enabling people to move into homeownership, and as nets, catching them in times of hardship. The system emphasizes that housing policy should guarantee continuity in access to dignified living conditions, even in adverse circumstances.

Housing solutions must not lead to a deterioration of the urban fabric. Instead, policies should promote upgraded building standards, modern architectural design, and integrated infrastructure in new zones. This improves residents' quality of life and helps rebalance city density by encouraging voluntary movement from overcrowded urban cores.

Tax policy also plays a role: shifting from one-time property transaction taxes to annual property taxes can reduce barriers to mobility and ensure a steady revenue stream for governments. To facilitate this transition, interim arrangements like tax holidays or phased implementation may be necessary.

Lastly, the outward migration to new urban areas should be used as an opportunity to *revitalize historic city centers*. Freed-up space in these areas can host cultural, commercial, and financial hubs, preserving urban heritage while fostering economic growth. In the long term, this migration cycle—if managed carefully—can enhance tourism, create new jobs, and reinvigorate urban economies.

- Improving Public Health Through Prevention, Governance, and Innovation

Improving public health requires coordinated policies beyond the healthcare system—such as those in housing, transportation, education, sports, and the environment. The preventive component of health policy is crucial and is deeply linked to environmental action, which involves five main pillars: GHG mitigation, climate adaptation, biodiversity protection, water management, and waste management.

To address environmental health risks, several key policy actions are required. First, reducing emissions from transport should be prioritized by investing in efficient public transit systems and encouraging the use of electric vehicles. Simultaneously, accelerating the energy transition is essential—this involves a strong shift toward renewable energy sources and nuclear power, while ensuring that solutions are tailored to each country's unique social, economic, and geographic context. Urban planning must also become more sustainable, integrating green spaces, and ensuring that housing, services, and employment opportunities are located in close proximity to reduce unnecessary travel and enhance well-being.

In addition, raising public awareness is crucial. Educational campaigns should focus on encouraging responsible consumption, reducing waste, conserving energy, and promoting healthier lifestyles. Investment in research and the adoption of innovative solutions will also play a critical role in mitigating both environmental and health-related risks. By funding scientific advancement, governments can better anticipate future challenges and develop effective preventive measures.

Beyond environmental concerns, health policy itself must evolve to address contemporary needs. Mental health should be supported through multiple accessible channels, including community associations, religious groups, and professional therapy. Health systems should also incorporate regular screenings, with artificial intelligence offering promising tools to identify risks early. Moreover, the promotion of physical activity must become a cornerstone of public health strategy. Cities should be designed in ways that make sports and physical activity accessible to all, regardless of age or income.

Effective public health policy requires a robust governance framework. This system must be both strategic and flexible, capable of identifying and responding to emerging health threats. It should be independent from private sector interests to ensure decisions are based on the public good. Internally, it must plan and maintain necessary infrastructure, while externally, it should coordinate closely with related sectors such as education, environment, and sports to ensure coherence and synergy across policies.

Finally, technological innovation presents new opportunities to improve public health outcomes. The emergence of self-driving vehicles could reduce air pollution, lower urban stress, and open up public space for green and recreational uses. Additionally, wearable technologies can track key health indicators, prevent chronic disease, and contribute to more personalized and proactive health-care systems, including dynamic health insurance models. By integrating these innovations into broader public policy, societies can build a healthier and more sustainable future.

The ultimate goal is to strengthen prevention to reduce pressure on curative services and build a healthier society.

The Milestones Related to the Economic Sector

– Monitoring the Social Cost

Inclusive economic development requires the implementation of mechanisms that promote equal access to economic opportunities and fair participation in the market, alongside mechanisms that reduce individual and collective vulnerabilities through effective social policies. In the global economic landscape, two distinct approaches can be observed. On one side, liberal economies—typically in the Global North—allow innovators to enter and compete in sensitive sectors, provided they meet legal and regulatory standards. These countries tend to update legal frameworks quickly to accommodate new ideas and alternative products, thus fostering competitiveness and fairness across sectors.

In contrast, overprotective economies—often in the Global South—are characterized by a complex legal environment that delays or restricts innovation, particularly in sensitive industries. In such settings, anything not explicitly authorized by law is effectively prohibited, and market entry is restricted to a limited number of players, often protected by entrenched lobby groups. Meanwhile, non-sensitive sectors are frequently unregulated, leading to economic disorganization and instability. This dual approach not only suppresses entrepreneurial initiative but also exacerbates inequality by favoring a small politically connected elite. As argued in my book "*The Unlearning Process of Nations*," this environment is shaped by lobbying practices and a "sky is the limit" paradigm that grants privileged access to a minority while excluding the majority.

Changing this paradigm would require a combination of dismantling protectionist practices and empowering the broader population through fair access to production resources. It also demands a deep reform of public institutions to eliminate lobbyist influence, which would pave the way for more transparent and open economic systems. Once these reforms are implemented, the private sector can be liberalized more easily, encouraging broader participation and innovation. Such transformation would generate more jobs, raise incomes, and increase the tax base. Crucially, if citizens and businesses perceive that they are benefiting from fair governance and visionary economic policies, they will be more inclined to pay taxes, even at higher rates. This leads to stronger public finances and a more dynamic, competitive economy.

At the same time, the government must invest in efficient public policies in social sectors such as education, healthcare, housing, and public transportation. These policies serve both as lifts—by enabling individuals and families to move up the social ladder—and as nets—by cushioning them during economic downturns. High-quality, accessible public services reduce household financial burdens and support social mobility. For example, a strong public education system reduces the need for costly private schooling and improves job prospects for future generations. Similarly, free or affordable healthcare protects families from financial shocks, especially in times of crisis.

These services also function as automatic stabilizers. During economic downturns, people often cut back on spending in areas like education and health. If the public sector guarantees access to these essential services, it mitigates the long-term damage to households and communities. Therefore, public policies should be coherent and mutually reinforcing, ensuring that positive outcomes in one sector are not undermined by shortcomings in another. When effectively coordinated, such policies improve quality of life, reduce inequality, and strengthen the resilience of the entire population.

Finally, the social cost—defined as the combined burden of essential expenses on households—must be carefully monitored and managed. Demographic shifts, such as an aging population, can increase pressure on healthcare systems, requiring anticipatory planning and reform. When governments are proactive and successful in lowering social costs, they reinforce their legitimacy and enhance their capacity to govern effectively. Examples such as cities offering free public transportation (e.g., Mulhouse in France or Hasselt in Belgium) demonstrate how reducing social costs can also boost business competitiveness and attract international talent. Over time, this creates a virtuous cycle where lower social costs lead to greater public trust, increased tax compliance, and stronger, more inclusive economic growth. Ultimately, reducing the social cost is key to narrowing the gap between population clusters and building a more equitable society.

Reducing Disparities through Risk Transfer Alternatives

This important step involves, among other things, connecting the unbanked to economic opportunities and gradually integrating them into the formal financial system. This can be achieved through:

- Creating specialized institutions such as mobile payment platforms, crowdfunding services, and microfinance institutions (MFIs). These should be independent of traditional banks to avoid mismanagement or loss of direction.
- Encouraging institutions that go beyond lending: they should also empower and support individuals in their financial and entrepreneurial journeys (e.g., M-PESA and M-KOPA).
- Promoting risk-sharing financial tools, such as Islamic finance and venture capital, to reduce the burden of losses on individuals.
- Using guarantee schemes to promote access to finance, particularly when they are part of effective public policies (for example, in housing and education).
- Offering lower financing rates for socially responsible investments, through mechanisms such as targeted refinancing or tax deductions.

These mechanisms play a crucial role in mitigating the consequences of financial collapse. Risk-sharing ensures that losses are not borne solely by individuals, except in cases of negligence, thereby spreading the burden more equitably and reducing personal financial ruin. Debt rescheduling offers borrowers a second chance during times of economic downturns, allowing them to restructure their obligations and avoid the loss of essential assets. In addition, grant programs provide direct support to individuals facing financial downturns, enabling them to meet their commitments and avoid economic decline.

This important step also aims to transform financial inclusion into long-term socio-economic progress by promoting a more strategic and inclusive approach to development. It involves supporting innovative sectors such as artificial intelligence, particularly when this support is coordinated with public incentives and national strategy, thus ensuring that cutting-edge growth benefits society as a whole. It also promotes investment in lagging regions, helping to reduce territorial disparities and ensure a more balanced distribution of opportunities. Furthermore, it aims to align with broader public policies aimed at strengthening the middle class and stimulating upward economic mobility, thus anchoring inclusion within a sustainable national development framework.

Ultimately, a balanced and well-sequenced combination of these mechanisms will reduce inter-cluster wealth transfer and create a more equitable and opportunity-rich society.

Conclusion of the Chapter

Building a middle-class nation is not the outcome of spontaneous growth—it is a deliberate political project requiring sustained commitment, institutional transformation, and strategic coordination across all sectors. At the heart of this endeavor lies the political will to transition from individual-centered governance to a mature, institutional governance model that is visionary, resilient, and responsive.

This vision demands the creation of empowered and accountable institutions guided by a long-term national strategy. These institutions must operate under simple, enforceable rules, transparent leadership, and robust oversight mechanisms—allowing them to adapt to emerging challenges such as artificial intelligence while maintaining alignment with national aspirations.

The government must also reclaim a strategic role in the social sectors—not necessarily as a direct provider, but as a regulator and enabler. In education, this means guaranteeing universal access while enabling private sector participation under fair, transparent rules. In housing, it involves designing inclusive urban zones with the infrastructure and financial tools that act both as lifts and nets. In public health, prevention and innovation must go hand-in-hand with cross-sector governance and environmental responsibility.

Economic policy must follow the same logic. By reducing the social cost of essential goods and services, governments can strengthen social mobility and economic competitiveness. A just and dynamic economy is one where innovation is encouraged, monopolistic practices are dismantled, and all citizens have access to production opportunities—not just the privileged few. This includes integrating the unbanked, supporting risk-sharing mechanisms, and ensuring that financial inclusion translates into long-term socio-economic empowerment.

Across all these domains, the ultimate objective is to forge a society where opportunity is not a matter of birth but a function of policy—where the middle class is not a narrow elite but a broad, stable foundation of national prosperity. Realizing this ambition requires a new social contract, where trust in institutions is restored, social investments are treated as engines of growth, and governance is anchored in fairness, accountability, and foresight.

This chapter lays the groundwork for such a transformation. It outlines not only what must be done, but how it can be achieved—through political courage, institutional reform, and a relentless focus on equity and inclusion. The path to a middle-class nation is clear. What remains is the will to walk it.

Chapter References

Acemoglu, D., & Robinson, J. A. (2012). *Why nations fail: The origins of power, prosperity, and poverty*. Crown Publishing Group.

Agence Française de Développement. (2018). December 26. *Tunisia reinvents its suburbs.*. https://www.afd.fr/en/actualites/grand-angle/tunisia-reinvents-its-suburbs

Ahalya, R., & Paul, S. B. (2024). *Middle class and development: A study of Indian state*. Gokhale Institute of Politics and Economics.

Birdsall, N. (2010). The (indispensable) middle class in developing countries. *Center for Global Development Working Paper, No. 207*.

Birdsall, N. (2016). Middle-class heroes: The best guarantee of good governance. *Foreign Affairs, 95*, 25.

Easterly, W. (2001). The middle class consensus and economic development. *Journal of Economic Growth, 6*(4), 317–335. https://doi.org/10.1023/A:1012786330095

European Commission. (2024). Education and training monitor 2024: Sweden. *Publications Office of the European Union.*. https://op.europa.eu/webpub/eac/education-and-training-monitor/en/country-reports/sweden.html

North, D. C. (1990). *Institutions, institutional change, and economic performance*. Cambridge University Press.

ODI. (2016). Service delivery and accountability in international development: Constraints and incentives. *Overseas Development Institute.*. https://odi.org/publications/6767-service-delivery-accountability-international-development-aid-contraints-incentives

OECD. (2020). International migration outlook 2020. *OECD Publishing.*. https://doi.org/10.1787/ec98f531-en

UN-Habitat. (2022). Morocco: Affordable housing and slum upgrading. https://unhabitat.org/morocco-affordable-housing-and-slum-upgrading

UN-Habitat. (2023). Housing affordability and basic housing provision in Tunisia. https://unhabitat.org/country/tunisia

World Bank. (2018). Tunisia: Improving urban living conditions through housing and neighborhood upgrading. https://documents.worldbank.org/en/publication/documents-reports/documentdetail/180121531634383377/tunisia-improving-urban-living-conditions-through-housing-and-neighborhood-upgrading

CHAPTER 10

Conclusion of the Book

This book promotes a new perspective that consists of linking successful nations not solely to their economic output or geopolitical influence, but rather to their capacity to reinforce and sustain the ***middle-class feature***. This concept goes beyond the traditional economic definition of the middle class; it defines the societal organization where various clusters are sufficiently integrated, and where opportunities, expectations, and institutional responsiveness are broadly aligned.

The Concept of Middle-Class Nations

Middle-class nations are distinguished by their internal coherence. They encourage a sense of collective belonging, reduce socio-economic polarization, and reinforce the legitimacy of public institutions. In such contexts, political stability is not the product of coercion or elite negotiation, but rather the natural outcome of a widely shared investment in the national identity and vision. Nations that achieve this condition possess not only more resilient democracies but also more sustainable economic trajectories.

A further implication of the middle-class nation framework lies in its capacity to simplify and rationalize the public policy process. In countries where socio-economic conditions are relatively homogeneous across the majority of the population, it becomes significantly easier to design

A. Tahiri Jouti, *Building Middle Class Nations*,
https://doi.org/10.1007/978-3-032-02134-2_10

policies that are both effective and equitable. Such environments reduce the need for excessively complex compensatory mechanisms, targeted subsidies, or fragmented governance approaches.

Conversely, in nations with large disparities, the policymaking process is often inefficient and ineffective. Thus, the government is called to act as a mediator between entrenched interests, while dealing with institutional fragility and public distrust. In such a context, policies are less likely to win sufficient trust and legitimacy, and more likely to increase disparities. The emergence of a strong, inclusive middle-class mitigates this dynamic by anchoring state action in a broad consensus.

While Gross Domestic Product per capita remains a commonly used indicator of national wealth, it is not a sufficient measure of true development. Many nations can boast high levels of income or economic output without having the internal mechanisms in place to ensure equitable distribution and inclusive growth. In the absence of such mechanisms, even the wealthiest societies remain vulnerable to political instability, social fragmentation, and institutional erosion.

Development must therefore be assessed not only in quantitative terms, but also in qualitative dimensions—in particular, the degree to which a nation has succeeded in institutionalizing socio-economic inclusion. A high GDP per capita without a cohesive middle class is akin to a structurally unsound but shiny building: impressive at first glance, but ultimately fragile. The true test of a nation's progress lies in its ability to maintain a stable, self-reinforcing, and equitable societal order.

The lessons drawn from this analysis call for a recalibration of development paradigms. Policymakers, academics, and practitioners need to turn their attention away from narrow measures of growth and focus on the broader, more sustainable goal of building middle-class nations. This means investing in education, social upgrade mechanisms, institutional equity, and access to quality public services, all of which contribute to forging a coherent societal core.

The middle class is not simply a by-product of development, it is a prerequisite for it. It represents the critical mass of citizens who are economically secure, civically engaged, and institutionally represented. Their presence guarantees the legitimacy of governance, the resilience of democratic norms and the sustainability of economic systems. In this sense, building a middle-class nation is not just a desirable outcome, it's a strategic imperative.

In conclusion, this book invites everyone to reflect on a profound but often overlooked truth: a nation's ultimate strength lies not in its wealth, military might or technological prowess, but in the depth and vitality of its social contract. Only nations that succeed in nurturing a strong, inclusive and self-reliant middle class can hope to achieve lasting peace, prosperity, and stability in the twenty-first century.

- Toward a Middle-Class Nation

Building a middle-class nation is not defined by economic growth alone, but by a country's ability to offer its people equitable access to opportunity, security, and dignity. This ambition rests on three interdependent pillars: institutional reform, inclusive public policies, and equitable economic development. Combined, they constitute the essential steps to foster a sustainable, cohesive, and future-ready society.

– *Political Commitment and Institutional Reform*

A middle-class nation begins with the political will to shift from the individualistic governance to a system based on competent and accountable institutions. This change implies a national vision that spans several decades, ensuring strategic continuity and guaranteeing that public institutions do not operate in isolation or in contradiction to each other. Institutions must be designed with clear missions, solid accountability frameworks and adaptable mandates to meet new challenges.

Leadership appointments must correspond to each phase of development, with performance-based appraisals guaranteeing continuity and progress. Effective governance also requires simple, enforceable rules and a comprehensive control system to uphold legality, discourage misbehavior, and reinforce public trust. Institutions must strike a balance between stability and agility, ensuring that they can innovate and evolve while remaining rooted in public service and national priorities.

In short, political will must manifest itself in resilient institutions that transcend individual ambitions and serve as a sustainable backbone for national development.

Public Policy as a Tool for Inclusion

Public policies in education, housing, health, and transportation are not just social services, they are the structural underpinnings of the middle class. In education, this means shifting the state's role from provider to regulator, guaranteeing universal access while encouraging innovation and accountability through performance-based school classification, public–private partnerships and adaptive learning models. Special attention must be paid to rural areas and marginalized populations through mobile and digital solutions, personalized learning, and alternative education pathways.

Housing policy must go beyond building units—it must offer access to dignified living conditions through targeted financial tools such as subsidies, guarantee schemes and crisis response mechanisms. Under this approach, social housing becomes a flexible financial framework rather than a building standard. New urban areas need to be supported by public infrastructure, especially public transportation network, to reduce hidden costs and encourage voluntary urban migration. At the same time, policies should revitalize historic centers and reconfigure taxation to promote mobility and balance.

Health, too, needs to be reconceptualized with an emphasis on prevention, sustainability and innovation. Environmental health risks, mental health, and chronic disease prevention require an integrated approach involving education, urban planning, and technology adoption. Public health systems must remain independent, forward-looking and strategically coordinated across sectors. By investing in preventive care and harnessing digital tools, governments can improve well-being while easing the pressure on curative systems.

In all areas, public services should serve as both a lift—helping people to rise economically and socially—and a net—protecting them in times of vulnerability. When well-designed, they reduce inequalities and reinforce public trust in the social contract.

Economic Inclusion and Risk Mitigation

A middle-class nation must adopt an economic model that balances competitiveness and fairness. Liberalizing markets while protecting the public interest ensures that innovation is not stifled and that access to opportunities is not reserved for a privileged minority. Unlike over-regulated and protectionist systems, open economic frameworks encourage broad participation, improve productivity, and foster trust in public institutions.

Moreover, it is essential to monitor and reduce social costs—the cumulative burden of essential expenses such as housing, education, and healthcare. This means improving the quality of public services, making them more affordable, and ensuring access to care during recessions. When households are freed from exorbitant basic costs, they are better positioned to invest in their future, contributing to a virtuous cycle of growth and resilience.

At the same time, financial inclusion must be strengthened. Risk-sharing models such as Islamic finance, venture capital, and targeted guarantee schemes can democratize access to capital. New financial institutions must not only lend, but also support individuals in their entrepreneurial, professional, and educational transitions. These tools also protect individuals from the long-term consequences of failure by offering second chances and stabilizing social mobility.

Investing in lagging regions, supporting innovation sectors, and aligning financing mechanisms with public policies can significantly reduce disparities. The goal is to shift from a survival paradigm to one of empowerment, where individuals are able to take risks, pursue their ambitions, and contribute significantly to the nation's progress.

Becoming a middle-class nation is not just a matter of economic status: it is a societal transformation. It means building a nation where institutions are reliable, policies are inclusive, and opportunities are abundant and accessible. This path requires vision, discipline, and a deep understanding of the interdependence between governance, equity, and sustainability.

By following these steps, nations can create the conditions for long-term prosperity, political stability, and social cohesion. More than a development strategy, it is a promise to future generations: progress will not be the privilege of a few, but a shared journey for all.

Index

A. Tahiri Jouti, *Building Middle Class Nations*,
https://doi.org/10.1007/978-3-032-02134-2

The manufacturer's authorised representative in the EU is Springer Nature Customer Service Centre GmbH, Europaplatz 3, 69115 Heidelberg, Germany. If you have any concerns regarding our products, please contact ProductSafety@springernature.com

Printed and bound by CPI Group (UK) Ltd, Croydon, CR0 4YY
21/09/2026
02219945-0009